The
WAR
Against
WOMEN

Ment HHx

MARILYN FRENCH

The WAR Against WOMEN

Ballantine Books • New York

This edition published by arrangement with Summit Books, a division of Simon & Schuster, Inc.

Library of Congress Catalog Card Number: 92-82995
ISBN: 0-345-38248-X

Cover design by Ruth Ross

Manufactured in the United States of America

First Ballantine Books Trade Edition: March 1993

10 9 8 7 6 5 4 3 2 1

ACKNOWLEDGMENTS

Although I alone am responsible for the content of this book, Ann Jones and Barbara Greenberg read the manuscript and offered very helpful suggestions; James Silberman edited it with his usual grace and good advice; Robert French, Ann Volks, Carol Jenkins, and Andrea Dworkin provided important research materials. I thank them. I also thank Isabelle de Cordier, Naomi Backer, Annaville Petterson, and Betsy Chalfin for their valuable assistance in innumerable ways.

CONTENTS

INTRODUCTION

In the popular view of human history, humans have progressed from a state of "savagery" in which we lived like predatory animals and men dragged women into caves by the hair, to a "civilization" in which men open car doors for women. But the reality may be the reverse. Evidence suggests that for three and a half million years, humans lived in small cooperative communities in which the sexes were equal but women had somewhat higher status and more respect than men. Archeological remains from about ten thousand years ago reflect goddess-worshiping communities living in egalitarian harmony and material well-being.[1] War may have begun about ten thousand years ago, but not until about the fourth millennium BCE did men begin to build what became patriarchy—male supremacy backed by force—probably first in the Middle East. Men began to assert themselves as "bigmen," appropriating the labor and resources of others. Over thousands of years, gods superseded goddesses as king-priests began to rule over formerly autonomous communities and spread domination over the globe. After the rise of the state, peasants, the main producers in agricultural societies, bore the major tax burden: their labor on the land supported parasitical elites and they were drafted to work (without pay) on state projects. They even had to pay for the instruments of their own repression: soldiers and weapons.

For women, it has been downhill ever since. Women were probably the first slaves, and while elite women had considerable power in early states, they were subject to men of their class. Women not only did not "progress" but have been increasingly disempowered, degraded, and subjugated. This tendency accelerated over the last four centuries, when men, mainly in the West, exploded in a frenzy of domination, trying to expand and tighten their control of nature and those associated with nature—people of color and women. European men had built ships capable of circumnavigating the globe for at least a century before they began to use them for that purpose in the late fifteenth century. Their explorations, motivated by curiosity mixed with greed for wealth and fame, generated some of the most tragic chapters in human history. By force and subversion, Europeans exploited Africa, Asia, the Middle East, the South Pacific, and the Americas, killing, enslaving, or subjugating their people and appropriating their resources.

In the next century, men reached out intellectually too, defying church restrictions to create the beginnings of an experimental science, justifying their efforts by biblical sanction of human dominion over nature. Their work provided a basis for a new technology they thought would benefit the human race, which eventually produced the industrial revolution. Industrialization did bring benefits, especially to a small group, but it also propelled most humans into new depths of destitution and misery. As feudalism gradually ended and capitalism began, a propertied elite in England thrust huge numbers of peasants off the land and locked them out of any share of society's goods. The industrial revolution began in England partly because of the existence of this class, which Marx later called the proletariat. For varied reasons, people were displaced from land throughout Europe, joining the proletariat, a faceless mass of dispossessed people, the majority of whom were women and children.

Those who benefited from capitalist industrialization became a new elite, a fluid, dynamic class. Individuals might rise or fall in wealth and power: what was constant was that the elite was composed almost entirely of white males. The women attached to them may have benefited from their wealth, but did not share their power. By the nineteenth century, most humans across the globe were workers or indigents subject to a small elite, and almost all women were subjugated to men. By then, unremitting male effort over centuries had succeeded in thrusting women's position to its nadir: women possessed almost no human rights—

to a political voice, to inherit, to own property, to do business on their own. They even lacked rights over their own bodies.

But subjugation generates resentment, and the last two centuries have been dominated by revolutions. Workers' and women's rights movements inundated Europe and the United States like a tidal wave in the nineteenth and early twentieth centuries, inspiring nationalist rebellions in Asia and Africa in the midtwentieth.[2]

Workers protested the unfair division of the world's resources, exploitive systems granting the people who produced goods little share of them. Most resources were and are owned by a small elite, whose economic control gives them political power. The workers' movements were largely inspired by socialist ideas, widespread in the nineteenth century. The first socialist experiments, the Owenite communities of early nineteenth-century England, were concerned with women's lot. But early European socialism was dominated by artisans' guilds concerned above all with protecting their own prerogatives. By the time Marxism came to dominate socialist thinking, few socialists cared about the problem women bear alone—responsibility for childrearing and maintaining the family while working to support their families—alone or with a husband's help.

Economic hardship and lack of political voice drove women to rise up in the nineteenth century—middle-class women through feminism, working-class women through labor agitation rooted in anarchist, socialist, or communist principles. Since for a woman even to speak in public violated gender rules, these women were making a feminist statement even if they disavowed feminism.

Socialism had wide-ranging consequences in the twentieth century. In some states, socialist revolutions overthrew autocratic governments to set up "dictatorships of the proletariat." In other places, fear of socialism led the elite to support repressive autocratic rulers who seized power and benefited the military and wealthy interests. In so-called democratic states, fearful elites assimilated workers' demands and legalized unions to negotiate them.

Socialist states removed legal discriminations against women but made no effort to teach men they must share the responsibility for taking care of themselves and their homes or raising the next generation. Fascist governments tried to solve the "woman" problem by reimposing extreme male controls on women and constricting them within the domestic realm. Capitalist governments and male-dominated labor unions colluded in keeping women in the lowest-paid, most marginal work. Everywhere, women were denied the right to work for decent pay on grounds that men supported them. Since not all men did, women and their children were thrust into even deeper impoverishment. And men who did support women treated them like property.

Feminist ideas had been articulated for centuries by writers like Christine de Pisan, Mary Wollstonecraft, George Sand, and a host of others, and a feminist movement arose during the French Revolution. But feminism as a widespread political movement dates to 1848 and the Seneca Falls movement in the United States. Smaller and more fragmented than workers' movements, feminism was even more threatening. It distressed all men, not just the elite, by creating discord at home, and unlike workers' protests, by challenging men where they are most vulnerable, in their self-definition. In this century, feminism has achieved striking successes in gaining women access to education, political rights, and jobs and in eliminating laws enforcing a double standard, mainly in industrialized and socialist states. Feminism has so many forms that many scholars refer to feminisms. I define as "feminist" any attempt to improve the lot of any group of women through female solidarity and a female perspective. Considering the power and solidarity of the forces arrayed against them, feminists' success in improving women's lot in so brief a time is dazzling.

Elite men kept seeking ways to defeat organized labor, moving their factories to regions and, later, countries where labor was not organized. Forming transnational corporations, they built factories in countries without protective laws where they could also buy cheap raw materials. Corporations huge enough to control governments (some of which, notably in England and the United States, tried to wreck unions) set out to bring labor to its knees.

After World War II in the United States, wages and working conditions improved for blue-collar men, whose average earnings leaped from $15,056 in 1955 to $24,621 in 1973. But by 1987 their average wage, adjusted for inflation, was $19,859, a 19 percent decline. By the 1980s, many married women had entered the work force to raise family income, but in 1988 two salaries brought in only 6 percent more than one in 1973. Business policies are gradually eradicating well-paid jobs protected by union contracts. As one economist puts it, "One well-paid smokestack job with health insurance has been replaced by two service jobs without benefits.[3]

The capitalist elite wanted to defeat labor and especially socialism but, ironically, socialism was defeated by the very governments supposed to enshrine it, socialist elites as oppressive and exploitive as those they displaced—even more so, embattled as they were from outside. The late twentieth century has witnessed what seems the final defeat for our age of workers' movements: as socialist governments fall, socialism itself seems discredited. Still, workers go on struggling: the labor movement is not destroyed. It if catches up with the new strategies of a global economy, we can expect to see continued conflict.

In the same vein, men-as-a-caste—elite *and* working-class men—continue to seek ways to defeat feminism, by rescinding or gnawing away at its victories (legal abortion), confining women to lower employment levels (putting a "glass ceiling" over professional women), or founding movements aimed at returning them to fully subordinate status ("fundamentalism"). As kin-group and community controls erode, men everywhere increasingly fail to support the children they engender, and use violence against females—daughters, wives, lovers, mothers, sisters, and strangers. Men are adapting new technologies to old purposes, for example, using amniocentesis to detect a fetus's sex to abort girls or new fertility techniques to create children they claim as their own ("surrogate" motherhood). These actions amount to a global war against women.

This war is aimed at reasserting or tightening men's control over female bodies, especially sexual and reproductive capacities, and women's labor. Although not all women are or want to be mothers, most women are mothers, and *only* women are mothers.

Mothering means taking responsibility, and since the beginning of human life, women have taken responsibility for the well-being of the human race. *This is their choice:* they do it not because they are programmed to by genes or hormones, but because it is necessary. One has only to glance at a newborn baby to understand the necessity. Besides, women have always done it, it is customary. But as industrialization, ideas of equality and freedom, and technology make it possible for women to repudiate this often thankless task, more and more women are doing so. Seeing this, men panic. Knowing that someone must fulfill this role or the race will perish, they face several alternatives: they will have to take on this role (unbearable); they will have to reward women for what they do (unpleasant); or they can use every means at their disposal to urge, demand, and force women to continue in their role and their subordination.

Most men choose the last, although they have not considered its costs. Just as men war against other nations without considering long-term consequences, they persecute women without recognizing they are destroying the human race. Men want to make sure that women go on taking all responsibility for producing and rearing children and caring for them economically and personally. (This statement may nettle men who do support their families economically, but the reality is that huge numbers of men in both industrialized and nonindustrialized countries do not. No statement in this book is directed against any individual man. It is based on global information and is an indictment of a system invented and maintained by men-as-a-caste.)

I believe patriarchy began and spread as a war against women. At first, humans did not recognize the male part in procreation and men were marginal in community life: women did everything, as they still do in many societies. They bore and reared the children, gathered or raised most of the food, and probably had the major voice in group decisions. Humans probably lived this way for two million years, until they invented projectiles and hunting began. While early people hunted as a group, men gradually took control of hunting. They may have been better at it, having more upper-body strength, and they were expendable in a way that women, the life-givers, were not. Hunting gave men a role in society and a base for solidarity. Even after people realized that men fathered children (that recognition is suggested by artwork in Anatolian villages dating to 9000–7000 BCE), social arrangements remained the same.

Evidence and common sense suggest the following hypothesis. Several enormous changes occurred: people (probably women) began to raise crops instead of gathering them, which enabled the population to grow; as an increased population spread out across the world, the supply of game dwindled. Hunting became undependable, men's single known ground of importance began to fade. To regain their status, they created hunting cults, excluding women (whom they may have blamed for the lack of game, still believing all life flowed from the female), and gradually began to worship male deities. (All hunting societies have exclusively male hunting cults.) But boys who grew up not as hunters but farmers lacked the old male solidarity. Men, imitating the onset of puberty in the female, devised puberty rituals for boys to teach them male solidarity. With the exception of certain Australian aboriginal groups, gathering-hunting people do not hold group initiations of boys. Most group initiations occur among horticulturalists. Male solidarity came under threat when gathering gave way to horticulture—it then had to be contrived, or it would have vanished as each man worked his plot alone. To keep it alive, men began to initiate boys into maleness.

Because the only ground of male solidarity is opposition to women and because its aim is to replace the primary bond to the mother, with whom men associate life-affirming qualities like nutritiveness, compassion, softness, and love, building male solidarity always involves some form of brutalization. Male initiations teach boys to have contempt for, to eradicate "feminine" traits, replacing them with hardness, self-denial (not self-sacrifice), obedience, and deference to "superior" males. It creates a bond different from love, an instrument for a "higher" good, a transcendent goal: power. Many puberty rites specifically require boys to reject their mothers—and with them, the "female" world.

Women-as-a-caste have never defined themselves in opposition to men and lacked female solidarity, forming their main bond with their children. And knowing themselves absolutely essential to the life of the group, they may not have been threatened by male solidarity. They may even have encouraged rites they believed would increase their sons' well-being and men's sense of responsibility. But probably under the direction of male priests avid for power, once men discovered their vital role in procreation they began to insist that children carry their name and form patrilineages. In order to ensure a male line of descent, in some places (like Africa) men enslaved women, capturing them and separating them from their own lineages, to which they owed obligations and who communally owned their children. Even so, to claim parentage, a man had to guard the woman's sexuality. Men began to demand a wife move to her husband's clan at marriage, isolating her from kin, placing her under the surveillance and control of her husband's lineage. Only at this point did men start to abuse women. These steps were taken at different times in different places, but had spread almost everywhere by about five thousand years ago.

Women fought these changes: myth and legend preserved in the Bible and other ancient works testify to a struggle between the sexes over the centuries. But women's defeat was also a defeat for men, who lost the relative autonomy and equality of kin-group life. The Sumerian word for "freedom," *amargi*, means "back to the mother." The idea of domination caught the imagination of certain men who, to impose their rule over larger regions, introduced innovations—large-scale war, tribute (taxation), bondage, prostitution, and two new crimes, treason and adultery. While women were soldiers in many societies, fighting gradually became a predominantly male activity—probably for the same reason hunting did. Conquerors forced defeated peoples into bondage, taxed them, and sometimes appropriated their land. The state was born. Women had high rank in early states, but only as they were related by blood or marriage to the male ruling class, and usually as men's subordinates. *All* early states decreed in law that women's bodies—their sexuality and reproductive capacity—were men's property and made it difficult or impossible for women to own or transfer property.

Patriarchy—that is, institutionalized male supremacy—probably arose in Mesopotamia in the fourth millennium BCE, and gradually spread across the world. Many revolutions have challenged ruling elites since patriarchy arose, but feminism is the first ever to challenge patriarchy per se. In virtually every country in the world today, women are organizing small grass-roots or professional political action groups. They are demanding to be treated as human beings with rights: the right to keep their own wages, to keep their children after divorce, to own property, to education, to paid work at a wage sufficient to ensure that they can live independently, to a voice in public decisions, to marriage at choice, to bodily integrity. They are demanding men not feel free to beat, rape, mutilate, and kill them. Feminist theorists challenge the patriarchal arrangement of society into stratified classes, each with different access to resources, some privileged, some disadvantaged from birth, and patriarchists' worship of domination. Women are central in global peace and ecology movements. Women form female networks and organizations based in cooperation and sharing, with only pro-tem leaders.[4] Women are creating an alternative definition of themselves, human nature, and experience.

Men imbued with patriarchal values are mustering all their forces to defeat this challenge. The social and political movements of the last two centuries were based on Enlightenment ideas that justified the revolutions that brought present elites to power. For that reason, elites cannot repudiate these principles and sophisticated men cannot openly admit they believe peasants, workers, and women are inferior species ordained by nature to serve them. While some people still use such arguments privately, the idea of natural inferiority is not legitimate in late twentieth-century Western discourse.

But patriarchy never announced its real purposes—at least, no such announcement is recorded in history, although myths of many cultures celebrate or justify a male assault on female dominance. Wherever and however men subjugated women, they justified it by declaring god or nature *made* women subordinate to men—by endowing men but not women with certain traits (reason, logic, intellect, souls) and women but not men with traits (chaotic emotionality, unbridled sexuality) subversive of good and proper order. Men treat women as marginal to the real business of life, not the essential maintainers they are. Even when feminists force men to hear them, politicians threat them as a "special interest group"—as if their concerns affected a small fraction of the population, not all women (51 percent of the population in most countries) and the children for whom women take almost sole responsibility.

Today, when governments or religious leaders articulate policies extremely injurious to women, they rarely mention women directly, focusing on other issues and cloaking them in euphemisms. The euphemism usually used to promote female subordination is "protection of the family." This is ironic: after all, which sex has always maintained the "family" and taken responsibility for children? But many men, in groups with political clout or as individuals with guns or fists, need no euphemistic sanction to injure women. As a result, in much of the world, women—and the children always with them—have become an endangered species. Charlotte Bunch writes that if one ethnic or national group were attacking another, killing and maiming them at the same rate as men attack and kill women (and she is speaking only of attacks by intimates), the situation would be held to constitute a state of emergency or even war.[5] But domestic violence is only one campaign in what amounts to a widespread war against women.

Because men mask their intention by omitting women or granting them superficial inclusion, we have to demystify their aims by looking at effects, not rhetoric. It may be objected that effects may be accidental or incidental, or occur without animus. But it cannot be an accident that everywhere on the globe one sex harms the other so massively that one questions the sanity of those waging the campaign: can a species survive when half of it systematically preys on the other?

Humans are the only species in which one sex consistently preys upon the other. Men claim male predation is "natural," rooted in genetic or hormonal coding and therefore unalterable: men are *by nature* driven to abuse and dominate women. If this is true, humanity is doomed to extinction. But history suggests men did not always prey upon women, that the sexes once lived in relative equality. Patriarchy may have evolved to overcome female dominance, but if women were dominant, they never institutionalized that dominance in matriarchy (no matriarchy has existed that we know of), never tried to constrict male sexuality and reproduction, minds and work. In historic periods when women had considerable power (there have been some), they never united against men. Nor is it conceivable they would. Men's need to dominate women may be based in their own sense of marginality or emptiness; we do not know its root, and men are making no effort to discover it. But men's long-standing war against women is now, in reaction to women's movements across the world, taking on a new ferocity, new urgency, and new veneers.

The essay that follows is divided into four parts. Part I deals with systemic wars against women, ways women are disadvantaged by overarching international and religious systems which individuals cannot change. These disadvantages ramify differently in different countries, but there are some universals. Everywhere in the world, men place all or most of the burden of raising children and maintaining the home on women, but pretend this burden is not work: they do not reward it as work or count it as work in global accounting, in either developing or industrialized countries. Systemic economic disadvantaging of women inevitably creates systemic political discrimination. Women overburdened by work lack leisure to pursue political activities; and those who do face systemic barriers. As a result, the women of the world have little voice in running the world—which perpetuates men's power to subject them economically. To keep women out of political life, men refuse to credit their contributions to it, and obliterate them from history. We will discuss one recent example of this long-standing and wide-scale problem.

Religions are major vehicles for subjugating women. To keep women from having political power—power within churches, a voice on public issues—religions concentrate mainly on women's bodies, treating the female body as if it incarnated the morality of the entire human race. Thus some focus on women's appearance, dress, and habits, as if all human virtue depended upon them (yet men's appearance, dress, and habits are seen as irrelevant to virtue); others focus on women's potential for motherhood, as if women alone had the duty to perpetuate the human species. Religions do not require men to support or reward or help women in this task, but they demand that men control it.

The discussion of religious war against women moves on to state efforts to dominate women by passing laws governing female bodies, either in alliance with a religion or independently of it. Tied to religion and to the notion that women bear the burden of human sexual morals is a practice promoted under the aegis of many religions, genital mutilation of women, which an estimated twenty million women in the world today have undergone. Finally, we will discuss war against the very existence of women, in parts of the world that selectively abort female fetuses, turn a blind eye to female infanticide, or neglect female children to the point of starvation.

Part II deals with institutional discrimination, focusing mainly on the United States. Here, too, the effort is across the board: institutions try to keep women from economic self-sufficiency, a political voice, and control of their own bodies. Institutions sometimes try to justify this treatment of women, and the section opens by discussing one current scientific justification: sociobiology. It moves to some recent examples of prejudice against women in various professions. The medical profession in general is unconcerned with women's medical problems; many doctors try to control female reproduction or take pleasure in mutilating women's bodies. The legal profession injures women in myriad ways, treating female lawyers contemptuously, making biased divorce and custody judgments. In education and business, males are given preference. Only occasionally and with difficulty can individuals challenge the bias of these institutions.

Part III offers some examples of woman-hatred in culture, in language and the arts. Cultural products are disseminated by institutions, and may even be created by them, but culture is too amorphous to be attributed to any given institution. Culture is built from form, style, and image; its surface may mask its politics just as rhetoric masks the politics of governments, religions, and businesses, but uncovering, "demystifying" its politics requires a somewhat different kind of analysis. For this reason, I have assigned it a section to itself. It includes discussion of the language of high-ranking men in the military and the weapons industry and of soldiers' songs, the policies of advertisers in women's magazines, and random observations on male depictions of women in the arts. It concludes with a discussion of male sadomasochism against women in the arts and some thoughts on the issue of censorship.

Part IV discusses assaults on women's bodies in daily and domestic life. The media treat male assaults on women like rape, beating, and murder of wives and female lovers, or male incest with children, as individual aberrations. But they are so widespread as to be systemic: male violence against women could not flourish as it does without the support or at least toleration of institutions like the courts and police; and psychological studies show the preponderance of men who rape or commit incest to be within the range of what is considered "normal" for men in American society. Thus the violent acts of individual men are intrinsic parts of the cultural context. Indeed, in many countries of the world men still have a legal right to beat, torture, imprison, or kill the women they "own," and elsewhere men had such legal prerogatives right up until the *twentieth century*. Governments, religions, institutions, and cultural groups that do not openly condone male violence toward women countenance it as a private act outside their provenance.

The pretense that this violence is not protected by institutional aegis means that humane groups like Amnesty International, for example, cannot intervene to protect women from beatings, imprisonment, mutilation, torture, starvation, rape, and murder *within the home* unless these acts are explicitly allowed by law. Indeed, many men even within humane movements refuse to acknowledge that the issue of "human rights" includes women. Moreover, statistics are not kept on male predation on women *in general*. Each category of crime is separate, obscuring the fact that all male violence toward women is part of a concerted campaign. I do not have the resources or knowledge to analyze the relation between individual male violence toward women (and children) and governmental, religious, and institutional policies in any given country, so I did not include this area in the sections on systemic or institutional war on women. And I want to stress the vital importance of ordinary men in waging male war against women. If individual violence could not be as widespread and devastating without broad-scale support, neither could global wars against women continue without the support of individual men.

Only feminist analysts treat male violence toward women as a global crisis. By treating violence toward women as individual acts, journalists, social scientists, and social workers conceal the politics underlying it: they whitewash men, and in the process preclude public discussion of the real situation. Yet without public discussion, we cannot plumb the reverberations on the male psyche of feeling permitted to abuse women in ways few would abuse animals, nor seriously discuss human morality.

Any discussion of the repression of women is complicated by several factors: the circularity of women's problems, the difficulty of proving discrimination, and men's obsession with female reproduction.

THE CIRCULARITY OF WOMEN'S PROBLEMS

Any instance of discrimination, in property rights, say, affects not just a woman's economic power but her political voice, her body, and her children. If a system grants property rights almost exclusively to men (as many African countries do), a woman, to survive, must either marry and farm her husband's land or find work in a city. Most African women are pushed into marriage; but marriage brings children and many African men do not support their families. If a man's land is insufficient to support them, or if her husband divorces her, a woman must seek work in a city, but *she* has the children; they may bear their father's name, but he takes little or no responsibility for them.

Having children makes it harder for the woman to move from place to place in search of work—she cannot simply leave them alone. And by rule or custom in Africa, few women are educated enough to do office work and few factory owners hire women. An impoverished woman with children can find work only in a marginal occupation—domestic service, petty trade, or prostitution. Women are hired as domestic servants in a few African countries; female domestic servants are often sexually appropriated by the men of the house. Petty trade is often illegal—as is prostitution. (Since patriarchy began, prostitution is the only work for which men pay women enough to support themselves.) But she still may not be able to earn enough to survive, or she may fall ill. If she does, her children starve. If they fall ill, she has to tend to them, which means she cannot work, and they starve. Society blames her for both her work and her children's condition: she grieves and blames herself. This is a common scenario. Economic factors affect women's bodies; "family" law is primarily aimed at controlling women's (not men's) bodies but also affects women economically—in negative ways. And whenever women are harmed, so are children.

The circularity of women's problems is reflected in this text, where one subject regularly spills over into others: it is sometimes as impossible to distinguish a particular injury as to separate those who are inflicting it (male-dominated governments, churches, corporations, and institutions). I want to stress, though, that almost always, when women are harmed, children are harmed, and when women are helped, children are helped. Thus policies damaging to women essentially damage the entire human race.

THE DIFFICULTY OF PROVING DISCRIMINATION

It is hard to *prove* discrimination in societies pervaded by prejudice. It is always possible to find something to attack if you look for it—in any human being. Anyone determined to find another person or group inferior can always find whole lists of grounds that demonstrate inferiority because we are all inferior to the ideals of humanness we have erected.

If we set out (for a change) to prove men inferior, we could cite the fact that men die at a greater rate than women in every decade of life, that they are emotionally stunted, unable to provide emotional support, cannot have babies or raise them, or even make their own dinners. Subject to hormonal swings that cause them to flare into rages that threaten life (their own and other people's), they are also fascinated by toys, particularly adept at inventing structures that give them the illusion that they are in control.

They have certain redeeming features: they are sexually passionate, and their irresponsibility frees them to be playful or brilliant about matters unconnected to the real business of life. Surely, such a species should be set in a playpen to amuse itself while women take the burden of responsibility for managing society, raising children, and cooking dinner. If this were the prevailing ideology, individual acts that challenged the definition could be fit into it, and protests by male groups would be seen as resulting from hormonally caused mood swings.

Whites *see* black men in white neighborhoods or expensive shops as predators. Whites *see* black women in rich white neighborhoods as maids or nannies but as prostitutes on city streets and shoplifters in expensive shops. In Moscow, women cannot enter hotels without proof they are guests because the government *assumes* that any nonresident woman entering a hotel is a prostitute. (This may have changed since my last visit in 1990.) When I was young, good restaurants would not seat a woman unescorted by a man: women without men were *seen* as prostitutes.

This is prejudice, prejudgment of people based on their inherent, unchangeable sex or color. It may be overt, or it may exist on a level beneath consciousness, among people's assumptions. All societies entertain prejudices which do not need to be spoken to be shared. Thus they are hard to prove. Many societies encode their prejudices in their laws. The feminist movement has brilliantly succeeded in removing discriminatory laws from the codes of most industrialized nations, but men now use more sophisticated techniques to exclude women. Few make sweeping statements of female inferiority, but many continue to act as if only men mattered. Company men insist no discrimination was involved when a certain woman was not promoted; the problem was the guys didn't like her, she didn't fit in. The operative word when people disparage women is "too." Women's voices are too loud or too soft, they are too aggressive or too passive, dressed too dowdily or too gaudily, are too old or too young. Every human trait annoys someone. In woman-hating societies, *everyone* finds women more annoying than men.

Women are seen as deviant whatever they do. A recent book, *The Trapped Woman: Catch 22 in Deviance and Control*, demonstrates the catch-22 situation trapping women.[6] One article lists some characteristics that mark a woman as deviant: not having children, or having children, working for wages, and using child care; or having children, working for wages, and not finding child care.[7] Women who have children and need welfare aid to support them are found guilty, as are women who divorce, who are battered and do not fight back, or who leave their batterers or fight back. Women are castigated for being sexually free or for being "uptight" about sex; for clinging to virginity or for having extramarital lovers; for being raped. Women are deviant if they are assertive, or if they are meek and subservient; if they do not devote themselves utterly to their husbands and children, or if they selflessly sacrifice themselves to them. Society condemns women for being ambitious, or for lacking ambition; for being rich or poor, fat or thin, with careers or without them.

In all patriarchal cultures, woman-hatred is common currency, the small change lying in every man's (and many women's) pocket, easy to pull out to pay for—justify—any action. Because women are blamed for being whatever they are, discrimination is difficult to prove. We must study its effects to prove its existence.

MEN'S OBSESSION WITH FEMALE REPRODUCTION

Men too are oppressed, everywhere, by racial, religious, economic, and political factors. Women share these problems equally (except that of male identity, a serious problem few men ever really face). But men do not share most of women's problems. The root of the problems men do not share with them is women's reproductive capacity: women's situation would be unique even without patriarchy because the human race is re-created through their bodies. But the patriarchal system locks women in their bodies. Because women bear children, men try to control or appropriate their bodies; the male-dominated system takes the position that women do indeed (as was thought for millions of years) reproduce all by themselves, miraculously. The attitude that women alone produce children pervades all societies and all levels of mentality, from the simplest to the most sophisticated.[8] Since women alone bear children, men assign them alone the responsibility for raising children. Men claim ownership of children, demanding they bear *their* names, but act as if women alone choose to have children and so have the exclusive duty of raising and, often, supporting them. Because women bear children, their problems are always circular: what men do to women's bodies often affects their child-bearing, and motherhood has an enormous and enduring impact on a woman's entire life. No treatment of a man's body—including castration and fatherhood—burdens him equally for the rest of *his* life; he does not bear children for whom he will be responsible for decades. Men can therefore compartmentalize their experience in a way women cannot. Because women bear children, men persist in seeing all women as mothers owing them caretaking service. Exclusive responsibility for reproducing and socializing the human race might conceivably be bearable if women were given the power to achieve these goals. But men expect women to perform the most important of all human tasks with no reward, without much help, and with almost no consideration.

History suggests that men envy women's reproductive capacity: it was the first female power they tried to appropriate, turning women into commodities for exchange and use even before states began. And their efforts to control it remain nothing short of obsessive. In the following discussion, efforts to control women's reproduction crop up repeatedly. It will quickly become apparent that the drive to control female reproduction is a silent agenda in every level of male activity.

This book is a survey. It is not exhaustive. Global statistics on male violence against women—battering, rape, incest—are either not available or not reliable. We have yet to discover the dimensions of incest. The treatment of women in courts of law, the arts and media, and in customs and habits is barely touched here. But what is here should alert you to look for yourself.

Part I

SYSTEMIC
DISCRIMINATION
AGAINST
WOMEN

If you travel around the world, especially in rural regions, you will notice that everywhere (except in Muslim countries) women are doing most of the work. Two women gather seaweed on the Indian coast near Ahmadabad: they bend and rise, bend and rise, pulling up the greens, adding them to their pile. When they have as much as they can carry, they lug the pile up the beach to a wagon pulled over on the side of the road, dump it in the wagon, and return for more. They continue in this for hours, until the wagon is full. All the while, a man sits in the wagon, head nodding in the sun, holding the reins of his horse. He does nothing.

Everywhere in the Indian countryside, you see adult women so thin you would worry about them if they were your children, trudging barefoot along the dusty roads with eighty-pound jugs on their heads. You spot their bright saris dotting fields where they bend weeding. But under a broad leafy tree, on a patch of grass, twenty or so men are sprawled out talking, in gleaming white shirts you know they did not launder themselves. The grog shop, being Hindu, sells only soft drinks, but they are expensive for these poor people. Only men sit on the boxes that serve as seats in this Indian version of a sidewalk café. In Ethiopia, you pass a woman with a very aged body who could be any age, bent under a load of firewood twice her size. Beside her rides a man, unencumbered, on a donkey.

On the other hand, in many cities, few women appear on the street during working hours. If you enter a Dublin pub during working hours, it is filled with men. In Italy, you become aware that a young man is following you. You stop and confront him. He has been following you all day, he says, and tells you where you have been for the last few hours. He is well dressed, works for an insurance company. He wonders if you want to have a drink. You understand he will not pay for it. In Moscow even in the days of full employment, men loitered outside hotels, in airports and railroad stations, waiting to sell rubles to a foreigner on the black market, waiting for something, a deal. There are more of them now. You don't see women except on the block-long food queues; the only queues men stand on are for vodka. You don't see women on the streets of Athens either, except in

the evening shopping hours. You don't see women because they
are all working—at home, in offices, in factories. But you know
that the men, whatever they do, however little work they do, earn
more than the women. And you know that the women spend the
evenings working just as hard at home, while the men sit back
expecting to be waited on.

ECONOMIC DISCRIMINATION

The statistics presented at the United Nations Conference on
Women in Copenhagen in 1980 remain true today: women do
between two-thirds and three-quarters of the work in the world.[1]
They also produce 45 percent of the world's food. But they are
still granted only 10 percent of the world's income and 1 percent
of the world's property—and part of that 1 percent masks male
ownership hidden for tax purposes. (In the United States, property
ownership is murky because most people own only a residence,
usually placed in the names of both husband and wife. But the
U.S. Census Bureau estimates that 16 percent of the property in
this country is owned by women in their own right as female
heads of household.)[2] And women's situation is worsening because a new world order created by a new global economic system
puts men in power everywhere, even in places where women had
some voice until recent decades.

The entire world is linked today: few communities exist in
isolated autonomy. What links us is economics, world-scale trad-
ing. Today, almost everyone is affected by a rise in the price of
oil. Droughts and crop failures have more limited impact, yet
touch areas far beyond those immediately affected. All states are
part of a world market to various degrees controlled by global
agencies—the World Bank, the International Monetary Fund, the
United Nations. The annual reports of these bodies and of national
governments are based on national statistics that claim to represent a country's economic performance. In her book *If Women
Counted*, Marilyn Waring explains the significance of such accounts, which with the UNSNA (United Nations System of National Accounts) contain the information the UN uses to assess
each nation's yearly contribution and evaluate the success of de-

velopment programs. These reports are used by aid programs to identify nations most in need of help, by businesses to locate new areas for investment and choose markets, and to guide internal policies.[3]

Everywhere in the world, analyses of these statistics determine what has happened and what should happen in the future. Like a single graph claiming to contain everything important, they guide national and international plans and programs. They do not dictate policy; they are the data on which policies are based. But they are narow, quantitative, and linear; they are guides only to economic and political exploitation. Omitting more than they include, they cannot guide users to broader social goals like well-being. They reflect not a country's actual production but its *cash-generating* capacities. There are two constants about these statistics: men make the decisions based on them; and what they omit are women, children, and the environment. The current state of the world arises from a system that puts little or no value on peace, preserving natural resources, women's labor, or the unpaid job of reproducing and maintaining human life. As Waring stresses, the system cannot respond to values it refuses to recognize.

At the end of the U.N. Decade for Women in 1985, a report on the state of the world's women concluded that women made some gains in education, health, employment, and politics during the decade, but still bore most responsibility while men had most power. The report stated that 35 percent of married European women work for wages; in Africa, women do 75 percent of the agricultural work over and above their work fetching water and firewood, cleaning, cooking, and tending children; in Malawi, for example, women put in as much work as men raising cotton and doing domestic chores, but also do twice as much work as men growing corn. In Burkina Faso, people lose weight during the rainy season because the women work such long days in the fields they are too exhausted to cook (and evidence suggests it is as hard for a man to prepare his dinner as it is for him to have a baby). In industrialized countries, women work fifty-six hours a week in the home; women in nonindustrial countries spend even more time—besides taking responsibility for procreation.

Women's gigantic task reproducing the human race, supporting and maintaining it, is specifically excluded from both Gross Domestic Product (GDP) and Gross National Product (GNP) statistics. (Gross National Product measures production that generates income *for* a nation's residents; Gross Domestic Product measures production that generates income *within* a country, even if the resources are not owned by its residents. U.N. statistics now use GDP, but the United States continues to favor GNP.)

Women are not counted as part of the labor force because they are not paid for their work, or because men take their wages, or because *their work is not considered work*. Waring offers the example of the Beti people living in the rain forest of southern Cameroon. The Beti practice slash-and-burn agriculture, clearing two new half-acre fields each year and cultivating them for two or three years. Food farmers (women are the farmers in most of Africa) always have four to six fields under cultivation, growing mainly groundnuts, cassava, cocoyams, plantains, and vegetables. Men too farm, but they raise cocoa, a cash crop and major export.

Beti men work seven and a half hours a day. They help the women raise food for an average of less than an hour a day; they work two hours on the cocoa plots, four hours making beer or palm wine or baskets, building or repairing houses, making housing materials or other simple commodities intended for sale, or in part-time wage work. Beti women work *at least* eleven hours a day: five hours raising food, and an extra hour to produce a surplus for city markets; three to four hours to process and cook food for the family, and two hours or more to collect water and firewood, do the washing, tend the children and the sick. Without women's work, the Beti could not live. Yet the International Labor Organization, a U.N. agency, counts the Beti man but not the Beti woman as an "active laborer" because she does not "help . . . the head of the family in his [sic] occupation."

After they won their independence from Western imperialist powers in the mid-twentieth century, many Third World countries, abetted by Western aid agencies and corporations, sponsored projects to "develop" their resources. Most development projects aim at enabling a population to earn cash by selling crops or manufactures for export or to urban national markets. In some countries, land appropriated by colonial powers was redistributed to the people. But it was almost always given only to men, and programs for raising cash crops (intended for market, not subsistence)—which involve instruction, gifts or loans of seeds, fertilizers, and tools—are established for men only. Women in developing countries work harder than men, but because they merely feed society and do not earn cash, their work is valued less than men's—or not at all.

After independence, African states named men "head of household" in census data and planning projects; this alone excluded women from national and international development programs. Men dominate the courts and legal practice, so the legal rights women do possess are rarely enforced. Kenya passed new laws protecting widows' shares in their husband's estate, but land is still commonly passed to the eldest son. Under apartheid, South African women are disadvantaged by laws confining them to overcrowded reserves, limiting their right to work and own land, and preventing them from moving to cities where they might find opportunities.

Almost all development projects in Africa focus on men. Although women are the farmers in most of Africa, very little help has been channeled to them. Land reform projects transfer land titles to men, which make them eligible for improvement loans and agricultural extension services. Without title to land, women are excluded from these. African women produce not only the food people eat, but most goods for domestic use or trade. Introduction of Western manufactured goods has weakened or ended their economic independence. When the West industrialized, working-class women were hired for factory work; however exploited, they could earn wages that enabled them to escape men's oppressive hold. But as industries spring up in Africa, they do not hire African women for wages or any job that allows them to accumulate capital. All African women get for backbreaking work on farms and providing goods and services in the casual exchange economy is—sometimes—bare survival, their own and their children's. Yet their work subsidizes corporate profits; women's work supports the men working in mines, on cash-crop farms, and in urban industry.

In 1984, an African woman farmer ironically remarked, "This one they call farmer; send in teachers to teach him to farm (while I'm out growing the food); lend him money for tractors and tillers (while I'm out growing the food); promise him fortunes if he'd only raise cotton (while I'm out growing the food). No, I daren't stop working, and I won't abandon that thing I was born for—to make sure my children have food in their bellies."

Farm women in Africa (and India) are the most overworked humans in the world, working ten to fifteen hours a day at a host of jobs. A typical Zimbabwean woman's day begins at 3:00 A.M. Every day she goes to the river for water, weeds the fields (breast-feeding her baby as she works), chases animals away from crops, pounds grain into flour, prepares meals, and gathers wood (steadily walking farther with these heavy loads because drought and over-cutting have depleted fuel wood). She helps her husband cultivate cash crops, processes food (threshes, dries, grinds), and carries it to market. She has weekly tasks like laundering. In the Ivory Coast, adult women's workload is twice men's; in Burkina Faso, women do all household work and still spend *82 percent* more time on farm work than men. A Tanzanian man complained, "Water is a big problem *for women*. We can sit here all day waiting for food because there is no woman at home. Always they are going to fetch water."[4] (Emphasis added.)

Women's traditional right to hold land varies from one to another African society, but in practice most women need living husbands to get access to land. Men hold such tight control of land that a woman who cultivates land owned by a husband who works in the city is not allowed to decide what crops to plant. Most Lesotho men work in South African mines, yet their wives need their permission to start a farming operation, hire a share-cropper, or get a loan from a credit union. Because they lack land rights, women cannot get credit. In many places, they cannot even join cooperatives that control credit, transport, and marketing. Nor do they have the right to the income from cash crops, *even if they raise them.*

Producing cash crops often raises family income, yet studies of projects that give men new technology to raise cash crops show that despite increased income, the family eats less and poorer food. Women's and children's nutritional levels fall because the income belongs to the men, who use it to throw "prestige feasts" or buy transistor radios. Men in Cameroon at least pay their children's school fees, but in Kenya, writes Irene Tinker, men gamble, buy liquor, and rent prostitutes, while their families starve— women can no longer raise food for the family because their work and the family land are given over to the men's cash crops.[5] In India, researchers estimate, men spend about 80 percent of their earnings on themselves: motorcycles, radios, watches, television sets, movies, alcohol, and prostitutes. African migrant workers send home a mere 10 percent of their earnings on average; women residents in the hostels in Cape Town roll their eyes at the men's "toys," as they call them—cars in various states of disrepair that clutter up the space around the hostel. In the United States, too, huge numbers of men desert wives and the children they have fathered, spending more on themselves while the family is forced onto welfare.

Studies also show that when women have resources or earn income at all, children's nutritional levels and well-being improve. Indian women, for example, consistently spend 95 percent of their earnings on their children. Indians have a saying: "A penny to a woman is a penny for the family; a penny to a man is a penny for the man." Yet when a Zambian tax code was amended in 1986 to give women half of a child allowance that had formerly gone to men, Zambian men complained women would waste it on "perming their hair, buying makeup and expensive dresses." Yet most Zambian men earn little and appropriate their wives' wages as their property, and most male employers exclude women from wage labor. Such lopsided systems increase male dominance and make it hard for women to negotiate or demand what they need to support themselves and their children. Because men rarely take responsibility for children, the children of the world are at risk.

The most blatantly exploitive form of development is what is called sexploitation or sex-tourism, a new business, tours for men to Third World countries to visit brothels created specially for them, womaned by virtual slaves—girls, often just children, sold into bondage by poor peasant fathers. *Sex-tourism was proposed as a development strategy by international aid agencies.* Maria Mies writes that the sex industry was first planned and supported by the World Bank, the IMF, and the United States Agency for International Development.[6] Thailand, the Philippines, and South Korea are the present centers of Asian sex-tourism. Parties of Japanese businessmen are flown to one of these centers by their companies as a reward. American workers at a construction site in Saudi Arabia, totally fenced off from the culture around them, were flown to Bangkok every two weeks to be serviced by Thai women working in massage parlors. Another part of the sex industry is marriage brokerage: private companies, most in what used to be West Germany, sell Asian or Latin American women as wives, openly advertising them as "submissive, nonemancipated, and docile." Both industries are maintained by a support network of multinational tourist enterprises, hotel chains, airlines, and their subsidiary industries and services.

The global accounting system reveals the profundity of male contempt for the necessary in human life, treating not just women's work but the environment as insignificant. In a damning indictment, Waring describes international environmental policies that directly affect all of us. Consider: economic statistics calculate the value of "undeveloped" rain forest in Brazil at $0. A standing tree offers shade and coolness, prevents erosion, and returns oxygen to the atmosphere. But it has no value in the GDP until it is cut down. Industry has polluted the earth irrevocably; many of us or our children will die from cancers caused by environmental poisoning, or will suffer miscarriage, stillbirth, blindness, organ damage, or insanity. But unless such poisonings become widely known, as at Love Canal or Three Mile Island, such illness is invisible to the UNSNA.

In fact, while common sense dictates that illness should be listed as a debit in national income accounting, medical care and medicines are given *positive* value. Economists say market prices (of medical treatment, in this case) are reflections of actual wants, but there is no way quantitatively to express wants for clean air, safe water, or standing forests. Nor is permanent damage to water, air, or ecosystems included in the accounting. The only item subtracted from the GNP is depreciation on the stock of capital goods—the cost of maintaining stock like nuclear bombs. The cost of cleaning up an ecological disaster is considered an expression of society's "preferences."

The most devastating indication of our values is that while producing and raising children, maintaining families, and preserving the environment count for nothing in global economic accounting, war is treated as productive and valuable. In 1988, the nations of the world spent over $110 for each man, woman, and child on military expenses—overwhelmingly more than on food, water, shelter, health, education, or protecting the ecosystem. Waring explains that militarization can be measured nationally as the share of the GDP devoted to the production of military goods and services or as the military share of a nation's budget. It is measured globally by the military share of global production and the share of international trade occupied by armaments. From 1980 to 1984, world military spending grew from $564 billion to $649 billion (in 1980 prices), a growth rate of over 3.5 percent. Over 5 percent of the production of the world, 27 times more than was spent on overseas development, was spent on the military in 1983, most by industrialized countries. Global military expenditures in 1985 were $900 billion, more than the income of half the human race. Military expenditures surpassed the combined GDP of China, India, and all of sub-Saharan Africa—a sum comparable to the combined GNP of all of Africa and Latin America.

Waring cites an estimate of over 70 million people engaged, directly or indirectly, in military work, work counted as contributing to the GDP of their countries. Military work is counted as a valuable contribution to society; raising children is not. Nor do we value keeping them alive. In the twentieth century alone, the world has fought at least 207 wars that killed 78 million people. And while states glorify the soldiers who fight the wars, most of those killed in them are women and children. In each minute that passes, thirty children die from want of food or inexpensive vaccines; in that same minute, the world's governments spend $1.3 million of wealth produced by the public (between two-thirds and three-quarters of it by women) on military expenditures. This, Waring asserts, is the real war.

A billion human beings go to bed hungry every night of their lives in chronic undernourishment: the majority are women and children. An average of 50,000 people a day die from starvation and the effects of malnutrition: the majority are women and children. Even in rich countries, chronic malnutrition afflicts millions, mainly old people and families headed by unemployed women with dependent children. In the United States, 12 million children are without medical coverage and 5 million teeter on the edge of homelessness. Poor prenatal care in what may be the richest country in the world means, writes economist Sylvia Hewlett, that "a baby born in the shadow of the White House is now more likely to die in the first year of life than a baby born in Costa Rica."[7]

Such problems are commonly viewed as personal—abandoned women are blamed for not being able to hold on to their husbands, for aging, being unattractive, or whatever faults their husbands may claim. But the problem is really systemic: Western society requires women to rear children in the isolated confines of the home. The economic and moral system of the United States requires women to take care of their families without pay, pension plan, or medical insurance of their own. The force of moral opprobrium was (and to some degree is still) exerted on women to force them into this position, backed by rules excluding them from wage work, or confining them to such low-paid jobs that they cannot afford to pay for child care. Even without external pressure, it is very difficult to earn enough to support a family and raise children at the same time. *The system forces mothers into dependency on men.* But neither fathers nor the state are forced to support the women who maintain society. Judges may award divorced women child support or alimony payments, but the majority of men in fact pay little or nothing, and welfare assistance is both demeaning and insufficient. And the system treats older wives whose children are grown, and who may have been out of the work force for thirty or forty years, as owed nothing—despite their years of work and responsibility for others.

This discounting of "women's work"—which is essentially taking care of all of society—has disastrous effects on women in industrial as well as agricultural societies. Women in socialist nations have long maintained that they hold two jobs to men's one. But this is the case in all industrial states—it is just more of a burden in countries lacking food, consumer goods, and labor-saving appliances. Women in rich Western states have the same problems. When they protest, men say "What do women want? They say they want jobs, then decide they want a baby or complain about being overworked. We *told* them it wasn't a tea party out here in the real world." But women are overburdened not by being in the "real world," but by having two jobs. It seems never to occur to men that taking care of themselves and raising their children should be everyone's work, not solely women's. That overworked women have less energy and time for demanding jobs legitimates men in excluding women from them. The circle again.

Transnational corporations hire Third World women to work for low wages in factories, and co-opt their men by making them "bosses." Western women workers too are affected by the increasing tendency of business firms to create systems requiring almost no intelligence or skill from (mainly female) workers in order to pay them minimum wages for mindless work that deprives them of any autonomy. And economic analysts predict that in the future most women will be hired only in low-paid jobs.[8]

Men exclude women almost completely from managerial positions. In Bangladesh and Indonesia, women hold 1 percent of such posts. In Norway and Australia, male managers outnumber females by 3 to 1. In the United States, women hold less than one-half of 1 percent of jobs in the highest echelons of corporate managers and only 3 percent of the top five jobs below CEO at all Fortune 1000 companies. Women earn less than 75 percent as much as men doing the same or similar work; they are still 60 percent of the world's illiterates—and these figures are *improvements*.[10] In societies that value primarily money and power, the value of a group is shown by its financial reward. Below is a breakdown of figures from the Bureau of Labor Statistics on median income in the United States in 1987, when for the first time women earned 70 percent as much as men.[11]

	Median Income
Entire population	$381 per week
All men	445
All women	309
Whites	391
Blacks	306
White men	462
Black men	334
Hispanic men	316
White women	312
Black women	283
Hispanic women	253
Male managers and administrators	667
Male professionals	628
Male technicians	501
Female professionals and mechanics	475
Female executives, administrators, and managers	421

This is after fifteen years of feminist agitation, begun when women earned only 59 percent of male wages. Demands for equal pay for equal work are a mockery when most people remain clustered in segregated jobs: of 504 occupations listed in the 1980 United States Census, 275 were dominated by one sex (by 80 percent or more). And male occupations *always* pay more than female occupations.

Partly because of job segregation, men reach their peak in earnings and prestige between the ages of 45 and 64, but women reach their peak earnings at 44 and decline immediately afterward. The most recent statistics show that in 1989 the median annual income of women between 45 and 54 was $20,466, only 59 percent of the median income of men the same ages, $34,684; and women between 55 and 64 earned 57.7 percent of male wages—$18,727 compared to $32,476. These statistics, drawn from Labor Department, Census Bureau, and other agencies' data, appear in a report by the Older Women's League, which adds that "less than half the wage gap could be explained by differences in education or work experience."[12]

The figures are even more depressing if we factor in race. There has been some convergence in work experience for black and white women, who now join the labor force at an almost identical rate. Black women have increasingly left domestic and service jobs (like janitoring) to join white women in clerical occupations, but they continue to earn less even than white women, and their unemployment rates are twice white women's. Black women are far more likely than white women to live in poverty, because of their lower earning capacity and because black men earn much less, on average, than white men.[13]

Political analysts in the United States, discussing a swing to the right in recent decades, suggest that one factor in this shift is whites' resentment of laws that redress traditional discrimination against people of color. No analysis I have seen links it to an element that became apparent in the same period, a "gender gap" in voting as women increasingly vote as a bloc against conservative candidates. Yet removing barriers to full citizenship for women affects men more intimately than removing them for people of color. Men's motivation to shift to conservativism may well be their opposition to women's increased economic power and political voice. Clearly, both women and people of color are aware of the nature of the battle, even if it is not publicly discussed; both tend to vote for liberal candidates. The "gender gap" is also a "color gap": one could say the gap is between white males and everyone else. But white males remain dominant.

A major force in impelling the swing to the right is the New Right. Marilyn Power describes this group as social revolutionaries whose doctrines center on a return to patriarchal family structure by forcing women back into economic dependency on men and rescinding legal abortion.[14] The New Right, which draws lower-middle-class whites by stressing a free market and (white male) individualism opposed to the state, helped elect the conservative administrations of Ronald Reagan and George Bush.

Reagan and Bush proclaimed ideological agreement with New Right anti-woman policies (under the euphemism "protecting the family") but found them too disruptive to pursue directly. But over the last decade, their administrations undermined the gains made by people of color and women. Reagan's main agenda in office was to restructure the economy to make big capital more profitable and to reestablish the global political and economic dominance of the United States. His administration dealt with economic crisis by making massive cuts in social services, tax cuts favoring the rich and corporations, and undermining labor unions, but increased rather than cut military spending, generating a severe recession. The result was a redistribution of income from the poor working class (many of whom are now homeless indigents) to wealthy individuals and corporations (many of whom have since collapsed under the weight of their own greed): 60 percent of the cuts in federal entitlement programs in fiscal 1982 came from programs for the poor.[15]

Since women were already the bulk of the poor (women and children made up four-fifths of the poorest class in America even before Reagan), they bore the brunt of these cuts—especially women of color. In 1978, one out of five families in the United States was supported and maintained by a single parent (compared with one in nine in 1970), usually a woman. Families of women raising children alone are 5.5 times more likely to be poor than those with a man present; a family raised by a black woman alone is 10.5 times as likely to be poor as the family of a white man.

So these cuts only seemed sex-neutrally directed at "the poor," not at women. They were in fact rooted in patriarchist theory, which is woman-hating. The idea that poverty is a result of human inferiority is rooted in the beliefs that aggressive pursuit of wealth is a characteristic of superior human beings and that economic inequality, stratification of classes, is adaptive, beneficial to the human race. This is essentially to worship domination. Conservatives like Reagan believe that poverty is a result of personal failure and that programs aimed at ameliorating poverty actually increase and perpetuate it by encouraging sloth in the poor. This belief masks an implicit agenda on women, which Power finds most clearly articulated in George Gilder's *Wealth and Poverty*, highly praised by Reagan and his director of the Office of Management and Budget, David Stockman.

Asserting that the keys to success in a capitalist economy are work, family, and faith, Gilder claims the poor are poor because they lack these. Defining "family" as the patriarchal nuclear family with male "head" and economically dependent female "homemaker," he disapproves of women working for wages because their economic power disrupts this "ideal" arrangement and may lead to its collapse. Dismissing the huge numbers of hungry children in this country, Gilder vehemently attacks social programs like Aid to Families with Dependent Children (AFDC) for their supposed effect on *men*. He blasts AFDC for "making optional the male provider role" and demoralizing low-income men who, unmanned, "cuckolded by the compassionate state," tend to leave their families. Families without men are doomed to poverty because women inevitably earn low incomes. By this logic, he would eliminate all options allowing women to live independently of men on the ground that *female wage-earning is responsible for poverty, urban decay, and crime.*

A broader logic would focus on male responsibility—not just in poor men, but those who control most of the country's resources—but blaming the victim is always safe because she can rarely fight back. An equally cruel bit of economic persecution was revealed in a study directed by Ian Ayres, a professor at Northwestern University School of Law. Six people between twenty-four and twenty-eight, college-educated and well dressed, were taught the same script and body language. The testers—one black man, one black woman, one white woman, and three white men—visited ninety car dealerships in Chicago. Despite the fact that a few of the salespeople were black or female, across the board white men were given the best deal on the cars. The people who could most easily afford a car were charged least; those who could least afford one were charged most. The testers found that white women were charged $150 more for a car than white men, black men $400 more than white men, and black women *$900* more than white men.[16]

POLITICAL DISCRIMINATION

Historians call ancient Athens the seat of democracy because it was the first state to establish a system allowing all citizens to vote. *But only about 6 percent of the population were citizens;* women and slaves could not be citizens, and law kept women in near-slavery. We are taught that the political revolutions of recent centuries have advanced democracy, that more people have a voice in government than in the past. This may be true, although most contemporary "democratic" systems mask the fact that the real power in the state is held by anonymous men who run huge corporations and important institutions. In any case, "democratic" rule, supposed rule by "the people," the citizens of a country, never included women at all until this century.

Discussions of women and political power often confuse two very different situations: an extraordinary woman coming to power as an individual in a mainly male governing establishment; and political power held by women-as-a-caste, women-in-general. Since the rise of the state, no state has ever allowed women in general to have a voice. But women could rule in many systems, especially monarchies. The first states were ruled by a single man supported by his clan, who appropriated the production and sometimes the land of those they dominated. But men in clans were surrounded by women—mothers, wives, sisters, concubines, and slaves. Within families, women matter, hold personal (as opposed to formal) power, and often rise to power. Most have held power behind the scenes, influencing the male ruler, or acting as regent for an underage male ruler, but many ruled directly in their own right, from the earliest Sumerian and Japanese states to the monarchies of medieval Europe. But most ruled along the male model: elite women may hold political power without any change in the situation of women-as-a-caste. They do not speak in women's voice.

That is because where they can hold power, women rulers are

women only incidentally, seen as extraordinary, able to overcome the "weaknesses" of their sex. Nevertheless, all are subjected to special attack because of their sex (the Chinese blamed emperors' concubines for the fall of dynasties). It may be ironic that a woman, Indira Gandhi, ruled a nation that more than any other kills its females, but the two factors are unrelated. That Indira Gandhi, Golda Meir, or Margaret Thatcher held power does not mean their countries have less contempt for women than others. Today, women usually come to power in countries with traditions of inherited elite rule: elite men may allow women of their own class to hold power if they have the potential to unify a country, counting on their being malleable to male control (as Indian Congress Party men mistakenly thought Indira Gandhi and Israeli Labor Party men thought Golda Meir). Whether or not such women defer to male control, men can usually count on them to uphold class interests. Women need servants more than men do, not having wives. And they know they govern by men's sufferance.

India elects more women to top political posts than other countries because it has a tradition of rule by an elite linked by blood: it is still a feudal nation. Few monarchies remain, but countries ruled by elites that are clans, extended families, within which women can hold influence, run on similar principles. In India, class (caste) distinctions are of huge importance and difficult to overcome. In 1990, there was a larger percentage of women in the lower house of India's Parliament (7.9 percent) than in the American House of Representatives (6.4 percent); women comprise 9–10 percent of the Indian upper house, but only two out of 100 U.S. senators are women. Economist Amartya Sen notes that more women were tenured at Delhi University than at Harvard, where Sen teaches now.[17] However, as the Indian caste system gradually erodes and becomes less constricting, elite women will no longer be privileged over lower-class men; indeed, fewer women of this generation have important government jobs than in the first generation after independence.

In both governments and economic institutions, as supposed merit succeeds blood as a standard, systems become more impersonal and more male-dominant. Women have the least access to power in systems supposedly based on merit, where rank is earned, not inherited. This is not, as some men claim, because women are less competent, but because they are foreclosed from the avenues by which it is earned. In systems controlled by male cliques—military oligarchies or so-called democracies—rank is earned by military combat service (which excludes women), work experience, or political experience (from both of which women are largely excluded). When educated men began to have a voice in Europe in the fourteenth century, women were forbidden to attend most universities, and few had even a rudimentary education. Simply by this single exclusion, men kept women out of political and religious life and all professions except midwifery. (They soon barred midwives as well—or burned them.)

Today, women are educated in most industrial countries, and can work in a variety of (but not all) areas. But male superiors, reluctant to advance them, rarely place them on a track to higher office. In nonindustrial or developing countries, women hold about 6 percent of government posts; in most European nations, they hold 5 to 11 percent. But in 1989 the Inter-Parliamentary Union reported that the percentage of women in the world's legislatures had *fallen*. In 1975, at the outset of the U.N. Decade for Women, women made up 12.5 percent of the world's parliaments; in early 1988, 14.6 percent; but by 1989, they had dropped again to 12.7 percent.[18] Women's voice is being voided in newly emerging Eastern European states too: top government posts in Hungary and Romania are held exclusively by men; in Poland a woman was minister of culture in Tadeusz Mazowiecki's cabinet, but Lech Walesa has not appointed even one.

On the other hand, many women occupy high political positions in the Scandinavian countries and some tiny countries like Dominica and the Netherlands Antilles. Gro Harlem Brundtland has several times functioned as prime minister of Norway, and several states have female presidents (a largely honorary position). A Norwegian research institute commissioned a study, called Scenario 2000, to delve into the causes of this seemingly feminist shift. Norway is (in my experience) one of the most feminist countries in the world; men as well as women support equal rights at least in principle. But the scholars, business executives, and politicians involved in the study suggested that one reason women were gaining prominence in public life was that men were leaving it. Like the American men who ruled New England Protestant churches when church and state were unified but deserted in large numbers (leaving religion to the women) when capitalism opened a route to greater power, Norwegian men are deserting the fairly narrow field of Norwegian politics for the more profitable and powerful transnational corporations. The report concluded: "Women may be moving from a marginal minority to a marginal majority."[19]

This is not yet the case in the United States, where, as of 1990, two women sat in the 100-seat Senate and there were 29 women out of 435 Representatives (6 percent). Here in the heartland of feminism where, we are told, women rule men, women have less voice in government than in nonindustrial countries. In 1986, 151 women held posts in state cabinets—17.9 percent.[20] In 1990, three women won governorships in the fifty states; they won 18 percent of state legislature seats; 54 hold state executive offices. It could be worse: in April 1990, men in the Swiss canton of Appenzell Inner Rhoden voted to continue to bar women from voting at all.[21]

Moreover, the few women who do operate in the public realm are subjected to a kind of attack rarely leveled at men (although the first black mayor of New York City, David Dinkins, has come in for criticism of his dress and manner—but not his sexuality). When Margaret Thatcher was prime minister of Great Britain, journalists regularly impugned her sexuality, her husband's "virility" (read dominance over her), and criticized her dress and manner. Yet she was the most extraordinary world leader of her time! While criticism of Margaret Thatcher's policies was legitimate, such personal attacks function forcibly to remind female leaders that they are under the constant surveillance of men who will pounce on any move to alter government policy toward women. It is doubtful if a strongly feminist woman could win major political office in any nation, but even if Golda Meir, Indira Gandhi, Margaret Thatcher, or later, Benazir Bhutto had had the inclination to ease women's lot, they would not have dared to do so. With a few exceptions, only male leaders dare to eliminate laws constricting women.

Men's hatred for women in the public realm extends even to the wives of political leaders. Barbara Bush escapes criticism by presenting herself as motherly. Pat Nixon was the object of considerable sympathy in later years, but when her husband was President journalists attacked her for brittleness. Wives who are perceived as having minds that might influence their husbands come in for the worst attacks. Journalists spewed contempt at Rosalyn Carter, an intelligent, dedicated, and hardworking partner to President Jimmy Carter. They viciously stabbed Nancy Reagan for her taste for luxury, her weight, and her clothes, but hated her for her influence on her husband (which seems to have been mainly positive: for instance, she opposed his going to Bitburg and wanted him to restrain CIA director William Casey). Being far more serious than Nancy Reagan does not exempt Raisa Gorbachev from attack. Soviet men resent her assertiveness and style. A deputy in a government forum even attacked her on prime-time television.[22] Asserting (falsely) that Napoleon was "tempted" into tyranny by "sycophants and his wife," he accused Mikhail Gorbachev of showing imperialist tendencies because he too was "incapable of avoiding the adulation and influence of [his] wife."

THE OBLITERATION OF WOMEN FROM HISTORY

One way men perpetuate women's exclusion from political life is by obliterating evidence of their participation in public affairs. Men close ranks to appropriate women's projects or attribute them to men; male historians present a united front in omitting women from all kinds of history. Few people know about the many female rulers, philosophers, scientists, artists, writers, and inventors of the past, yet some were highly influential and many contributed to human knowledge and well-being. We cannot remedy this lack here, but we can describe a recent case in which women founded a very important organization, only to be thrust out of it and their record expunged.

The organization was Poland's Solidarity, which was begun by two women. Anna Walentynowicz joined the Lenin shipyard in Gdansk as a welder in the Rosa Luxemburg Brigade over thirty years ago[23]. In 1953, after she had the temerity to complain that women were given lower financial incentives than men, she was arrested and interrogated for eight hours. In 1968, she protested corruption in government trade unions and was fired. She was later allowed to return to work but began in the 1970s to agitate for free democratic trade unions. Subjected to constant harassment and intimidation, she endured, earning her fellow workers' respect.

In 1980, working as a crane operator in the Lenin yard, she fell ill. While she was on leave, she was dismissed. The yard went on strike in protest, demanding her reinstatement and that of Lech Walesa (who had also been fired), a wage increase, and a promise to build a monument to honor workers killed in the December 1970 strike. Other shipyards struck in sympathy. In two days, the Lenin yard acceded to its workers' demands, and they prepared to go back to their jobs. But Walentynowicz and a young nurse, Alina Pienkowska, objected to what they saw as a betrayal of workers at the other yards, whose demands had not been met. They ran back to the hall to stop the return, but the microphones had been turned off. Walentynowicz explains, "The shipyard loudspeakers were announcing that the strike was over and everyone had to leave by six P.M. The gates were open and people were leaving." Everyone, even Walesa, was willing to go back to work. The two women ran to the main gate; Walentynowicz called out urging a solidarity strike, reminding the workers that the manager had met their demands only because the other yards were on strike. If they were defeated, the Lenin workers might be too.

The tired workers either paid no attention to her or challenged her authority. Tired too, she began to weep. But Alina Pienkowska leaped up on a barrel and cried out, "We have to help the others with their strikes because they have helped us!" Someone shouted, "She's right!" Someone else closed the gate. The workers returned to the hall to continue the strike. Out of their negotiations, Solidarity was born in September 1980. In December 1981, the Polish government invoked martial law. Safe in southern Poland, Walentynowicz nevertheless returned to the yard to help organize. The workers erected barricades and set up a hospital.

They had no weapons. At six in the morning, ZOMO, the Polish riot police, began to push in. "I tried to walk in front of them but the workers stopped me. They smuggled me out and I stayed in a private flat." But ZOMO found her. She was seized and imprisoned, along with Pienkowska and other leaders.

The government held Walentynowicz under cruel conditions, in a men's ward with no privacy, until 1983; then she was released but forbidden to return to the shipyard. She smuggled herself in and was arrested and sent to a prison hospital for psychiatric observation: "They wanted to prove I was insane." Jane Atkinson, interviewing her, asked about a rumor that the government released the women prisoners because they constituted no political threat. Walentynowicz laughed: "They always said Alina was a better negotiator with the government because, unlike Lech, she never compromised and she always got what she wanted." Walentynowicz could not return to work at the yard (Walesa did), got no pension, and lost everything while she was in prison (her flat was looted). Men took over Solidarity. She shrugs: "The men are the public speakers; they have the authority and power. It's part of their makeup to feel they are first and they don't want to share it." She was poor and unemployed; Walesa became president of Poland.

The men of Solidarity did not just appropriate a union Walentynowicz started, they pushed her out of it, impugned her sanity (a common way to attack women), and obliterated her from history. If it were not for *MS.* magazine, we would not know she existed. Yet this irrepressible woman is now rebelling against Walesa's government: she founded a new labor organization, the Independent Trade Union, and in March 1991 led a strike at the same Gdansk shipyard, for higher pay and quicker privatization of the yard.[24]

RELIGIOUS WARS AGAINST WOMEN

Although every country erects barriers to women in its economic and political systems, and women's political and economic situation is worse than men's in every country in the world, the figures on political representation cited earlier show improvement over two decades ago, before feminism organized women globally. But major international institutions are working to revoke these gains, to return women to a more subordinate and subjugated position. These institutions are religious, the repositories of many women's trust and faith.

All major world religions are patriarchal. They were founded to spread or buttress male supremacy—which is why their gods are male. But there is nothing inherently patriarchal about the religious impulse; religious people define god in their own way, and under pressure from feminism, many churches are trying to eliminate the more egregious patriarchal elements from their symbology. In response to this, other churches have become more rigidly, even fanatically, patriarchal in a movement called fundamentalism. Jewish and Muslim thinkers insist the term "fundamentalist" does not describe the new movements in Judaism or Islam, but journalists tend to call all zealous right-wing religious movements "fundamentalist."[25] That outsiders apply the term to groups that share few or no religious principles but which are all equally ferocious about strong male control over women indicates they have picked up the subtext of these movements, their real if tacit agenda. Writers on fundamentalist sects rarely discuss women, but the only characteristic shared by all religions called fundamentalist is their war to dominate women even more totally.

PROTESTANTISM Women were important to the founding and spread of Protestantism. But men seeking power in America found anti-hierarchical Protestantism less attractive once industrial capitalism offered them other paths to power. As men deserted it, Protestantism became largely a church of women. The fundamentalist revivals of both the nineteenth and twentieth centuries were intended to reassert male dominance over the churches and the family and prevent Protestant women from being drawn into the orbit of feminism—but they were mounted under very different, exalted, banners.

American Protestant fundamentalists claim to uphold the fundamentals of Christianity. They imply that other Protestants have abandoned these tenets, otherwise all Protestants would be "fundamentalist" and no separate group would adopt the label. A fundamentalist authority who was Jerry Falwell's mentor wrote:

> The fundamentals of the Christian faith include the inspiration and thus the divine authority of the Bible; the deity, virgin birth, blood atonement, bodily resurrection, personal second coming of Christ; the fallen, lost condition of all mankind; salvation by repentance and faith, grace without works; eternal doom in Hell of the unconverted and eternal blessedness of the saved in Heaven.[26]

These ideas are accepted by Christians who do not consider themselves fundamentalists, but most American Protestant fundamentalists also accept evangelicism—a belief that the Bible was dictated by god and is the highest authority, that eternal salvation was won only by Jesus' atoning for human sin, and that the greatest act of charity is to inform others of this gospel promise of salvation. Thus fundamentalists are militant, ready to fight for their religion. Whether attacking modernist theology or secular humanism, American Protestant fundamentalists are religious warriors. Combativeness is a characteristic they share with "fundamentalist" Jews and Muslims.

Most fundamentalists also believe in dispensational premillennialism. Dispensationalism is the belief that human history is divided into seven ages or dispensations, each ending with dramatic divine intervention and judgment after the human race fails a test from god. The last age will be inaugurated by the return of Jesus, who will establish his kingdom and reign for a thousand years—the millennium—in Jerusalem: literally. We, in the sixth age, are about to be destroyed, but believers will be exempted from destruction by "the secret rapture." Dispensational premillennialism is thus both a counsel of despair (humans are doomed to destruction) and an exemption from responsibility (the saved are not responsible for the evil of our age; having remained true to fundamentals, they will be saved from destruction). And because fundamentalists are not responsible to society outside their own churches (until very recently, hard-core fundamentalists made separation from mainline denominations a test of faith), any means they use to impose their beliefs is justified.

But to get to the heart of fundamentalism, we must leave the exalted realm of abstract belief and focus on concrete particulars. Fundamentalists are militant about the Bible, doctrine, and daily behavior; they forbid smoking, drinking, dancing, card playing, immodest dress, and any sexual behavior outside marriage. Richard Hofstadter finds them anti-intellectual, paranoid, militant, and oppositionalist, yet devoted to populist democracy. Hofstadter's fundamentalists cannot tolerate ambiguity and are phobic about sexuality: they bar sexual behavior outside marriage, and even any verbal reference to sexuality, and would like to extend the taboo to the entire society.[27]

Psychiatrist Mortimer Ostow agrees that fundamentalists are subservient to charismatic male leaders and believe women should be segregated from men, assuming their "natural state" in society and the family. But Ostow feels Hofstadter exaggerates when he describes fundamentalists as having a "thoroughgoing . . . fear of normal sex and deviation," because fundamentalists marry and have sex within marriage.[28] But—as we shall see—the family is the primary site of female subjection, which is achieved largely through sexuality: women are indoctrinated into their supposed "natural state" by male control of their sexuality in the family. To forbid sexual discussion outside the family is to maintain the privacy in which this subjection is imposed. For deeper understanding of fundamentalism's basic agenda, we must turn to a feminist scholar.

Betty DeBerg, who studied fundamentalism from its late nineteenth-century emergence, asserts that most analysts of fundamentalism interpret it mainly as an intellectual or theological response to modernist biblical criticism, evolutionary theory, or social science, and that only a few see it as a reaction, only incidentally religious, to significant changes in American society.[29] Theologian H. Richard Niebuhr saw it as a regional (Southern) rural protest against urbanization and industrialization, but most scholars today agree that it arose in middle-class white urban culture outside the south. While noting the great social changes that occurred between 1880 and 1930—industrialization, urban-

ization, immigration, a consumer economy, and World War I—
DeBerg argues that none of these factors affected as many Americans as intimately and intensely as changes in sex roles in the same period.

The men who dominated fundamentalism, and those they appealed to, were living through a revolution that threatened their self-definition as superior by virtue of sex: they were losing control over women. After 1850, as more and more girls were educated and took jobs that expanded their worlds beyond the home, their new economic and social resources placed them to some degree beyond their fathers' control. Men with less control over fewer children, DeBerg remarks, had to depend largely on subordinate *wives* to reflect their superiority at home. But subordinate wives were getting harder to find: women gained more power within marriage over the century: acts guaranteeing married women's property rights were passed in many states, and after 1870 a precursor to today's fight for legal abortion emerged—the voluntary motherhood movement. Linda Gordon studied this movement, which was closely associated with the purity movement, and became part of the agendas of suffragist, moral reform, church auxiliary, and free-love or marriage reform movements.[30]

In an age in which contraception was illegal, the voluntary motherhood movement supported women who tried to control the frequency of sex and stop rape and other sexual abuses within marriage, encouraging them to avoid unwanted pregnancies by asserting control over their own bodies. Daniel Scott Smith considers the movement a major factor in the steady decline of the birth rate throughout the nineteenth century despite the inadequacy or unavailability of artificial contraception and the fact that most American women were married—89 percent to 96 percent of those over forty-five.[31] The movement was part of a larger tendency of American women to claim the right to control their own sexuality, whether to avoid pregnancy or to express desire: statistics show that half the married women born between 1900 and 1920 and two-thirds of those born between 1910 and 1920 had sexual relations with at least one man before marriage.

Women were claiming the right to control the use of their bodies to the point that many (mainly "New Women," educated women with careers) refused to marry at all. This was shocking defiance—in patriarchy, marriage is always compulsory for women. Speaking of a "revolt" against marriage, Carl Degler estimates that a quarter of all female college graduates and half the women with doctorates remained single in 1900.[32] Moreover, women who did marry divorced at a startling new rate. Between 1870 and 1930, the U.S. divorce rate jumped fivefold; during the 1920s, two-thirds of divorces were initiated by women. Many observers felt the institution of marriage itself was under attack— by feminism.

DeBerg shows that at the turn of the century, as women moved into independence and rights over their own bodies, fundamentalist rhetoric became obsessed with domestic relations, sexual identity and behavior, and "proper" gender spheres. A set of books, *Fundamentals*, published between 1910 and 1913, laid out the basics of the movement, but preachers focused as much on women's behavior as on religious precepts. James H. Brookes, founder of the premillennialist Niagara Conferences, called Elizabeth Cady Stanton's *Woman's Bible* (1898) a "miserable abortion . . . the impudent utterance of infidelity." A popular evangelical preacher gave a sermon ("The Choice of a Wife") declaring that any woman who attended lectures like Stanton's was *"an awful creature*, and you had better not come near such a reeking lepress. She needs to be washed, and for three weeks to be soaked in carbolic acid, and for a whole year fumigated, before she is fit for decent society."

Battle cries for a return to the Victorian ideology of separate spheres flooded popular fundamentalist literature. In 1921, a major fundamentalist journal advertised "Wanted—More Mothers: We are short on homes; *real* homes. We are short on mothers; *real* mothers . . . God designed woman as the *homemaker* but somehow she seems to have gotten sidetracked."[33] As always, the emancipation of women was equated with the destruction of the family. The fundamentalists knew how to "save" the family: the church had become too "feminized" and had to be returned to male control. Men must be in authority in every sphere, they said, and women must suffer subordination within the domestic sphere.

There is a full-fledged rebellion under way not only against
the headship of man in government and church but in the
home. Statistics of Yale and Harvard show that women of
the better homes are not having children, the average showing less than one child to a family. . . . The cultivation of
the modern's woman's idea of "my individuality" is bound
to be a destroyer of the home life.[34]

With perfect assurance that this was sanctioned by god, these
men ordered women to give up ambition and personal well-being
for the sake of their families, especially their husbands and brothers; ministers told women their true mission and fulfillment lay
in "self-sacrificing service." Woman's lot was suffering, "one of
the great privileges of the Christian life," a female path to em-
ulating Jesus.[35] Woman suffrage would destroy True Womanhood
and threaten the home, which was sacred: evangelist Billy Sunday
called it "the most sacred spot on the globe." They bemoaned
that few men attended church, and campaigned to attract them
first by diminishing women's influence and power (by impugning
the legitimacy of women speaking and holding positions of authority within the church), and second by replacing the feminized
rhetoric of Christianity as a church of compassion and nutritiveness with a masculinized language of virility, militarism, and
Christian heroism.

The King's Business (cited several times above) was published
by the Bible Institute of Los Angeles, which, with the Moody
Bible Institute, trained women lay ministers and publicly en-
dorsed women's right to speak and teach. All writers and editors
of fundamentalist journals, however, opposed ordaining women
to traditional parish ministry on the grounds that god's and nature's order would be disrupted if women were given authority
over men. But women had been virtually running the churches
for nearly a century, as men abandoned them. Twentieth-century
fundamentalists were far less tolerant of any female leadership in
churches than their nineteenth-century counterparts—yet the religion had not changed.[36] One journal having already admonished
its readers in 1895 to protest "whenever an 'advanced' woman
attempts a harmful innovation in one of our churches," by 1917

was striking a more strident tone, warning that feminism, having "wrought such evil in social and domestic life," was now "invading the sacred realm of the church."[37] When the Independent Fundamental Churches of America (formerly the American Conference of Undenominational Churches) was founded in 1930, it officially excluded women from membership. In the same year, fundamentalist A. J. Gordon's Gordon College voted to limit women students to a third of the total. The Moody Bible Institute stopped accepting women in its Pastor's Class: the last woman graduated from it in 1929.

Casting aspersions on religions in which women were central—theosophy, spiritualism, Christian Science, and Pentecostalism—and drumming into their audiences that female authority in churches was illegitimate, fundamentalists began to campaign to rid the church of Christian symbols and doctrine characterized as "passive," "soft," creating "a very chicken-hearted set of people," in favor of "muscular Christianity." Even male historians note "an overwhelming fear of effeminacy and an exaggerated attention to masculinity" in the fundamentalism of this period.[38] Seeking to return men into American religious life and reassert male authority in the church, one fundamentalist minister would praise another for being "a real man," a "manly Methodist," for having fought in a war. The words "man," "manhood," and "masculinity" become an obsessive refrain in fundamentalist sermons and writings.

Many attributed the huge popularity of Billy Sunday to his exaggeratedly "masculine" (I would call it pugnacious) demeanor. He reveled in threatening physical violence, even murder, praying, "Lord save us from off-handed, flabby-cheeked, brittle-boned, weak-kneed, thin-skinned, pliable, plastic, spineless, effeminate, sissified, three-carat Christianity." A male historian feels he "spoke intuitively to the deepest confusion of his age and to the realities most troubling his evangelical audiences."[39] Fundamentalists praised their own virility, militancy, militarism, hardness, and inflexibility, seen as elements of control, declaring modernist theologians "women," college professors "effeminate," "sissified," "effeminate ginks," and modern theology "emasculated Christianity." And conservative evangelicals did draw unusually large numbers of men; Sunday converted more men, especially young men, than women. (A militaristic morality always creates bigots: similar values and rhetoric pervaded late nineteenth- and early twentieth-century European thought, especially in Germany, where it nourished the Nazi movement.)

Fundamentalists also attacked cultural treatments of sexuality, castigating the theater, books, and movies for encouraging "social vice" and "laxity in the observance of the obligation of marriage relations." Film was one of the greatest dangers to public and private morality, fundamentalists said, because theater owners did not attend church, actors were moral degenerates, movie advertisements offered "passion and thrills," greedy producers produced trash rather than "wholesome" films, and movie houses were open on Sunday. But the main focus of their attacks was the woeful effects on women: movies, very popular with young women, contained "influences" that would destroy them; their "impure" plots familiarized girls with "sensual subjects," destroying their "proper delicacy," leading them into the peril of "present-day freedom." As in ancient Athens, women should not be discussed at all:

> When men begin to regard woman as a curious and complex social engima . . . they cease to pay her the old-fashioned deference which we like to regard as her unquestioned right. The less woman is considered as a "question" the surer she will be to fulfill her natural destiny.[40]

Fundamentalist propaganda especially condemned "cultivated Christian women" who patronized "frivolous and ofttimes sinful indulgences" like theater, cards, gambling, and mainly dancing, which "with its increased modern liberties of personal contact, breaks down personal barriers of safety." Dancing imperiled "purity" and "Christian character" because it "inflames passion [and] kindles salacious thoughts." Women's dress was a major theme in fundamentalist sermons in the early twentieth century. Ministers found flappers' dress indecent because their tight skirts did not uphold "the nice sense of the modesty which is the greatest safeguard of feminine virtue," but rather incited men, "arousing

the passions of the lower nature and causing impure thoughts."
Women were responsible for male sexuality: men are what they
are by nature and cannot be blamed for that. In sex and sex alone,
they granted Women control, since women were *by nature* in-
carnations of sex. As a minister explained in "The Word of God
on Women's Dress":

> Every man has a quantity of dynamite . . . in him. It did not
> come to him by cultivation, and it will not leave him by
> combatting. The frequent explosion of that dynamite and its
> result is a tragic part of the world's history. . . . Many men
> are made to commit sin in their hearts by the unclothed
> bodies of women who may be professed Christians and ig-
> norant of the evil they are doing in causing a brother to
> stumble and become weak.[41]

As today's fundamentalists oppose legal abortion, yesterday's
fought legalizing birth control on grounds that it was a sin and
would destroy the "race" (the white middle class). It was well
known, they argued, that the birthrate was declining faster among
native middle-class whites than among foreign-born, black, or
lower-class people. Abortion was also severely condemned, but
was not a major theme in popular fundamentalist literature of
the period despite soaring numbers of abortions between 1840 and
1888—performed mainly on married middle- and upper-class
white Protestant women.

Fundamentalists regularly blamed modernist theologies for
modern morality, which they of course found wanting, but for
them the word "morality" was code for traditional sex roles.
DeBerg's brilliant analysis of fundamentalist positions that seem
irrelevant to women—biblical inerrancy and creationism—shows
that fundamentalism arose *primarily* to counter feminism and
reassert male control (DeBerg claims only that it was partly so
intended).

No theological position is more closely identified with fundamentalism than biblical inerrancy, the claim that every word of
the Bible is absolutely true historically and inspired by god. The
Bible was compiled in a period when patriarchy was spreading,
and its editors altered early materials to eradicate signs of an

earlier female dominance and to make male supremacy a divine principle.[42] Like the *Iliad* and the *Aeneid*, the Old Testament is great literature that stresses war, male dominance, and murder (of enemies—but "enemies" always exist) more than compassion or tolerance. If it is god-given and without error, then its values, also god-given, are eternally right. Conservative evangelical Protestants use an inerrant Bible as a major weapon in their war to retain the separate spheres that guarantee male dominance.

Finding turn-of-the-century changes in family power structure a threat to the social order, fundamentalists attributed them to a loss of faith in the absolute truth of the Bible. They were sure that lower birthrates (read as women's "revolt against motherhood") and rapidly rising divorce rates (read as women's revolt against marriage) were inevitable results of a "revolt" against Paul's teachings in the Bible. The cure for divorce was "the restoration of the Bible to its proper place. . . . Let the husband and wife realize their God-appointed sphere and duties."[43] "Back to the Bible" meant "back to the home and the God-ordained family."[44]

The same subtext underlay creationism, belief in the biblical version of human origins. Fundamentalists abhorred (some still do) the theory of evolution because it offered a scientific explanation for the origins of life. Fundamentalist minister J. F. Norris told the Texas legislature that evolutionary theory "will destroy faith in the Bible" by contradicting the account of creation given in Genesis, which was "the foundation upon which everything rests." In fact, no religious tenet except male supremacy rests on the Genesis myth. Without explicitly linking evolutionary theory to women's revolt against male supremacy, Norris insisted that the main objective of anti-evolution legislation (barring the teaching of evolutionary theory in public schools, the grounds for the famous Scopes trial) was to defend the Christian home: "The home is God's first institution. . . . Let us do all we can to protect that institution, pass . . . laws to protect it and let none invade its sacred precincts."[45]

Fundamentalists also opposed the theory of evolution on grounds that it denied the personhood of the deity (god *is* a white man) and destroyed morality by degrading human beings to the status of animals or machines, obliterating their responsibility as moral agents. Evolution, they felt, precluded the existence of free will and thus moral responsibility. Again, to understand their real message, we have to locate the kind of moral responsibility they had in mind, and, of course, it was sexual and gendered. Norris made it explicit: evolution "breeds free-loveism. The apes . . . have never had a marriage license. . . . They change mates frequently."[46] Evolution leads to "liberalism of the Sabbath, liberalism of the law, liberalism on love, liberalism on divorce, liberalism on morals, liberalism on doctrine."[47] Fundamentalist morality, translated, meant almost solely female behavior: discussions of "morality" treat divorce, crimes committed by women, and girls drinking and smoking.

DeBerg concludes that fundamentalists were bothered not by evolution as scientific, philosophical, or theological principle, but by its anticipated effect on the conventions governing family life and sex roles. She believes creationism had a wide appeal because its rhetoric was permeated with arguments supporting Victorian sex roles and domestic conventions, arguing that people unable to follow complex intellectual debates on Darwinian theory could understand the significance of changing social mores—"their own understanding of who they were as men and as women and what they were to do." Changes in sex roles underlay their opposition to modernism in general: Christendom was declining into heathenism because family life was being "desecrated." The "revolt of youth" appalled them, not because youngsters were committing crimes or violence but because they were abandoning conventional Victorian domestic patterns and sexual mores.

Most analysts of nineteenth and early twentiety-century fundamentalism have concluded that it was not a political movement, because it dealt only with "personal ethics." Like political commentators today who dismiss feminism as a political movement (even as feminist novels pour from the presses, male critics deplore the dearth of political novels in our age), male analysts of fundamentalism ignore its major agenda—female subordination and separate spheres of activity—a "thoroughly political" agenda, DeBerg remarks. Analysts of the fundamentalism resuscitated in the 1970s as a major political and social force continue to censor this agenda. The few who note fundamentalists' opposition to the women's movement, abortion, and divorce believe this is a new theme; George Marsden wrote that their alliance with the Roman Catholic church on gender issues was new, and Douglas Frank, who praised the new fundamentalists for focusing on homosexuality and the Equal Rights Amendment, believed these concerns were innovative. But they are as old as fundamentalism itself.

The same men who are blind and deaf to feminism are acutely sensitive to what threatens their dominance and privilege. One of their responses is to join fundamentalist sects; another is to ally with them, as Reagan, Bush, and other conservative politicians have done. The new fundamentalists are extremely vocal and have increasingly entered the political realm in the past two decades, violating their own rule of segregation. Nancy Ammerman analyzed strict fundamentalists and found their main characteristic to be rigid separatism: out of an intense desire to avoid compromise and accommodation, each sect holds itself separate from all others and from political parties.[48] The only faction that does not demand strict separatism swelled to a majority in the Southern Baptist Convention in the 1970s and 1980s and now dominates the fundamentalist movement. Militant biblicist conservatives, they uphold separatism but justify their engagement in political activism by their desire to reform society. Their leading exponent in the 1970s, Jerry Falwell, founded the Moral Majority, a self-described special interest group linking millions of Americans who shared the same moral values and wanted to influence government. Falwell explains what triggered his activism:

Back in the sixties I was criticizing pastors who were taking time out of their pulpit to involve themselves in the civil rights movement or any other political venture. I said you're wasting your time from what you're called to do. Now I find myself doing the same thing and for the same reasons they did. Things began to happen. The invasion of humanism into the public school system began to alarm us back in the sixties. Then the Roe vs. Wade Supreme Court decision of

1973 and abortion on demand shook me up. Then adding to that gradual regulation of various things it became very apparent the federal government was going in the wrong direction and if allowed would be harassing non-public schools, of which I have one of 16,000 right now. So step by step we became convinced we must get involved if we're going to continue what we're doing.[49]

This engaged fundamentalist sect transmuted into the Moral Majority, which transmuted into the extreme right wing in American politics. Whether as the New Right, the Radical Religious Right, or the New Conservatism, it has become enormously powerful and has abandoned the position articulated by Falwell of wanting to *influence* government, aiming now to control it. It helped defeat the Equal Rights Amendment and has removed many liberals from office; it works to criminalize abortion, censor liberal ideas in the media and public education, and introduce "pro-family" laws. Most of its efforts in the last decade have been unsuccessful, but its propaganda and support contributed to the elections of Ronald Reagan and George Bush, and the swing to the right of the American electorate in general.

At the same time the electorate moved right, a pronounced "gender gap" appeared. The New Right rhetoric of morality masks its real agenda: to relegitimate and reimpose subordination on the working class, people of color, and women. A majority of blacks and women oppose it, but many white working-class men support it, men whose own interests it actually threatens, who have nothing to gain but their spurious "superiority" over blacks and women. Sheila Ruth points out that beneath a rhetoric of family values, patriotism, and the "American way," fundamentalists are trying to revoke fundamental principles of American government—separation of church and state, First Amendment rights, the political party system.[50] She quotes some of their major spokesmen:

We've already taken control of the conservative movement. And conservatives have taken control of the Republican Party. The remaining thing is to see if we can take control of the country. [Richard Viguerie, major fundraiser and strategist, Religious New Right]

Groups like ours are potentially very dangerous to the political process . . . a group like ours could lie through its teeth and the candidate it helps stays clean. [Terry Dolan, chairman, National Political Action Committee]

We're radicals working to overturn the recent structure in this country . . . we're talking about Christianizing America. [Paul Weyrich, director, Committee for the Survival of a Free Congress][51]

The fundamentalist movement jettisoned its religious image for a political one that claims to be "pro-life" but supports "tough" foreign policy and opposes gun control laws. Though pro-Israel (because of belief in millenarianism), it is anti-Semitic. Professing to hold the family sacred, it opposes AFDC (Aid to Families with Dependent Children), shelters for beaten women, and child abuse legislation. Ultra-nationalistic, militaristic, authoritarian, racist, sexist, driven by "a mystical principle of mission" requiring "absolute devotion," Ruth writes, the movement has "the shape of fascism, American style."

The New Right grew even stronger during the 1980s, as conservative judges named to the Supreme Court effectively halted affirmative action programs and modified reproductive rights. Grass-roots activists intimidate educational institutions by attacking curricular materials, sometimes burning or banning them. The movement is very rich and can support right-wing journals attached in fact or by association to major universities, some of which publish viciously bigoted material, and organizations like Accuracy in Academia, which seeks out and attacks "secular humanism" in universities. The New Right has succeeded in diverting funds from pro-female to "pro-family" agencies, cutting back funds for social programs, and increasing those of the military. Besides First Amendment rights, it threatens the rights to privacy, sexual freedom, and perhaps all civil rights in the United States.

The leadership of the Southern Baptist Convention has become too extreme even for some *conservative* members, many of whom began to separate from it after it dismissed two editors of its news service, upheld a ban on financial support to churches with female pastors, and destroyed a history of its Sunday School board that the leaders themselves had commissioned. In May 1991, this less conservative wing, comprising about six thousand Southern Baptists, set up a new organization, the Cooperative Baptist Convention. They reject a literal reading of the Bible and accept the ordination of women.[52]

The Southern Baptist Convention incited the movement, led by Senator Jesse Helms, to coerce artists receiving grants from the National Endowment for the Arts to pledge not to create "obscene" work—although no one can define "obscene" (even the Supreme Court makes it a matter of local sensibility), and such a pledge violates the First Amendment to the Constitution. The SBC backs or fosters any number of agencies besides Accuracy in Academia, among them the Coalition on Revival (COR), which is agitating to transform the United States into a fundamentalist Christian state. The Reverend Don Wildmon, who triggered the NEA censorship campaign, is a major figure in COR, working to abolish public schools, the IRS, and the Federal Reserve System (among other things) by the year 2000.

Indeed, a strong faction within COR, Reconstructionism, seeks to impose "biblical law" on American society, to establish what it calls the "kingdom of God." Its head, R. J. Rushdoony, wants to execute (preferably by stoning) homosexuals, adulterers, astrologers, blasphemers, and incorrigible children. The leader of COR, Dr. Jay Grimstead, who describes himself as "less extreme" than Rushdoony, wants boys trained as "warriors" in Christian "green beret" boot camps. COR's strategy, Grimstead explains, is to take over city councils and school boards and elect sheriffs and county officials. Once in power, it will establish county "militias" to wage spiritual wars, the first against "Communist Mexico." COR urges members to run for office as Christians without acknowledging their connection to COR or their real agenda. In this way, a COR candidate recently won election to the city council of Gilroy, California: a *woman*, Sara C. Nelson.[53] Women are not immune to the fundamentalist message, and the extreme right often places them in visible positions, usually in movements aimed at impeding or revoking women's rights.

ISLAM Movements with similar agendas have emerged in Catholicism, Judaism, and Islam. A black Islamic movement founded in America by Elijah Muhammad, now called the Nation of Islam, is led by Louis Farrakhan. This movement too is primarily defensive: like fundamentalists, blacks feel assaulted by American society. But black Americans *are* persecuted: fundamentalists are not. White male Protestants believe their prerogatives are being eroded by economic policies, feminism, and civil rights laws; blacks are singled out for prosecution for acts performed with impunity by whites. Anywhere in the United States black males are regularly stopped and even arrested simply for walking or driving in white neighborhoods. They may be beaten; sometimes they are killed. The percentage of black men in prison in America is shockingly larger than in apartheid South Africa. A black male has a one in three chance of being imprisoned before he reaches twenty-one.

Whites' unremitting drive to persecute African-Americans is reflected in the number of prosecutions of black political leaders, which is especially striking given their low number in the population and the corruption of white political leaders. A double standard is applied to cultural figures, too. Adolph Reed Jr. notes that while black music group Public Enemy is publicly censured for racism and misogyny, white heavy metal Guns N' Roses offers unremitting, unapologetic misogyny, homophobia, racism, and xenophobia; black rap group 2 Live Crue is put on trial for obscenity, but the bigoted and violently woman-hating Andrew Dice Clay is given television specials and film contracts.[54] I would add that black mayor Marion Barry was prosecuted for *taking* drugs (by white men who coerced a black woman into betraying him), while important white men in the Reagan administration either escaped prosecution or were punished lightly for subverting the Constitution by selling arms and *importing* drugs to support a private war against tiny, impoverished Nicaragua. Rich white men are lightly punished or will escape punishment for swindling

the public of billions of dollars through savings and loan manip-
ulations.

This intense scrutiny of blacks who rise to political or social
leadership, this need to cut them down, added to the pervasive,
systematic discrimination imposed on African-Americans,
amounts to almost a genocidal policy. A militant response to it
is understandable; it is understandable that Farrakhan should be
racist, admirable that he offers racial pride to replace racial shame.
What is not understandable is the rest of his ideology. He does
not attack systemic discrimination—poverty, ghettoization, exploitation—but black "social pathology," a slave mentality that
leads to crime and drugs. Farrakhan claims blacks "as a people
are sick." In this, he echoes white fundamentalists who, despite
their designs on the state, are most concerned with private life,
family structure. Jews contributed enormously to the 1960s civil
rights movement and were never part of groups like the Ku Klux
Klan, yet Farrakhan is anti-Semitic: why? And he unabashedly
favors male supremacy and female subordination in accordance
with the laws of Islam.

Reed (who like male analysts of Protestant fundamentalism
pays little attention to Farrakhan's insistence on male domination, merely noting it) writes that Farrakhan uses a militant, radical style to promote bootstrap capitalism and private, individual
responses to social problems that *cannot* be solved individually.
Farrakhan's program is familiar: private virtue, hard work and
discipline, male authority, racial essentialism. If he were white,
he might add to this list the training of black boys into "warriors"
in black "green beret" camps. Being black, he would likely be
killed for such a message, like other black leaders of both nonviolent and militant movements in the United States. But the
ideas are the same whoever espouses them: militancy, competi-
tiveness, a contempt for victims (even if ones own group is among
them) because victims are "feminine"—like Jews in nineteenth-
century ideologies. Virtue is a private affair—but private virtue
means "female virtue" defined and enforced by male dominance
of the sacrosanct family.

Militant Islamic movements (called Muslim Brotherhoods; the
Western press calls them Muslim fundamentalists) are more ex-

plictly woman-hating than African-American Muslims. Men form these brotherhoods in response to real economic and social ills in their societies, many of which have been impoverished by centuries of colonial rule. Leaders thought industrial development would ease some of these ills, but (as always) it brought terrible dislocations—crowded cities with their inevitable social problems, and changed work arrangements in families. The problems of industrialization revived colonial resentment of Western policies and customs, the main target of the Muslim Brotherhoods. Like Mussolini and Hitler and a host of less successful leaders, they believe that the past was "pure" and happier and can be revived in the present. But they put responsibility for reviving the past on women. In Muslim countries, many men see militant Islam as the only nationalistic movement, the only alternative to westernization. And for many in the Middle East, westernization means the results of development—wealth and privileges for a few, but also high unemployment, urban unrest, and a change never publicly claimed as a motive—more independence for women—which is in fact the most threatening.

The Muslim Brotherhoods direct most of their animus at women, as if women caused the present problems and changes in their behavior could solve them. No party runs on a blatantly anti-woman platform, but everyone knows the tacit agenda of the brotherhoods is to force women in Western dress back into the veil and out of the workforce. No overview of the Muslim Brotherhoods has yet been written, but wherever they exist, they are fiercely nationalist and religious, anti-modern, eager to fight "religious" war; and all concentrate obsessively on women. We will focus on the militant movements in various Muslim countries.

Iran. Many Iranian women opposed the Shah's autocratic rule and his use of a cruel secret police, SAVAK, which tortured many women who joined underground anti-government guerrilla groups. In 1978, militant Muslim supporters of Ayatollah Khomeini incited massive demonstrations against the Shah. To placate the religious leaders of the revolutionary movement, he banned abortion. But in 1979, the militants drove him out. Khomeini, who had been propagandizing from exile in Paris, returned to Iran in triumph. In March 1979, 100,000 women gathered at the University of Teheran to celebrate the overthrow of the Shah and the Ayatollah's victory. But almost at once, Khomeini suspended reformed family laws, barred women from becoming judges, issued his first order on the veil, passed a series of laws to segregate schools, buses, beaches, and other public areas, and established theocratic rule.

Disregarding women's support, the Ayatollah abolished all laws granting women rights and showed no reluctance to kill women who upheld them. He established a "morals police"—made up, in a rare exception, of women, called the Zeinab Sisters—to exercise surveillance on women's dress and behavior and harass or arrest them. One of his first acts was to prosecute the first woman member of the Iranian cabinet, Farrokhrou Parsa. Tried by judges in hoods, allowed no defense attorney and no appeal, she was in fact declared guilty before the trial began. Parsa was charged, writes Mahnaz Afhjami, with "expansion of prostitution, corruption on earth, and warring against God." Her actual offenses were to direct schoolgirls not to veil and to establish a commission to revise textbooks to present a nonsexist image of women.[55] In December 1979, Khomeini had Parsa executed; she was wrapped in a sack and machine-gunned.

Women protested the new rules in massive marches in Teheran and other Iranian cities; men beat, stoned, and even stabbed them as they marched.[56] Men purged women from the public realm, then passed laws severely restricting them from taking jobs and making it almost impossible for them to talk to or deal with men at work. In 1981, Khomeini had fifty schoolgirls shot and thousands of girls and women arrested for "counterrevolutionary" or "anti-Islamic" activity. None were given trials, and reports indicate that 20,000 women, including pregnant women, old women, and young girls, were executed. In 1982, Khomeini set the legal minimum age for execution at ten years (or puberty) for girls and sixteen for boys, banned women from most sports events, and launched a new campaign of arrest, executing 15,000 people. That same year, he intensified government persecution of religious minorities, especially Jews and Baha'is. In 1983, he made veiling compulsory for women, and had ten women hanged for refusing to convert from Baha'i to Islam: three were teenagers; others included the first Iranian woman physicist, a concert pianist, the former personnel director for Iran Television, and a nurse. He recruited children to clear minefields during Iran's war against Iraq; hundreds of thousands were killed.

In 1989, a woman interviewed on a television program said she would rather model herself on a contemporary woman than on Muhammad's daughter, the self-sacrificing Fatima who has been held up as a model for women for thirteen hundred years. Ayatollah Khomeini ordered those responsible for the program arrested and executed. When his advisers assured him the producers had made an innocent mistake, he granted pardons—but by then Iranian women had surely gotten the message.

Algeria. The success of militant Islam in Iran spurred on groups in other countries. Neither Algeria nor Jordan has ever been a militantly Islamic state, but as economic pressures cause hardship and their governments impose austerity measures, Muslim Brotherhoods gain adherents by blaming the hard times on Western influence and women taking "men's" jobs and adopting Western dress and habits (so do the men!). Algeria's problems were not solved by independence from France, and the industrialization introduced by President Houari Boumedienne produced urbanization, unemployment, and economic crisis. Some Algerians had already begun to call for a return to the old, "pure" Islam when the 1978 Muslim revolution in Iran inspired a young British-educated graduate in physics to form a Muslim Brotherhood. They demanded women be segregated from men and forbidden to work or travel without escorts. Militants prowled the streets targeting young women in Western clothes and threw acid at them, blinding one; they stabbed boys who tried to help them. Operating underground, they spread fear among women everywhere.

Peter R. Knauss reports that the Algerian police marked their files in red ink, as if for a crime, that a woman—but not a man—had divorced.[57] "Morals police" spied on women and charged them with prostitution if they were found alone in a café, renting a hotel room, at the beach, or if they went out with more than two men. Women seen with foreigners after dark could be questioned, even beaten. Kissing in public was forbidden, and women were held responsible for it. More women wore veils—to placate men *and* to protect themselves from them. The government tried to undermine the Muslim Brotherhood by allying with orthodox Muslim clergy, and tried to placate the clergy by naming them to a committee to reform the family code, which at the time mingled *shari'a* (Islamic law) and French colonial law.

No women were named to the revision committee; they protested but were ignored. During debate over the code, one legislator proposed specifying the length of the stick a husband may use to beat his wife. In January 1981, the government forbade women to leave the country. When women denounced such "revolting discrimination," the minister of the interior asserted that no such decree existed. The women managed to get a draft of the revised family code and found that it returned them to the legal status of minors. In September 1981, the Council of Ministers accepted the revision; in October, women held major demonstrations in Algiers with a lawyers' collective, labor union representatives, and former freedom fighters. They launched a national campaign, obtaining 10,000 signatures on a petition opposing the code. Tacitly comparing the Algerian government to the former French colonial regime, they paraded heroines of the war of independence, whose presence forced the police to avoid brutality. They filmed their protest and declared their demands (monogamy, an unconditional right of women to work, equal inheritance rights, identical ages at marriage, identical divorce conditions, and the best possible protection for abandoned children). It was never broadcast.

The government withdrew the code and did not resubmit it until June 1984. But the new version was *worse* than the earlier one. It gave husbands the right to divorce wives for almost any reason and eject them from the family home. Divorce by mutual consent was eliminated, as was the right of a divorced wife to demand housing from her former husband (unless she had custody of the children). Both permitted polygyny, but the 1981 version had maintained the *shari'a* condition that a man had to provide separate houses for each wife and allowed a woman to exclude polygyny in her marriage contract. These conditions were eliminated in the 1984 version. The 1984 family code confines women in the family as in a "cell" to protect and preserve them from "social ills." It requires a husband to support his wife; in return he may marry more than one woman "if he can justify his action." Wives who object are allowed to divorce. A man may marry by proxy and divorce at will; a woman may divorce only under specific conditions or can pay her husband to grant her a divorce. Women are required to "obey" husbands, "respect" their in-laws, and "breastfeed their children if they can."

Some provisions remained the same: Muslim men but not women may marry outside the faith, and children must be raised in the father's religion. Marriage is arranged, but the man gives the woman a dowry which she keeps if he dies or repudiates her. A father may restrain a daughter from any marriage he considers not in her "interest." Boys reach independence at eighteen, girls at marriage (when they fall under a husband's domination). The single improvement was that the minimum age of marriage was raised from sixteen to eighteen for females, and from eighteen to twenty-one for males.

The code satisfied the orthodox clergy but not the Muslim Brotherhood, who took it as a sign that persistence would be rewarded by more power. They incited student members to riot and attack progressive students with axes and bicycle chains, killing one, wounding several. Some of the militants were arrested, but they had read the political climate accurately. After initially suppressing the Brotherhood, the government, initiating a policy of greater "democracy," gave it the status of a political party, the Islamic Front of Salvation (FIS). The FIS demands that an Islamic ethic be imposed that bans Western secular customs. This ethic focuses almost completely on women: the militants insist women wear a *hidjab* (a raincoat-like garment, ankle-length, with a scarf completely covering the hair); some press women to give up their jobs. They demand that the government continue to ban birth control information, contraceptives, and day care. Government legitimation of militancy encourages men to treat women high-handedly. In 1990 in the city of Mascara, a

Muslim man, outraged that his sister, a nurse, treated male patients, doused her with alcohol and set her on fire.[58]

Although the women's association is a government mouthpiece, Algerian women are trying to organize and fight for rights. But men increasingly support the FIS, which in June 1990 received almost 65 percent of the popular vote (40 percent of the population did not vote at all, and over 60 percent—mostly women—are illiterate). It is now working to prohibit women from working outside the home. One woman said, "Algeria's 500,000 working women are not going to march to the slaughterhouse silently, even if it means a civil war."[59] A civil war of women against men?

Egypt. In 1956, Egyptian President Gamal Nasser granted women the vote, legitimating their existence as citizens. After oil prices increased in the early 1970s, President Anwar Sadat let men travel to the oil-producing states on the Persian Gulf to find jobs. Women, left behind, took on the responsibilities of handling the money their husbands sent home, hiring workers, and deciding local issues. Middle-class women increasingly entered the work force. Poor families migrated to cities to find work, forcing rural women to find new ways to bring money into the household. Many sold small goods or food on the street—a public space.

Islamic militants were enraged at women's new role and for entering public space. A female leader of the Wafd Party explains that militant Muslim men believe women have no right to occupy public space and should be at home with their children—women's place "is not in public life, not to be seen but to be a spectator." The secretary-general of the National Council for Childhood and Motherhood adds, "If there's unemployment [the militants say] it's because women are taking jobs. If there's delinquency, it's because women are leaving the home to work. If there's no room on the buses, it's because women are filling them on their way to work."[60]

Men angry at women for appearing in public commonly molest them on public transport. The problem became so severe that authorities in Cairo established segregated railway cars in the rapid transit system. Some opposed establishing a "harem on wheels," arguing that women would not use them, but they have become very popular: women use segregated cars to escape unremitting sexual harassment by men. The police find it necessary to enforce the rule—men often insist on entering the segregated car, which is sometimes less crowded than the others. But harassment on the Metro is not as severe as on the buses—which are cheaper and not segregated.

The militants have also worked to increase the authority of men, who use purdah strictures to hinder women's advancement and keep them out of the public realm. In 1985, the Egyptian supreme court struck down a 1979 law giving women the right to divorce husbands who take second wives.[61] In 1987, the government altered its electoral practice to reduce the number of seats designated for women in the 448-member legislature from thirty-three to eighteen and brought women's political organizations under official control, stifling the growth of an independent women's movement.[62]

Afghanistan. When the Soviet Union swallowed Afghanistan within its sphere of influence, it demanded that the Afghans educate women and allow them to participate in local "town hall" meetings. The Afghans resisted Soviet pressure in all areas but especially on women's rights, and in 1979 the Soviets invaded the country and installed a puppet government in Kabul. The Afghans rebelled, and war broke out. The Soviet Union supplied and supported the Kabul government, and the United States and other Western nations armed the *muhajadeen* guerrillas. Afghan women were caught in a no-win situation between supporting their men and the possibility of personal liberation under a Soviet aegis. As women (and workers) tend to do, most sided with the nationalist cause despite Afghanistan's prejudicial laws. Schoolchildren led by a girl, Naheed, demonstrated against the new government, chanting slogans and throwing bricks; government soldiers killed seventy of them. Naheed became an instant heroine and Afghan women thronged almost universally to the rebels. Demonstrating almost daily, they formed the Afghanistan Women's Revolutionary League to organize girls and women into the resistance. A League leader, Farida Ahmadi, was imprisoned and tortured in 1981, but escaped.

In 1983, the puppet government released all female and some male prisoners of the nearly 100,000 incarcerated. In 1989, the Soviet Union, near bankruptcy and worn out, left Afghanistan, but the Russian-backed government still stands—it clearly has some popular support. The rebels, the *mujahadeen,* who continually squabble among themselves, are united only on one issue: militant Islam, which mainly means sending women "back to their bags" (the *burka,* a head-to-toe shroud). The government tries to gain points with Muslims by renovating mosques and prefacing its proclamations with invocations to Allah; it also hints ominously about the policies of any *mujahadeen* government, especially toward women.[63] Although Afghan women supported them in protesting the Soviet invasion, the *mujahadeen* want not only to force them back into the *burka* but to eliminate female education and expel from wage work the quarter-million employed urban women and the 80 percent of rural women who work in the fields.[64]

The U.N. estimates that three million refugees fled Afghanistan between 1979 and 1984; those in Pakistan, many in the border city of Peshawar, are under *mujahadeen* control. The *mujahadeen* strictly confine female refugees to their houses or tents and forbid them to take advantage of the medical care and education offered by international agencies. In June 1990, eighty mullahs from all seven *mujahadeen* parties issued a *fatwa* (religious ruling), posting it throughout Peshawar. It ordered women not to wear perfume, noisy bangles, or close-fitting, decorative, or masculine clothing. They must cover their bodies with veils at all times, and *clothes must not be made of fabric that rustles!* Women may not walk in the middle of the street, swing their hips, or talk, laugh, or joke with strangers or foreigners. They may not attend school, even Muslim schools: "if such knowledge is necessary . . . it is better that women learn from cassette tapes," the *fatwa* advises. And it is unnecessary for women to go out to work: men will provide for them (although thousands of men have been killed in the war).[65]

Mujahadeen gangs in Peshawar harass Afghan women who

work with foreign relief agencies (one of the few employers in the area), intimidating female doctors, teachers, and nutritionists.[66] They distribute pamphlets signed "Protectors of Islamic Purity" or "Afghan Islamic Youth"; one charged that fifty "Western Christian women" with AIDS had been sent to work on projects in Afghanistan and Pakistan to infect the guerrillas. They send threatening "night letters" to working women, warning against Western influence; they make threatening telephone calls; they sent an envelope to one woman's office containing five bullets and a note informing her one was for her, the others for her colleagues.[67]

These men wrecked a school for Afghan girls run by the Pakistani government, and in April 1990 a Muslim cleric instigated five thousand Afghan refugees to destroy a women's center. Run by an Australian religious charity, Shelter Now, the center offered lessons in sewing and gardening and a child-care facility to widows of Afghan men killed in the war. The men claimed it gave the women birth control pills and Bibles and *allowed them to relax!*—to sit on the children's swings outside the center and use its bathroom and soap! The women who ran the center and those who used it adamantly denied that birth control pills or Bibles had been handed out.[68] A group of armed men shot at the male director of Shelter Now in his car. Many of the women have quit their jobs in terror; others travel with armed bodyguards; one teacher changes her clothes several times a day to confuse men following her.[69] The *mujahadeen* have disappeared over a dozen Afghan women who worked in women's centers or for foreign aid organizations.[70] The United States continues (at this writing, May 1991) to send aid, including arms, to these same *mujahadeen*.

Jordan. In Jordan, the Muslim Brotherhood won almost half the seats in Parliament in the 1989 election and was effective in defeating all female candidates.[71] The 1989 election was the first general election since women won the right to vote in 1974 and the first in which they ran for office. Thirteen women were courageous enough to do so; the Brotherhood targeted all of them, but especially Toujan Faisal, who had written in an article for an Amman newspaper that the Qur'an grants equal rights to men and women. For this sin, the Brotherhood tried to have her declared mentally incompetent, annul her marriage, and exonerated before the fact anyone who killed her. Some political commentators blamed women themselves for losing, arguing they should have presented themselves as advocates for everyone, not just women. But Faisal explained, "I am fighting for human rights and when you fight for human rights, you find yourself often fighting for the rights of women and children." Jordanian women are highly influenced by men, and vote as they are told. The ballot is secret, but some men might have punished their wives if any woman candidate had won.

JUDAISM When the term "fundamentalism" is applied to Judaism, it refers to the new political prominence of religion in Israel, especially of two Orthodox groups, one nationalist (Gush Emunim), one anti-nationalist (Agudat Israel).[72] Leon Wieseltier believes the term really denotes a change in the relationship of religion to politics in Israel, because of "a great reaction . . . to what some people consider . . . the excesses and the exaggerations of the separation of religion from politics."[73] Approving of religion's impact on politics, he scorns the Labor Party's "shallow, socialist, anti-clerical notion of the place of religion in human affairs."

Many people might approve the intrusion of religion into politics if religions offered a different message from political bodies, turning their adherents toward elements other than power—reverence for nature and living beings, human needs for affection, cooperation and toleration, respect for the unquantifiable in human experience. But the new militant sects are totally concerned with power and obsessed with subordinating women. Not only do they not urge affection, cooperation, toleration, and a reverence for the nonmaterial aspects of life, but their demands for female subordination are made in hatred. Some militant sects have a nationalist content, but for them even national autonomy seems to require total female subordination. So assured, so certain are they of their rightness that no one questions the connection among these elements: why must women be subordinate for a nation to define its own character? for virtue to exist?

Israel was founded with the dream of creating an egalitarian socialist state, and the young people who thronged to the early kibbutzim hoped to build lives that combined work on the land with work of the mind and imagination, subsistence and culture fostered in small, sharing, familial communities. And this dream was realized on many kibbutzim—up to a point. Gradually, men shunted women to kitchens, laundries, and nurseries; gradually, men pressured women to sit silent as men took over leadership. Many women left; and many of those I met during a brief visit live on in the kibbutzim feeling powerless and oppressed.

The strength, individuality, energy, and assertiveness of many Israeli women obscures the fact that they live in a country whose laws governing women are almost as repressive as those of Muslim states. The global prominence of Golda Meir as prime minister of Israel obscures the fact that she was one of only ten women in the 120-member Knesset, the only woman ever to hold a cabinet position, and no friend to women. Israel's founders established Jewish law—as repressive of women as any other ancient law—but for decades Israelis gave the Labor Party a majority, in accord with their socialist ideals. But Labor never won a large enough majority to set up a government without the support of the National Religious Party. These two parties dominated Israeli politics even before the state was founded. The importance of the religious right (which has always been extremely conservative) to a predominantly secular socialist state is puzzling, especially since many Jews are not religious. The reason for its importance may be the problem of determining Jewishness.

Jewishness is not a discrete quality. No ethnic or racial category is discrete. People who are citizens of Italy and speak Italian call themselves "Italian," even if some of their ancestors came from outside Italy. Citizens of the United States are called Americans, although most possess mixed ethnic backgrounds. Certain human qualities *are* genetically discrete: the world's four major races exhibit different skin colors, hair type and, sometimes, eye shape or other variable. Race is detectable through analysis of blood, but racial intermarriage over generations modifies and can eradicate the signs of racial ancestry. Jews do not constitute a race.

Nor do Jews have a common remembered homeland. Even when

they did, the ancient kingdom was constantly contested by native groups and invaders like the Philistines (Palestinians). Jews, who would not submit to foreign invaders, were transported as slaves, killed, or dispersed. Yet they did not vanish as a coherent group to become assimilated into alien populations like other ancient peoples. What held them together as self-conscious Jews in their wanderings across the globe was religion. Despite (surely) many defections and additions, enough Jews conformed to a religion with a strict written law to maintain group identity.

The touchstone of Jewishness—having a Jewish mother—harks back to a time before the law, when people were unaware of men's contribution to procreation. But what makes ones mother Jewish? Only consciousness of belonging to the Jewish community. Without a remembered common homeland or a common language, Jews have no defining characteristics except religion. But religious practice or belief does not make one a Jew: many Jews are not religious. Yet Jews absolutely needed to establish a Jewish homeland after millennia of persecution and the most horrifying event of a horrifying century, the Holocaust. A homeland for Jews should be open to all Jews, but Jews, fearing the lesson of history, want to limit citizenship to Jews.

Their problem then, was defining a Jew. Since religion held the people together over the ages, it is religion that provides coherent Jewish identity. So the Jewish state grants enormous moral weight to its tiny ultra-Orthodox party, which does not even support the Jewish state, refuses to serve in its army, and continues to uphold the law laid down in the Torah.

But the law laid down in the Torah was intended to order a society that has vanished, that had vanished even before Christianity and Islam emerged. The Jewish religious law that governs "family relations" in Israel, the Halachi, was last amended in the eleventh century. Like older Hindu law, it was intended to expand male dominance and make patriarchal ideas a standard. The driving force of "fundamentalist" religious movements is not to rediscover an intuition of divinity but to reassert patriarchy, the ideology that has brought the world to its present calamitous pass. These movements identify religion with law rather than spirit; their aims are not religious but political; their motive is not to seek holiness but to avenge the loss of a specious superiority.

Since Israel began as a religious state, its laws have always discriminated against women. In 1948, President David Ben-Gurion told women they could best serve the state by bearing at least four children, in what he called *aliya p'nimit*, internal immigration. Twenty-five years later, *aliya p'nimit* determined public policy, which banned abortion (unless pregnancy or childbirth threatened a woman's life) and even the dissemination of birth control information.[74] The government offered economic incentives to encourage large families and exempted married women from military service. Moral standards have not changed since ancient times: the ancient Hebrew word for prostitute meant "she who goes out of doors"; today, the rabbis still insist *C'vod bat melech p'nima*, "Honorable women remain indoors."

Even before the militant Judaic movements emerged, Israel oppressed women, as we can see in men's response to Jewish feminists. Trying to found a shelter for battered wives, rape victims, girls beaten or raped by male relatives, runaways who here as elsewhere had little recourse but prostitution, feminist Marcia Freedman discovered that although two billion pounds a year was allocated to the youth division of the Welfare Ministry, only one million pounds—*.005 percent, or one-twentieth of one percent*—went to distressed girls. The rest went to *no'ar b'm'tzukah*, boys in distress.[75] Only one ministry staff member and seven social workers were assigned to help teenage girls, although the ministry estimated—underestimating, as government agencies often do—that twenty thousand girls needed help. The Defense Ministry knew that every year 25 percent of teenage Israeli girls were rejected by the army for not having completed eight grades of school. Their male counterparts were taken into the army, placed in remedial programs, and educated; the girls were not. A quarter of Israel's prostitutes were between fourteen and eighteen. Strenuous efforts led to an increase in the budget for "distressed girls" from one to seven million pounds—*.035 percent, or seven-twentieths of one percent*.

Israeli marriage and divorce are under the jurisdiction of the rabbinical courts, presided over by the ultra-Orthodox who follow the Halachi. Thus, only husbands can initiate divorce, only men can bear witness, and all the judges are "fundamentalists." A wife can refuse to consent to divorce, but it is easy to force her consent. The Halachi decrees that "disobedient" wives can be declared *moredet*, rebellious, divorced against their will and deprived of all rights, including those to property and child custody. A woman is *moredet* if she leaves her husband's home, has sexual relations with another man, refuses conjugal "rights," or fails to provide domestic services. Ashkenazi women in particular are impoverished by divorce, allowed to keep only the gold teeth in their mouth, their wedding ring, and personal jewelry—if they have any. It is estimated that 10,000 *agunot* (the anchored) linger in a limbo state in Israel, unable to obtain divorces because the man refuses his consent. Many live in extreme economic hardship.

In the 1960s, women in some Israeli cities began spontaneously to organize women's groups. In 1974, Marcia Freedman was elected by an underground feminist vote, the single admitted feminist in the Knesset (some of the few women parliamentarians were sympathetic to feminism, but too fearful to support it on all issues). The women's groups began to agitate for change, in one instance supporting a wildcat strike of women factory workers in major cities demanding equal pay. Freedman was hooted and booed when she proposed a law against wife battering. Jews did not batter their wives, she was told.

Feminists had been demanding legal abortion since 1971. The Halachi prohibits abortion except to save a woman's life. Otherwise abortion was illegal, yet was unofficially sanctioned for those who could pay for it. Most Israeli gynecologist ran private abortion clinics in their offices, performing about 45,000 abortions a year illegally and another 15,000 legally in hospitals, allegedly to save the mother's life. Freedman led an effort to legalize abortion, collecting signatures on a petition, protesting at Rabbinical Court. In her account of her years in the Knesset, *Exile in the Promised Land*, she writes, "We demanded, rallied, petitioned, sat-in, or marched; there were only a few of us, and angry crowds gathered." Israeli doctors physically assaulted her at a physicians' convention.

Feminism spread as thousands of women joined women's groups and agitated on a number of fronts. Even Arab women began to speak out, if mainly among themselves. In 1975, at the end of International Women's Year, Freedman introduced a bill legalizing abortion and Shulamit Aloni introduced an Equal Rights Act. Both bills raised havoc in the Knesset. Labor, not wanting to *appear* anti-woman during International Women's Year, did not oppose the Equal Rights Act, knowing they could defeat it later. But its partner in the coalition government, the National Religious Party, was outraged: for a law to assert that the sexes were equal could open the door to civil marriage and the military drafting of their daughters: *equal rights threatened the Jewish family and therefore the Jewish state.* The NRP threatened to leave the Labor-led coalition, thereby toppling the government. The next morning, Prime Minister Yitzhak Rabin announced that the Equal Rights Act was dead.

Despite enormous effort, the women's movement was unable to get a law legalizing abortion by choice, but a new bill was passed. Deferring to the desires of the dominant religious party and the gynecological establishment (who earned huge sums from illegal abortions), the Knesset restricted abortion to rape and incest victims, single and menopausal women, teenagers, and the medically or mentally ill, with a poverty clause, a *sa'if sotziali*, extending the right to poor mothers with large families. And at the end of the year, the government established the Prime Minister's Commission on the Status of Women, in what Freedman calls the most significant, long-lasting result of the women's campaign.

But as feminism grew, so did a nationalist Orthodox group, Gush Emunim (the Bloc of the Faithful). The Gush movement was founded by an Ashkenazi rabbi who believed Zionism was a prelude to the coming of the Messiah, and that the conquest and settlement of Judea and Samaria (the West Bank) were a necessary precondition. In the mid-1970s, this small vocal group, risking their lives for their principles, began to settle in the West Bank and Gaza. With "passion and tenacity," they set up campsites in the West Bank, dotting it with tiny Jewish enclaves.[76] The land they settled had been claimed as military zones by the state, or purchased by the Israel Land Authority, and did not legally belong to them. They threatened to resist removal, and the state hesitated; the military, without clear orders, refused to act.

Gush Emunim is driven by religious fervor like the Zealots of the New Testament period. They are nationalist religious fanatics, unconcerned about "the humanity of others . . . almost as if they don't exist," explains Leah Shakdiel, a religious feminist who left Gush and now supports the religious peace movement. Yet the Gush movement has determined Israel's course in the last decades, and for the foreseeable future. Its ideas—and the fact that women were beginning to fight for themselves, to speak out—shifted Israeli men strongly to the political right. Two years after the modified abortion bill was passed, the conservative party, Likud, was elected to power for the first time since Israel was founded. One of its first acts was to rescind the *sa'if sotziali* allowing poor women with large families to have legal abortions.

The climate for Israeli feminists grows ever more hostile. Local religious councils—secular bodies that issue permits for all essential personal services from marriage to burial—have been monopolized by religious parties that exclude women from membership. Shakdiel, elected to the council in Yeruham, was denied her seat and had to petition the High Court of Justice to obtain it. When Rina Shashua-Hason was chosen by several political parties to serve on the council for Ramat Hasharon in 1986, the rabbis refused to seat her on grounds that she was not strictly observant—yet many men on the councils are secular Jews. She too petitioned the high court, which referred the matter to the government, which dragged its feet for two years. In 1989, the parties replaced her with a male candidate.[77]

Women are in the forefront of the Israeli peace movement: they demonstrate and endanger themselves by making contact with Palestinian women. Like Iranians, Israeli men attack demonstrating women, hurling names—and objects—at them. In December 1989, Israeli, Palestinian, and European women joined together in a large peace march from west to east Jerusalem. When they entered a courtyard, someone raised a Palestinian flag (it is unclear whether the person was one of the marchers). The Palestinian flag is outlawed in Israel, and its raising allowed the police to become violent. They hit the women with sticks, kicked them, dragged them off by their hair, and fired tear gas—at three thousand nonviolent women marching for peace! The police claimed that when they tried to remove the flag, they met resistance.[78]

The so-called Wailing Wall in Jerusalem is intersected by another at one end thus: ⊤ . The larger section—about three-quarters of the wall—is reserved for men, the remainder for women. Orthodox men will not worship beside a woman and post a man to stand guard, threatening any woman who even glances into their section. Women do not challenge this segregation, but on several occasions in 1989 groups of women trying to legitimate female worship marched to their own section of the wall, wearing prayer shawls, with a female rabbi carrying a Torah. Orthodox Jewish men insist women are forbidden to wear shawls and even to touch the Torah. Each time the women appeared, Hasidic men physically attacked them (paralleling the Muslims who physically attacked Iranian women marchers): they ran at the women, knocking them down; one hurled a heavy metal chair at their heads, wounding a woman in the neck.[79]

Israel, surrounded by enemies, has become an extremely militaristic state: soldiers are everywhere, especially in Jerusalem, and males are exalted even more than before. During the 1990–91 American-led war against Iraq, Israeli men were forced to sit on the sidelines. This triggered their machismo, Israeli feminist Alice Shalvi explains: they pulled female reporters from television news broadcasts, allowing only men to report and comment on the war—although women headed all political science departments at Israeli universities.[80] But employers other than the television network demanded female workers appear. Knowing that schools and day-care centers were closed (for almost four weeks), employers still threatened to dismiss women who did not come to work because their children were at home. When Iraq was sending missiles into Israel, all Israelis were ordered to stay home for three days. Then people returned to work, but hastened home in the late afternoon to the "safe" rooms women had sealed against a poison-gas attack. But the rooms, Shalvi points out, were not safe for women: during this period, rape decreased on the streets but reports of sexual assault within the home, incest, and sexual assault on minors rose dramatically, and the number of women who reported their husbands for beating them *tripled*.

CATHOLICISM The teachings, structure, and rituals of the Catholic Church are built on the same thinking as that of simple horticultural societies in which adolescent boys are "made" into "men" by the adult males of the society. Although both sexes are initiated at puberty, the rites differ: when a girl begins to menstruate, she is isolated, usually deprived (of food, drink, or comfort), and often demeaned. Men initiate boys in groups. In a ritual that imitates birth through the mother, men force boys to undergo a "second" birth through men. This second birth is brutal and intimidating; the men may beat or otherwise injure them; they may cut their penises, spilling the boys' blood in imitation of female menstruation, or send them through a frightening human tunnel that mimics the vaginal canal. Whatever the ritual, it teaches boys that to be men they must renounce the mother, be reborn through men, and maintain male solidarity against women. They are taught men's secret ways of terrifying women (with the fearful sound of a swinging whip, say), taught that the essence of maleness is control of female power. The ritual teaches boys to war against women, to subjugate *them* as they are being subjugated, by male solidarity and intimidation.

The primary, founding mystery of the Catholic Church is a God who utters the word that becomes flesh (birth through a male); the mutual love of father and son issues in reproduction—a third figure, the Holy Ghost. Both these acts symbolically appropriate the exclusively female power of birth. (The mystery involves the belief that all three exist in all time and none precedes the other.) Beyond that, the hierarchy of the church imitates and appropriates the transmission of this power from mother to daughter. Men not only symbolically usurp a female power, but characterize their version of it as "higher," spiritual, and thus more exalted than mere "animal" powers. Gloria Steinem points out that the architecture of Catholic churches mimics the female body: the outer portals serve as the labia majora, the inner portals as labia minora, the side altars as ovaries, and the high altar the uterus at the heart of the swelling dome that holds the body of the faithful, the child.[81] Immersion in or sprinkling with holy water at baptism—a rite called rebirth—mimics the water in which the fetus lives. The god ingested at communion is a symbolic version of the actual nourishment a mother provides to her fetus and her newborn baby.

All Christian sects hold that the sexes are equal in the eyes of god. But actual equality is deferred to an afterlife, and leaders stressed equality only when they were first attempting to establish their churches. Women, major figures in the founding and spread of Christianity, were very powerful within the Roman church from its early years until the high Middle Ages. But once it had political control of Europe, the church excluded women from any form of power and shut up once-active nuns in cloisters.

Unlike Judaism, Islam, or Protestantism, Roman Catholicism is not a religion of (male) consensus changing over centuries in accordance with commentaries of important (male) religious figures on basic texts. Its forms and its dogma—the beliefs one must accept to be a member of the church—have not changed much over the centuries. The main shifts in its forms were forbidding priests to marry and, later, to keep concubines, ending certain fasting requirements, and reading the Mass in vernacular languages. The main changes in dogma were the consecration of the Virgin Mary, declaring her immaculate conception (1854), papal infallibility (1870), Mary's bodily assumption into Heaven (1950), the later deconsecration of some legendary saints (many of them female), and a hardening of its position against contraception by any means but abstinence (1968). Most of these changes were detrimental to women in some way, but the church's position on birth control and abortion is the most injurious. It is hard on both men and women—but while men are expected to support their families, there is no sin in failing. Women have to bear and raise the children; women are the ones who suffer most when children suffer, starve, die.

Because its stance has for so long been anti-women, denying women power both within the hierarchy and in local parishes, and because it has always opened an avenue for men to attain power-in-the-world, the Catholic Church has not generated a need for a fundamentalist movement. It never abandoned fundamental male dominance. But its patriarchal rules, like those of other religions, fell under siege during the 1960s by the sexual and feminist "revolutions." (While many blame the 1960s sexual revolution on feminism, it was surely instigated more by men like Freud and Havelock Ellis than by feminism.) The sexual revolution legitimated sex: once sex was recognized as a basic need rather than a taint, men felt legitimate in demanding it openly. Instead of "going over the fence," as they had earlier, priests of conscience began to press for the right to marry. Although the Catholic priesthood now accepts defectors from Anglicanism (which allows priests to marry), it continues to forbid marriage to its own priests. Far fewer men are entering the priesthood, but the church is immovable on the celibacy issue. The same steadfast opposition characterizes the church's treatment of women petitioning the Vatican to allow female ordination.

On the issue of abortion, the church has not been steadfast, but has become more militant and oppositional: in the United States, it has even allied with Protestant fundamentalists. Jane O'Reilly shows that the Catholic Church, not fundamentalists or the political right wing, is responsible for the drive to criminalize abortion in the United States.[82] Yet it has not historically been so opposed to abortion.

During its first six centuries, the church took the position that abortion was not murder because a fetus had no soul.[83] Augustine held that "one cannot be said to be deprived of a soul if one has not yet received a soul"; "the law does not provide that the act pertains to homicide, for there cannot be said to be a live soul in a body that lacks sensation, if it is not yet formed in flesh and so not yet endowed with senses." The early church accepted woman-hating Aristotle's pronouncement on the beginning of life—a male fetus becomes human forty days after conception, a female ninety days after conception. ("Becoming human" is not the same as quickening; it is not a biological but a symbolic quality, something simply *said* to occur.)

The church considered abortion wrong mainly because it concealed real sin—adultery and fornication. It not only was not murder, but was punished less seriously than illicit sex, bribery, theft, or divination. The seventh-century Irish Canon ordered fourteen years of penance for one who had intercourse with a "neighbor woman," and three and half years for "destruction of the embryo of a child in a mother's womb." The Irish Penitential Code (c. 800) ordered three and a half year's penance for willful miscarriage after the fetus was established in the womb, seven years' if flesh had formed, and fourteen years' if the soul had entered. An eighth-century penitential, possibly by Bede, ordered a year's penance for a mother who killed a fetus before the fortieth day. She was a murderer only if she killed her baby after birth, but even this was judged according to her situation—a poor woman who could not support a child was judged more leniently than a "harlot" trying to conceal her "wickedness."

The first authoritative code of canon law, compiled by Gratian in 1140, stood until 1917. It decreed abortion homicide only when the fetus was formed (again, at forty days if male, ninety if female). In 1588, Pope Sixtus V, a fanatical anti-sex puritan trying to rid Rome of all extramarital sex, issued a papal bull, *Effraenatum*, decreeing all abortion and contraception murder. But Gregory XIV annulled it in 1591, returning to the earlier position that abortion was not homicide early in a pregnancy because the fetus was not human. There were no further pronouncements until 1869, a year before the doctrine of papal infallibility was issued. *Apostolicae sedis*, issued by Pius IX, directing that abortion at any stage be punished by excommunication, became part of canon law in 1917, yet to this day the church rarely baptizes fetal miscarriages or even full-term stillborns—does not, in other words, treat them as living creatures with souls.

Thus only in the nineteenth century, after women had begun to agitate for rights, did the pope declare his own infallibility ex cathedra and the church firmly oppose abortion. It did not begin to wage war against abortion until *1968*, when feminism revived and women began to demand rights over their own bodies. In that year, Paul VI issued *Humanae vitae*, forbidding contraception and all abortion, even for therapeutic reasons. In 1974 (a year after abortion was legalized in the United States by *Roe v. Wade*), the Vatican issued a "Declaration on Abortion" that finessed any uncertainty about when life begins; claiming that to abort a fetus was to risk committing murder, it named it a "grave sin."

The Catholic church opposes abortion on the specious ground that it is murder *if* a fetus is a living being. Neither the Catholic church nor Protestant fundamentalists or their allies in the campaign to criminalize abortion have ever shown much compunction about murder. The clergy accompany soldiers to war and bless battles; "pro-lifers" ardently support executions and war, the murder of people who may be enemies today but will be friends tomorrow. If life is sacred before it exists, it should be even more so once it breathes in a person. Because churches have shown over the millennia that they sanction murder—indeed, on many occasions, Christianity and Islam have been its agents, killing on *religious* grounds (of all world religions, only the Quakers have ever held all killing wrong)—one doubts that reverence for life motivates the campaign to criminalize abortion. No church opposes capital punishment. Moreover, a study by Catholics for Free Choice shows that legislators who oppose legal abortion also almost across the board oppose economic and social assistance to poor women and children.[84] They want women to bear the babies they conceive: after that, they are on their own. This is not concern for life, but repression of women.

The real motivation of the Catholic Church is revealed by several of its positions. It denies women control over their own bodies by forbidding contraception and abortion and by teaching women they are subordinate in marriage. A subordinate woman does not have the right to refuse conjugal intercourse. In addition, its justifications for constricting women have often involved racism. This is a historic fact: men have justified imprisoning women in purdah during periods when an alien group was coexisting in the same territory.[85] Steinem cites Father Paul Marx, director of the Human Life Center, an anti-abortion think tank in Minnesota, who argues that "the white Western world is committing suicide through abortion and contraception." Pointing to the large families of the many people of color in his area, he insinuates that they would be unwilling to fight the Russians should that become necessary.[86] That particular threat has collapsed, but Marx is busily contriving similar arguments.

Abortion has always existed, whether it was legal or not, because it is necessary. Like infanticide, abortion has been legal when *men* controlled it. Those who oppose it may criminalize it, but cannot eradicate it. All they can do is send it underground, make it harder for poor women to obtain, and assure that more women die of it. Robin Morgan points out:

> Thirty to fifty percent of all "maternal" deaths in Latin America are due to improperly performed illegal abortions or to complications following abortion attempts. . . . Every ten minutes in 1980, an Indian woman died of a septic abortion. . . . Illegal abortion is the leading cause of female deaths in Caracas. . . . In Peru 10 to 15 percent of all women in prison were convicted for having had illegal abortions; 60 percent of the women in one Lima prison were there for having had or performed illegal abortions.[87]

If the "pro-life" campaign succeeds, far more women will die of illegal abortions and more women will have babies they do not want or cannot support, adding to the burden borne by welfare agencies. We must question the motivation underlying a campaign directed at such ends. The real motivation of the campaign to criminalize abortion is to establish the principles that women's bodies belong to the state and that women bear the responsibility for sex.

In October 1984, just before the presidential elections, twenty-four nuns and four priests joined in signing an advertisement in *The New York Times* protesting John Cardinal O'Connor's attacks on Democratic vice-presidential candidate Geraldine Ferraro for her pro-choice position. The Vatican immediately ordered the signers to recant or be dismissed. The priests were silenced in a matter of months; it took two years to silence the nuns. By May 1988, two still would not recant: Barbara Ferraro (no relation to Geraldine Ferraro) and Patricia Hussey, who had between them forty-seven years of service as Sisters of Notre Dame de Namur, working mainly with poor women and children. In July, they resigned from their order. But they remained in the church and now run a shelter for the homeless in Charleston, West Virginia.

Fundamentalist Protestants provide a façade in most protests against legal abortion. The Catholic Church is the power in the background, providing money and propaganda. That its animus is less moral outrage at murder than outrage at female autonomy is suggested by the fact that Catholic clergymen who denounce political figures target mainly women: they helped destroy Geraldine Ferraro, a Catholic for choice, for having the temerity to run for national office. But they have not seriously moved against New York governor Mario Cuomo, also a Catholic for choice who is nationally known, far better known than Ferraro before she ran for vice president. This, one might think, would be reason to make an example of *him*.

But the church prefers to hit women, who are less powerful and (presumably) can't hit back: a bishop excommunicated Lucy Killea, a Catholic for choice, when she ran for local office in California. (This backfired: women outraged by the act rallied to her support and she won.) Bishop René H. Gracida excommunicated Rachel Vargas and Elva Bustamente, who direct Texas abortion clinics. The only men I know of (I do not have comprehensive data on this) who have been persecuted by religious agents for supporting legal abortion are both members of minorities: Gracida also excommunicated Dr. Eduardo Aquino, an obstetrician at one of the Texas clinics, and a Catholic nurse in a Boston hospital accused Dr. Kenneth Edelin, a black obstetrician, of murder for aborting a fetus. He was acquitted, but only after a ravaging trial. If the church per se did not precipitate this event, its campaign did.

The drive to criminalize abortion is unremitting. Considering most men's disinterest in children, and their frequent abandonment of and failure to support their children, the fervor with which Catholic or Protestant fundamentalist men fund campaigns to criminalize abortion is nothing short of astounding. Moving from state to state to erode legal abortion, the church flooded state legislatures with nearly four hundred abortion statutes in 1990. Most were defeated, but four states and one territory passed criminalizing measures. The criminalizing campaign forces women to fight the same battle over and over again, when they would prefer to spend their energies on other struggles for women's rights.

Moreover, while the legal struggle fills the headlines, the anti-abortion forces are winning the battle in the trenches. By harassing doctors who perform abortions, picketing their homes, and verbally assaulting their familes, they have intimidated most of them. While abortion remains a legal right, only a minority of women can actually obtain them. Le Anne Schreiber reveals that from 1977 to 1988 access to abortion *decreased* by 51 percent, as more and more doctors refuse to perform them. Only 17 percent of counties in the country have some kind of abortion service. Half the urban counties and "a staggering 93 percent of rural counties had no known abortion services in 1988."[88] Hospitals, which used to perform over a third of all abortions, now perform only 10 percent; the rest are performed in clinics, many of them embattled. Some states (like North Dakota) have *no* doctors willing to perform abortions; South Dakota has *one*. A few courageous physicians fly from city to town to offer the service (yet do not escape harassment at home). As usual, women with money to travel can obtain legal abortions; poor women and girls are barred from legal abortion as effectively as if by law, in a circumvention of law by intimidation—terrorism.

Canada. The American campaign to criminalize abortion is being waged by an alliance of male-dominated fundamentalist Protestant churches and the exclusively male Catholic clergy, but the Catholic campaign is worldwide. On the heels of a feminist victory in Canada, the church initiated a campaign that may cause the rescission of legal abortion there. In 1981, the Canadian Charter of Rights and Freedoms (equivalent to the American Constitution) was due for overhaul. As legislators debated, women across the country rose up, grass-roots groups joining organized feminists to demand a statement of sexual equality. They succeeded: an equal rights clause was added to the Charter that year.

At that time, Canada had a law permitting abortion in principle: a woman had to petition a panel of three physicians for approval, and the operation had to be performed in a hospital—no clinics existed. Since many hospitals were run by the Catholic church, in practice abortion was hard to obtain.

Abortion became legal in Canada largely because of one man, Henry Morgentaler, an Auschwitz survivor who emigrated to Canada and became a physician. During the 1970s, he openly performed abortions in Montreal, where poor Catholic women, forbidden birth control, sorely needed them. He was arrested and imprisoned several times; in jail, overcome by memories of Auschwitz, he suffered a heart attack. But he was tried twice for the same act and acquitted. In this period, Québec province was quietly rebelling against the authority of the Anglo-Saxon Canadian government and the Roman Catholic Church; convinced that no jury would convict people for performing abortions, Québec announced that despite federal law, it would no longer prosecute such cases. Morgentaler opened clinics throughout the country in provinces where abortion was still illegal. He was again prosecuted. Women across Canada lobbied and raised money to help him when in 1988, a few years after the equal rights clause was passed, Morgentaler's case reached the Supreme Court. Declaring the abortion law discriminatory against women, the court struck it down, simply erasing abortion from the acts regulated by the state, essentially decriminalizing it.[89]

The conservative Canadian government immediately drew up a new law punishing pregnant women and physicians who participated in abortion with two years in prison unless the abortion was necessary for physical or psychological reasons—exceptions that always function to allow women with money, but not poor women, to get abortions. The Catholic Church helped fund the campaign to pass this bill and lobbied Canada's large Catholic population. During the debate, over three hundred physicians across Canada announced they would no longer perform abortions. A teenager who could not get a safe abortion tried to abort herself with a coat hanger and died. Found on the floor beside the bloody hanger, she became a symbol for CARAL, the Canadian Abortion Rights Action League, which fought to defeat the bill. But when it came to the Canadian Senate, which usually defers to the government, it was defeated by an odd alliance between male "pro-lifers" who opposed it as too lenient and women opposed to criminalizing abortion.

As of 1991, Canada had no law covering abortion; it may be the only nation in the world so situated. Moreover, the province of Ontario, for the first time in its history, in 1990 elected a social democratic government, the new Democratic Party, which has named eleven women to the twenty-six-member cabinet, many with economically powerful, high-profile portfolios. It funds abortion clinics *and* provides money for women to travel to them from outlying districts.

Still, abortion is not easily available in most of Canada, a huge country with a widely dispersed population. In northern regions and the Maritime provinces, the sole hospital is often Catholic and refuses to do abortions. Women without money to travel to large cities may have to resort to coat hangers. The Church will probably continue its efforts, pressuring the federal and provincial governments opposed to legal abortion to continue to deny funding to abortion clinics. The Church funds REAL Women, a female front organization like the American Eagle Forum led by Phyllis Schlafley; REAL Women lobbies against public funding for any agency that helps women by funding abortion clinics or women's centers that counsel battered women, incest survivors, rape victims, and poor women needing shelter or legal help. REAL Women also opposes publicly funded day care and equal pay for equal work. When a new bishop was named in Toronto in 1990, his first act was to remove laywomen filling priestly functions, and all altar girls. As Canadian journalist-author Michele Landsberg comments, "All orthodoxies are founded on the domination and control of women."[90]

Poland. The Catholic Church is also pressing to criminalize abortion in Europe, Africa, and Asia. Across the world, the Pope is strategically appointing extremely conservative bishops, especially in liberal urban centers. The church backs resurgent nationalist movements in many Eastern European states (which may be why so many of them have an anti-Semitic component), and where it is strong, as in Poland and the Yugoslav republic of Croatia, it is waging a battle to criminalize abortion. To understand its power in Poland, we must look briefly at Polish history.

Poland, partitioned throughout the nineteenth century, did not produce a strong women's movement. People with the courage and resources to rebel dedicated themselves to the struggle for independence: each generation mounted a new insurrection in Russian-controlled Poland. Partition kept Poland poor, and most women were beaten down by poverty (which is always hardest on women). Yet many took part in the uprisings, directly or by endorsing men's revolt, raising children and maintaining households without men, who were imprisoned, exiled, or killed. The "Enthusiasts," the first organization for improving women's education and status, were active in 1840–50. Members also worked in the underground independence movement; most were imprisoned or exiled by the Russians. The first Polish vocational school for women was created in the 1890s; women were admitted to universities in Austrian-controlled Poland (Galicia) in 1897. The Polish Society for Equal Rights for Women was founded in 1907, and when Poland regained independence in 1918 women won the right to vote and run for office. A women's movement suddenly emerged. Between the wars, over eighty women's organizations flourished in Poland.

Poland was devastated by World War II. A third of its people and 90 percent of its livestock died, bombed and shot by invading Germans, burned when they retreated, then bombed and shot by invading Soviets. After the war, the Soviets imposed a Communist system on a hostile population and banned independent organizations, replacing grass-roots women's groups with a mass organization, the Women's League. By law the sexes were equal, though as late as 1960 women made up less than a third of the work force. But in 1970, they were 40 percent of workers, and by the mid-1980s, 45 percent. They gradually increased their numbers in education too, and now have more education than men. In 1987, 30 percent of Poles had a secondary education or more— 27 percent of men and 33 percent of women. In 1989–90, women made up 51.3 percent of university students—but also 62 percent of registered (no doubt many more of actual) unemployed. In a shifting economy, firms reduce their staffs, and the first dismissed are women.

Poles never stopped squirming in Russia's fist, rebelling in 1956 and again in the 1980s, as the Solidarity movement spread across the country. In June 1989, Poland held the first free elections in Eastern Europe since 1939. These elections were not totally free: the Communist Party controlled 65 percent of the seats in the Sejm (lower parliamentary house); Poles voted on the remaining

35 percent of the Sejm and on the Senate, a newly created upper house. They elected six women to the one hundred Senate seats and *fewer* women to the Sejm than the Communists had. Indeed, when the people have a voice in elections, the number of women in the Sejm drops; during the 1956 uprising it fell from 17 percent to 4 percent; in 1989, from 23 percent to 20 percent. (Yet Poland never fostered segregation like all-male clubs until recently, when it began to imitate the West. Sexism varies in its forms.)

The Catholic Church was vital to the survival of the independence movement in Poland. The church flourished despite fifty years of Communist persecution, the only alternative institution to the party, offering a personal space within a totalitarian society and supporting traditional Polish values. But what are those values? the male-dominated family, irrevocable monogamous marriage, and regulated sexuality. Perhaps *the* major item on its agenda was to criminalize abortion, which it has fought fiercely since 1956, when abortion was legalized in Poland. In 1958, the PAX Catholic Association appealed to the Sejm to annul it and urged the faithful, especially medical workers, to sabotage it.

Most socialist states had legal abortion but also promoted a high birthrate. To encourage large families, they saw to it that contraceptives were both unreliable and in short supply—making abortion the major form of birth control. But abortions were performed savagely. Socialist states thus put women in an untenable position. Already overburdened with wage work, domestic maintenance, and child care, they could not afford large families and, in cities, had no room for them. Women without birth control but with the right to abortion were essentially punished for using it. Still, an estimated half of all pregnancies in Poland ended in abortion.

When the Poles courageously stood up to the Soviet Union, Solidarity sought the help of the Catholic Church, the prime institution of resistance in Poland. The male-dominated church offered support on the condition that male-dominated Solidarity criminalize abortion in an independent Poland. Solidarity agreed, and at independence Jozef Cardinal Glemp immediately launched a campaign to criminalize the termination of pregnancy under any circumstances. The Catholic Church also influenced Solidarity to curtail the availability of contraceptives.[91] It backed the creation of lay Catholic groups (Care for Life, Gaudum Vitae, Pro Familia), organized marches, and collected subscriptions in churches to fund the campaign. In 1989, the church proposed a law punishing anyone connected with "the death of an unborn child" by a prison term of up to three years, with no conditions or exceptions. Seventy-four Sejm deputies (eight of them women) submitted this extraordinary bill.

The bill not only bans abortion and penalizes mother and surgeon with prison sentences, but grants a fetus legal status from the moment of conception. Once born, a child may demand compensation for damages suffered *as a fetus;* the bill does not specify what kind of damages. Małgorzata Fuszara, a professor at the Warsaw Institute of Applied Social Sciences, writes that the rule is so broad a child could conceivably sue its mother for *any* act that may be construed as having affected it negatively.[92] The bill enjoins parents (whether married to each other or not) to care for the child from the moment of conception until maturity, placing duties on the father beyond those at present enjoined by Polish law. *But it does not provide women with means—legal or administrative—to establish a man's paternity before a baby's birth.*

The draft bill created a furor: parliamentarians and critics argued passionately. The issue split political alliances and allied erstwhile opponents. Solidarity supported it (promises, promises), as did both Tadeusz Mazowiecki and Lech Walesa during their presidential campaigns. Press silence on the bill leads Fuszara to infer the press disagrees but fears criticizing it. Ninety-five percent of Poles consider themselves Catholic, but most (57 percent) also believe one should not follow religious dictates one finds morally wrong. A greater number consciously make exceptions to rules of religious observance. The first outcry, against imprisoning women who aborted, was so vociferous that before the bill was sent to the Senate in August 1990, that clause was removed. The Senate heard it read in January 1991 and sent it to a committee for consideration, then asked people to write in with their opinions. In the last poll before the vote, 13 percent of the population would ban abortion entirely (as in the bill), 33 percent would allow it in special circumstances (endangerment of the mother's well-being or impregnation against her will), 26 percent would add economic difficulties to those conditions, and 23 percent wanted all abortion legal.

The Catholic Church had already won one battle. The socialist state had subsidized all drugs, including birth control pills. But in May, the government eliminated subsidies for birth control pills on the jesuitical ground that "avoiding pregnancy is not a sickness." Removing the subsidy tripled the price of birth control pills for an already impoverished population.[93] The decision was announced only days before the bill criminalizing abortion came to a vote in the parliament. In May 1991, the legislators rejected the total ban on abortion sought by the Catholic Church, but adopted a nonbinding resolution petitioning the government to ban abortions by private doctors (whom women prefer, so the abortion does not appear in public records).[94]

Consider the logic—and the consequences—of these policies. Poland is teetering on the edge of bankruptcy; it cannot adequately feed, house, educate, or provide medical care to its people. Instead of concentrating its energies on finding ways to improve the economic situation, the government caves in to the church and obsesses about women's bodies. In the process, it puts women in an impossible situation—deprived of birth control pills by their expense and (perhaps) deprived of abortion by law. Women will be forced either to deny themselves and their husbands sexual intercourse (and risk men's violence) or to bear more children than they can afford or can care for.

The situation is similar in other nations where religions dictate government policy. While sex is linked to having babies and fertility rates affect and are affected by economic and political conditions, economic and political problems cannot be solved by men controlling women's bodies. For men to focus on controlling women's reproduction to solve a society's problems seems nothing short of mad or, at best, superstitious. But men's superstition or insanity has real and dire consequences for the women who are its object. And states, too, home in on women's bodies, perhaps to create the illusion that men are in control of uncontrollable forces. Indeed, almost all governments try to control women's bodies and regulate their appearance in some way.

STATE DOMINATION OF WOMEN'S BODIES

Ancient states often regulated women's dress and adornment. The Greek lawgiver Solon (seventh century BCE) tried to codify the proper demeanor of women in every sphere of life—their dinner parties, their walks, and expenditures—and, like present-day Muslims, established a women's police to spy on them. In China, into the early years of our century, the feet of many upper-class women were crippled by binding; it is inconceivable that this be done to men. Chinese men were explicit about the reason for foot-binding: "Why must feet be bound? / To prevent uncivilized running around!"[95] The toes, twisted back under the instep as a child's bones grew, formed a kind of fist, which became a sexual fetish: Chinese pornographic art shows men using the open space in the deformed foot as an entry for the penis. As women began to move into the public realm in nineteenth-century Europe and America, fashion produced clothes that highly exaggerated the breasts and buttocks and so constricted their waists that they could not breathe. Girls grew up with deformed rib cages; some even died.

When Chiang Kai-shek entered Shanghai in 1927 at the head of the Kuomintang forces (KMT, the Chinese Nationalist Party), he targeted mainly women. His soldiers hunted down women who had bobbed hair, wore "masculine" clothes, or had chosen their own fiancés. Chiang's soldiers stripped to the waist women wearing men's clothes and paraded them publicly, so "every man in town may see she is in reality a woman," before killing them. They shot women with short hair for radicalism or wrapped them in gasoline-soaked blankets and burned them alive; everywhere KMT agents or troops physically mutilated suspected women, often hacking off their noses or breasts, and raping them before they killed them. One young woman was tortured for having freely chosen her fiancé, then shot seventeen times; KMT soldiers shrieked at young women they were about to behead, "You have your free love now!"

We may believe that today only Islam regulates women's appearance, but secular states also treat it as a matter for male judgment and regulation. In most countries, women but not men are forbidden by law from going into public without shirts. In an action by a business, not a state, but one on which state law will ultimately rule, Continental Airlines in 1991 dismissed a woman for refusing to wear makeup.[96] (Presumably, a man would be dismissed for wearing it.) Women's appearance has far more bearing on their employment in television and films than men's, and only women actors are required to maintain a skeletal weight.

Women's appearance is a matter of state importance in many newly independent states, where Western dress (on women, not men) is taken as a sign of Western influence, which is unacceptable (in women, not men). Samora Machel, the socialist revolutionary who became president of Mozambique, was dedicated to women's rights, yet warned against Western "cultural imperialism." He feared what he called the "mechanical" emancipation of women typical of capitalist countries: "An emancipated woman is one who drinks, smokes, wears trousers and miniskirts, who indulges in sexual promiscuity, who refuses to have children." Iranian feminist Azar Tabari remarks:

> What is culturally imperialist about women drinking, smoking, wearing trousers, miniskirts, indulging in sexual promiscuity and refusing to have children (what a crime against the nation!)? If someone had said that drinking, smoking, and so forth, *in general* (and not only for women) constituted "cultural imperialism," he or she would in all probability be accused of being totally ignorant of the rich cultural traditions of the Third World. Did not tobacco smoking come from American Indians, what about Khayyam's poetry about "a cup of wine and a loaf of bread and thou," and didn't our indigenous women in the rural hinterlands always wear trousers?[97]

SEXUALITY AND REPRODUCTION

Most countries try to regulate sexuality by regulating women; some enforce virginity before marriage and fidelity afterward. Almost all criminalize prostitution—but only for the prostitutes, who are usually women (men make up roughly 10 percent of prostitutes in most societies but sex-work is associated with women). Male temple priests in Sumer are believed to have invented prostitution in about the third millennium BCE, using priestesses to draw income to the temple. In probably *all* past patriarchal societies it was the only occupation in which some women could earn enough to survive; it is still the only one in which poor, uneducated women can earn a decent living. Men are also almost exclusively the consumers of this service, yet men outlaw prostitution and invented penitentiaries (harsh prisons in which to repent sin) to punish (under the guise of reform) those who followed it. Efforts to punish male customers by publicizing their names invariably draw such outrage in high places that they are rescinded. In societies like the Philippines and parts of southeast Asia, an important component of the economy is *based* in prostitution, from which men profit far more than women, many of whom are virtual slaves.

States long ago arrogated the right to determine whether women had access to contraception or abortion. States have never tried to stop men from obtaining condoms (although churches have), but years of lobbying by feminists was necessary before they allowed women to learn about or possess contraceptives. Not just Catholic states like Ireland but secular states as well intervene in women's reproduction. Socialist states like Romania or China imposed the most stringent controls on reproduction because they could, exercising almost total control over their citizens. Even after socialism collapsed in Eastern Europe, some states eager to placate men or churches continue to sacrifice women's special needs for legal abortion, maternity allowances, and parental leave with guaranteed job protection.

In some former socialist states, the Catholic Church drives the campaign to control women's bodies. But nationalist movements not directly linked to any religion show the same inclination. Many Eastern European nationalist movements are reviving the fascist ideals of militarism, a cult of "manhood"' and male dominance, discipline, obedience, uniformity, and cult of "folk" with a very narrow base of solidarity (like Hitler's "Aryanism"), which leads to xenophobia of all sorts but especially anti-Semitism, and to efforts to put women's bodies under male control (all militaristic societies repress women). Abortion has been a major item of contention in the unification of East and West Germany, the East having had a liberal abortion policy, and the West a severely restrictive policy. It is highly likely that abortion will be criminalized in eastern Germany, Hungary, and Serbia, where nationalism has taken a particularly virulent form, reporter Celestine Bohlen writes.[98] Serbs make up 70 percent of the officer corps of the Yugoslavian national army and seem to have a militaristic society. At present, the government is debating a punitive tax on married couples with no children, implying a strong pronatalist policy.

Romania. Until 1966, abortion was legal in Romania and women depended on it because contraceptives were shoddy and hard to find. (All socialist states produce poor-quality contraceptives in inadequate numbers, perhaps because they want women to bear many children despite the difficulties of raising them. But they also seem not to produce sanitary napkins or tampons—a shocking lack in the late twentieth century. Maybe anything "female" gets short shrift.) Romania had over a million recorded abortions and 274,000 live births in 1965: *80.3 percent* of known pregnancies were aborted.

Nicolae Ceauşescu, who ruled Romania dictatorially until the 1989 coup d'état, wanted more workers. In 1965, he decided the way to get them was to ban abortion. The next year, births doubled to 528,000 but factory production *fell*. Ceauşescu had forgotten, as men tend to do, that women work, and cannot work and give birth simultaneously. Impoverished Romanian women resorted to illegal abortion. Live births declined, but the maternal death rate rose from 85.9 per 100,000 live births (1966) to 96.2 (1968) to 139.9 (1981). (In England and Wales, 9 of every 100,000 mothers die giving birth, 15.5 in France.) In England, 22 percent of maternal deaths result from abortion, in Romania, 85.6 percent. Women ill from botched abortions often did not seek medical help because of the ban. But ban or no, by 1983 the birthrate was what it was in 1966: 14.3 per 1000 population.

Ceauşescu then required all women to have monthly medical

examinations to determine whether they were pregnant! He placed a high tax on unmarried people over twenty-five and on childless couples without medical certification of infertility, and barred contraceptive imports from the West. Women of child-bearing age without proof of the monthly exam could not get free medical care or drivers' licenses. Perhaps fertile women began to forgo sex to avoid pregnancy—suddenly the population showed a huge rise in stress; in addition the infant mortality rate rose, and the number of babies available for adoption swelled. In 1985, the official infant mortality rate in Romania was 25.6 deaths per 1000 infants under a year (the 1983 rate in Sweden was 7, France 9, the United States 10.9, Czechoslovakia 15.6). And this rate was achieved only by bureaucratic juggling: *New York Times* reporter B. Meredith Burke writes that the actual rate was 60 to 80 percent higher.[99] Even so, after the 1989 coup Romanian orphanages were overflowing with unwanted children. And while the new government has legalized abortion, it also seeks to curtail it.[100]

Japan. Capitalist states put indirect pressure on women to have or not have children—depending on men's perception of the need. High taxes and expensive education, medical care, housing, and food lower the birthrate. Men's perception in the 1980s that middle-class white women were not having enough children (control of women's bodies almost always has a racist component) led to a spate of movies and television programs stressing the joys of motherhood and the motherly capacities of men. Israel used financial incentives to increase childbearing, and Japan offered women a reward of 5000 yen a month ($38) for each child of preschool age and double for a third child.[101] Japan is overcrowded, but its ruling men are worried about the plummeting birthrate.

It is hard to say which is more outrageous—men's indifference to the conditions in which women raise children or the paltry sum they think will persuade them to have more. Japanese women told a reporter who bothered to ask them that their reluctance to have children was a rebellion against an oppressive system: education and housing are very expensive, day care nonexistent, and husbands never home. Japanese men return home exhausted about midnight. For recreation, they play video games or sports, or take sex-tours to Southeast Asia. The life of a wife and mother is not enviable, and many women defer or eschew marriage. Yuriko Marumoto, a physician and mother who has vocally opposed the bonus plan, explains, "Our politicians and business leaders only go home late at night. They don't know how kids are raised, or what family life is like. Our political system is controlled by men who know nothing about the kitchen or the home."

Before the church-driven campaign to criminalize abortion penetrated government, the United States quietly worked to *sterilize* populations it considered undesirable—mainly southern black (especially in North Carolina), Native American, and Hispanic women. In 1972 alone, clinics used federal funds to sterilize 100,000 to 200,000 people in the United States (Hitler managed to sterilize only 250,000 in his entire regime). Over 35 percent of Puerto Rican women of childbearing age were sterilized in the 1970s, and 24 percent of Native American women of childbearing age by 1976.[102] Now, a movement has emerged in supposedly liberal circles to control *the way* women reproduce. Powerful, widespread, but unadmitted, it is being conducted by groups with different agendas, which literally persecute pregnant women, mainly the poor, under the guise of medical, legal, or ethical concern. I will discuss it in Part II, "Institutional Wars Against Women," in the section dealing with women's treatment by the medical and judicial systems.

COMMUNITY WARS AGAINST WOMEN'S BODIES

As patriarchal ideas took hold four or five thousand years ago, and men created states, one of their first acts in every state was to define women by their sexuality and constrict them within it. They were not concerned with female but male desire; they also wanted to appropriate female reproductive capacities. They forced women into the position of domesticated animals which men could breed, train, buy, sell, and grow rich from. To this end, they used religious or philosophical propaganda to train women to be docile, tractable, penned in—like cows, pigs, or sheep. While training women to such subservience should have been easy if men's definition of women as an inferior species was accurate, it was immeasurably complicated by women's possession of minds, emotions, talents, and spirit. Not only did women continue to express themselves, but men sometimes loved and admired them, which added to the difficulties of control. A conflict within an individual man between affectionate respect for a woman and a drive to control her may reach any of a wide gamut of resolutions; but in organized society—communities, institutions, or states—the drive to control always wins.

Men's first step to control was the establishment of patriliny, which overturned the ancient tradition of naming children for the known parent, the mother. Tracing children's descent through the male line gave men an excuse to guard women's sexuality by forcing them into marriage and childbearing at very young ages (which Adrienne Rich calls "compulsory heterosexuality").[103] They killed or enslaved women for losing virginity (even if they were raped), put them in purdah, denied them rights to divorce or child custody, and killed them for abortion or extra-marital sex. *None of these constraints were ever imposed on men.* Men were killed for adultery in some societies, but only for having usurped another man's property—his wife—not for having sex with women other than their own wives.)

In many societies, men had the legal right to order abortions or to expose infants or have them killed after birth. In all societies, men could have multiple sex partners, sometimes multiple wives, could initiate divorce at will, and were given custody of children. Only patrilineal societies were exogamous (required marriage into a different clan) and only exogamous groups were patrilocal (requiring women to move to their husband's community). Patrilocality enabled men to isolate women among strangers, deprive them of the solidarity of their kin, and deprive them of property rights. In such an environment, men could abuse women with impunity.

As these customs spread, women increasingly became commodities for men's use: men exploited them, enslaved them, forced them into concubinage, or into sati or other kinds of disposal of widows that allowed men to keep their property. By depriving women of the right to own property, men forced them to marry to survive. The control was circular, and total.

We need this context to understand a form of control of women's bodies rarely discussed, and considered inflammatory: genital mutilation.

GENITAL MUTILATION Many people associate genital mutilation of women with Islam. Muslims resent this: Islam did not initiate the practice, which is also followed by Christians and animists. Indeed, in 80 percent of the present Islamic world— including Saudi Arabia, Iran, Lebanon, Algeria, Jordan, Tunisia, and much of Muslim Asia—girls do not undergo genital mutilation. Most Egyptians who practice it live in the Nile valley, suggesting a Pharaonic origin.[104] But it is also true that a large percentage of genitally mutilated women are Muslim, and while Islam as a religion does not encourage it, some Islamic leaders do. Moreover, infibulation, its most devastating and dangerous form, is practiced *only* by Muslims, so far as we know. Wherever it exists, it is systemic; and it exists in many places: scholars estimate that at present *over twenty million* women are genitally mutilated.

Female genital mutilation is sometimes called female circumcision, as if it paralleled male circumcision. But they are not parallel. Male circumcision does no good but usually does no harm. On rare occasions, the surgeon's hand slips and cuts a baby's penis or a baby dies from the operation. Though some believe that removal of the prepuce (foreskin of the penis) keeps the penis cleaner or protects a man and his sexual partners against cancer, there is no evidence that male circumcision produces any advantage whatever on any ground. However, circumcision does not deform a male's genital organs or impede sexual pleasure or any other penile function. But even the mildest form of female "circumcision" can kill a girl; in all forms, it deforms the female genital organs. It usually leaves women unable to experience orgasm or sexual excitation, and in its severest form often leads to agonized sexual intercourse and childbirth, illness, or death. There are several forms of female genital mutilation:

Circumcision (sunna). Removal of the sheath (prepuce) and the tip of the clitoris. *Sunna* means "tradition" in Arabic; this mildest of mutilations is called "sunna" in Muslim countries, perhaps because it was the form known by Muhammad.

Excision (clitoridectomy). In this operation, the entire clitoris is removed. Usually, parts of the labia minora (the small lips surrounding the vagina) are also cut away. Sometimes, cuts are made around the vagina to make childbirth easier. In fact, such cutting makes childbirth more difficult and painful.

Infibulation (Pharaonic circumcision). This operation is called "Pharaonic" because it was originally performed in Upper Egypt. The term "infibulation" comes from the Romans, who sometimes fastened a ring or clasp (*fibula*) through the large genital lips of slave women to keep them from having intercourse and bearing children. The practice may have been extended from animal husbandry, for exactly the same thing is done to female animals like mares and cows if their owners do not want them to procreate while they are free at pasture. The Romans also fixed such a ring through the foreskin of males they wanted to avoid sex, usually gladiators. Today, infibulation is practiced only by Muslims.

Infibulation of women involves removing the prepuce, the clitoris, and the labia minora, and scraping the flesh from the labia majora and sewing them together. Sometimes flesh is also scraped from the inside of the vagina. A tiny opening is left to allow discharge of urine and menstrual blood. Often a reed is placed in this opening and the girl's legs tied together until the wound heals. When she is married, the merged flesh has to be cut open to allow the penis to enter. Some groups make the opening tiny to increase male sexual pleasure. Whether it does that or not, it does increase female pain during intercourse. At childbirth the opening has to be made larger. A husband may order his wife resewn after each child, or whenever he goes on a journey.

In childbirth, the labia and inside walls of the vagina expand to allow natural stretch; if they are removed, childbirth is agonizing. Female readers can imagine what mutilation must mean during sexual intercourse. And removal of the clitoris in all except sunna circumcision means a woman never experiences sexual excitement, pleasure, or orgasm. (Some women claim to experience sexual pleasure after excision, but it is difficult to get firm information about this. In parts of the world that practice genital mutilation, women are taught to be modest and have trouble speaking about such subjects even to female researchers.)

These operations are usually performed with unsterile, even rusty knives, splinters of glass, or razors. Midwives or sometimes male barbers perform them. Physicians describe the following consequences from these operations.

Immediate consequences. Agonizing pain (no anesthetic is used); hemorrhage; shock; inability to urinate; urinary infection; blood poisoning or tetanus (from unsterilized instruments); fever; death from any of these. Some girls' bones are fractured by the force used to hold them down during the operation.

Later consequences. If the wound heals slowly, the girl may develop infection, anemia, or malnutrition; she may develop a pelvic infection, cysts, or abscesses, or may become unable to menstruate because of a scar covering the vagina. This leads to the accumulation of menstrual fluid in the vagina and uterus and can cause pelvic infection or congestion. She is likely to find intercourse painful because of a tight vaginal opening, pelvic infection, or injury to the vulval area. (In some societies, it it customary for the husband to thrust his penis violently into his bride's vagina as soon as she has been cut open. Quantities of *her* blood are considered a sign of *his* prowess.) Some women develop recurrent urinary tract infections and painful urination. If the vaginal opening is uncomfortably tight (or if a husband has had his wife sewn up after child-weaning), he may enter her anus, which can lead to anal incontinence and fissure. It is also the most efficient method of spreading AIDS, which is epidemic in Africa, where genital mutilation is most common.

Consequences for childbirth. Scar tissue is far tougher than ordinary flesh. If a woman's genital scar is extremely tough, the baby will not be able to emerge without a long, painful delivery; sometimes the baby's head will thrust through the perineum. Infibulated women experience agonizing deliveries because the natural easements of birth have been removed. Children may be stillborn or brain-damaged because of protracted labor and lack of oxygen. Sometimes the baby's head, unable to move downward in its natural course, bangs against the posterior wall of the bladder, leaving the mother with a damaged organ through which urine seeps, so that she constantly smells of it. This urine will kill later fetuses. If labor is severe enough, the uterus itself may descend into the vagina; sometimes other organs, the bladder or rectocolon, are also thrust through the vagina.

Genital mutilation of women is equivalent not to circumcision, but to castration. But horrible as castration is for a man, eunuchs suffer less than mutilated women because they do not later have to accept a penis into or give birth through mutilated organs. A woman's bodily structure allows her to reproduce even if her external genitals have been removed.

HISTORY OF FEMALE GENITAL MUTILATION We can only touch on the history of female genital mutilation here.[105] Its origins are essentially unknown: some scholars believe it began in Africa and was adopted by Islam when it conquered Egypt in 742 CE, others that it began in the Arabian peninsula, and still others that it arose in many places independently. Its spread follows that of Islam, down the coast of West Africa and eastward across the belt of the Sudan to Pakistan, India, Malaysia, and Indonesia. In many regions, it is practiced only by Muslims, but Islamic influence cannot explain its practice by some Australian aborigines. Some doctors claimed they found signs of clitoridectomy on Egyptian mummies of the sixteenth century BCE. Researchers have found no sign of infibulation in predynastic or later Egyptian mummies.[106]

A Greek physician, Aetius (502–575 CE), wrote approvingly of excision, saying the clitoris should be removed "before it grows too large." As he described the process, the girl sits on a chair, her legs held open by someone sitting behind her, and a surgeon, standing in front, seizes the clitoris with a large forceps and pulls it out. Paul (or Paulus) of Aegina, a seventh-century CE Greek physician, defended excision, saying an enlarged clitoris was a shameful thing that could "erect like a penis and could be used for lesbian coitus." A traveler in the Sudan in 1843, describing infibulation, reported that a wood or clay model measured to the husband's erect penis was given to the operator about to cut open the bride's infibulation. Anthropologist Ashley Montagu gives a more graphic and horrifying account of this:

> When a girl whose virginity has been preserved in such a revolting manner becomes a bride, further cruelties are practiced. One of the women who perform infibulation visits the bridegroom immediately before marriage in order to obtain exact measurements of his member. She then makes to measurement a sort of phallus of clay or wood and by its aid incises the scar for a certain distance *and leaves the instrument, wrapped round with a rag, in the wound in order to keep the edges from adhering again.* The wedding feast is celebrated with hideous din. The man leads his bride home—every step she takes means pain—and without giving the fresh wound time to heal or scar, he exercises his marital privileges. [italics mine]

Clitoridectomy was widely practiced in Europe and the United States, especially during the second half of the nineteenth century. Dr. Isac Baker Brown, one of the most prestigious gynecological surgeons in England, seems to have introduced the practice there mainly to "cure" masturbation.[107] Finding his claims fraudulent, most British doctors abandoned the practice by 1867. But physicians in the United States went on performing it and extended it to include oophorectomy (removal of the ovaries). E. Wallerstein writes that thousands of women had this operation in the 1870s.[108] Doctors maintained that excision cured "sexual deviations" like masturbation and "nymphomania" ("it was unthinkable that any decent woman should derive pleasure from sex").[109] They claimed "the venereal excitement incident to setting the [treadle sewing] machine in motion" could make women ill. (They probably also found women riding horses astride dangerous.)

After 1880, surgical removal of the ovaries declined, but clitoridectomy continued on a large scale, primarily to eliminate lesbianism—actual, a suspected inclination, or simply aversion to men.[110] Proclaiming that "the sexuality of the young woman does not reside in the sexual organs," a Boston surgeon in 1897 asserted that female orgasm was a disease and the removal of erectile organs like the clitoris a necessity. It was often performed in mental hospitals until 1935. Doctors in America were willing to perform even infibulation into the twentieth century to keep females from masturbating.[111] Holt's *Diseases of Infancy and Childhood* (1936) recommended cauterization or removal of the clitoris to cure masturbation in girls.[112] Fran Hosken, who first revealed the dimensions of female genital mutilation, cites a 1982 issue of *New National Black Monitor*, an American Sunday supplement, which published an editorial proposing using excision and infibulation to eliminate premarital sexual activity by teenage girls in the United States. Scholar Lilian Passmore Sanderson writes that both are still performed in the United States and Europe.[113]

Researchers have tried during the past few decades to learn more about excision and infibulation in Africa and Asia, but their efforts are often frustrated. Wherever it is practiced, it is secret: researchers are seen as intruders, infidels, or Westerners bent on converting the world to their own vision. Fran Hosken, who stumbled on a reference to it in 1973, has spent the years since trying to discover more about it, arousing the hostility of traditional Africans and Muslims by heroically insisting on pursuing her investigations and publishing her findings. That we know what we do about genital mutilation is due largely to her.[114]

JUSTIFICATIONS FOR FEMALE GENITAL MUTILATION Societies offer different rationalizations for excising females. Some say the vulva smells foul and makes the female body unclean. This justification arises from woman-hatred: the genitals of *both* sexes have an odor (indeed, odor may help arouse desire, as it seems to in animals). But only women's is found objectionable (by some male authors and advertisers touting vaginal sprays), when in fact men often have a stronger odor because they urinate and ejaculate from the same orifice and rarely clean it afterward— but there has never been a perfumed penile spray. It is possible that mutilated women cease to secrete the dewy vaginal fluid that signals sexual excitation, but infibulation probably increases odor or *makes* it foul by trapping body fluids in the created pocket of flesh. Thus mutilation may increase rather than eliminate women's odor, reversing the declared intention.

Many peoples justify mutilation on the ground that female genitalia are repugnant or ugly. Extreme largeness (hypertrophy) of the clitoris is often mentioned as a reason for excision, especially in Ethiopia. Yet a gynecologist who examined thousands of Ethiopian women over many years asserts that clitoral hypertrophy is no more common among Ethiopian women than any others, and workers at the largest family planning organization in Addis Ababa, interviewed by Hosken, had not seen *any* cases of clitoral hypertrophy. Some societies believe that an unexcised clitoris will grow as large as a penis. Others, like the Temnes, Madingos, Limbas, and Lokkos of Sierra Leone, the Bambara of Mali, and some Hausa of northern Nigeria, who know the clitoris will not grow to hang down between the legs, still find it ugly.

Extremely large clitorises may exist; but even if they were common, what makes a society see them as ugly? Is a penis ugly? Are testicles beautiful? What could be more ugly than the scars of mutilation? Men interviewed by Hosken intimated that they were upset by the symbolism of a large clitoris. Seeing the clitoris as analogous to the penis, they were unsettled by a large one, and threatened by women possessing the organ that was their seal of superiority. The real ground of their upset may be their knowledge that the clitoris is the superior organ. Women's sexual organ is compact, protected, and unique—it has no other function but producing sexual pleasure. Clitoral stimulation does not depend on a penis; it is in a woman's own control. Justifications on the ground of aesthetics make no sense; they conceal resentment and envy of the female's body, power, and autonomy.

An even more absurd set of justifications concerns health. For instance, the Mossi of Burkina Faso and some Nigerian groups believe the clitoris can kill a baby if its head touches the organ during parturition. Others believe that clitoral secretions kill sperm and that a woman cannot become pregnant unless she is mutilated. Nineteenth- and early twentieth- century western physicians taught that cutting out sexual organs improved women's health, curing masturbation, depression, melancholia, nymphomania, hysteria, insanity, epilepsy, kleptomania, and *truancy*! In fact, all women suffer horribly from the operation; it makes many ill for the rest of their days and kills some immediately or later.

It probably does "cure" masturbation—what is shocking is that masturbation should be considered a disease. Nor do babies die from touching (if they do) their mothers' clitorises at birth. And far from increasing fertility, mutilation impedes it—for reasons cited above.

However, mutilation does tend to preserve virginity, a prerequuisite for marriage in all traditional African and Muslim societies. Because men in some societies will not marry unmutilated girls, parents feel it necessary to mutilate them. Most mothers explain mutilation as *custom*, unquestioned, traditional: girls are mutilated because they always have been. Wholeness would make them separate, different, outcasts in the community. Even mothers who do not believe the justifications offered for mutilation, who know its pain and danger, inflict it on daughters to save them from being social outcasts.

Some groups believe mutilation increases male pleasure in sex. Other say a clitoris makes men reach orgasm too quickly, before they wish to, diminishing their control over intercourse—and control is a male prerogative. Though some hold that the tightness of the opening in an infibulated woman excites men, sometimes the opening is so tight that intercourse is impossible. In any case, if William Blake is right, what lovers want most from each other is "lineaments of gratified desire," something a man can never get from a mutilated woman. Most men interviewed in Sierra Leone said they preferred sex with whole women.[115] Of 300 Sudanese husbands interviewed by a Muslim doctor, 266 admitted they preferred whole women sexually.[116] Yet they would rather marry a guaranteed virgin guaranteed to remain faithful than a woman who gives them greater sexual pleasure.

Indian Muslim women in Delhi gave me another reason for mutilation: religious salvation. Extremely poor, they could not afford the ceremony to mutilate their daughters and lamented that the girls would never go to paradise. Were they sure of this? Oh, yes; the Muslim teacher had told them so. These women had no education, were illiterate. Were they "circumcised"? Yes, certainly. And was it not a loss? They were bewildered. Loss? What could possibly be lost? Pleasure, I explained to the translator. Pleasure during sex. Such embarrassment followed that no answer could be extracted, but from the astonished looks on their faces, I suspected they did not know women could enjoy sex. They finally declared: sexual pleasure is *male*. This was also the justification used by Christian Kenyans, whose girls, Hanny Lightfoot-Klein writes, submit to the mutilation at puberty, believing that if they do not, they will be condemned to eternal hellfire.[117]

Virginity, fidelity, and suppression of desire mean taming. Many people (the Nubians, for example) believe girls (but not boys or men) are "wayward," sexually wild; girls must be mutilated to make good wives. The operation teaches a female her place, makes her docile, passive. A man need not worry about a mutilated wife chasing other men, since she has no sexual desire: this protects "the family." M. B. Assad writes that Islam supports or sanctions the practice explicitly to attenuate women's sexual desire and to strengthen men's control of virginity and chastity.[118]

Millions believe that women must be protected not from their own "wildness," but from men. So a Muslim doctor defends ancient Arabs who practiced infibulation *to protect girls who were out alone sheepherding against attacks by men*.[119] Yet infibulation is far more savage than most rapes, and even an infibulated female can be raped by a man with a knife. "Protection" is a reason often given for mutilation, which, again, means protection of "the family."

All accounts of present-day genital mutilation in Asia and Africa describe women as in charge of the surgery, and supporting its necessity. They accept this horror because it gains them and their daughters acceptance by their society and their religion. But women only seem to be in control of the practice: men will not marry an unmutilated girl, and girls must be married to survive in these parts of the world. Ergo: mutilation is mandatory.

COMMUNITY WARS TO ERADICATE FEMALES

Amartya Sen describes a phenomenon that would be called genocide if it were aimed at an ethnic group: eradication of females.[120] In an article entitled "More Than 100 Million Women Are Missing," Sen calculates the number of females who would have existed if female fetuses were not selectively aborted and female babies given the same food and medical care as males in their countries. When the sexes are not given extremely unequal care, females outlive males because nature favors the female. From conception to birth and throughout life, females seem more resistant to disease and hardier than males. With the same nutrition and medical care, they live noticeably longer than males even though men are privileged by greater access to resources because of more education, better jobs, and higher prestige, and have fewer burdens—no menstruation, pregnancy, or childbirth or, usually, childrearing. In places where the sexes receive relatively equal care, like Europe, the United States, and Japan, the ratio of female to male is 1.06 to 1. Even in sub-Saharan Africa, where women are dying of hunger, they outnumber men by 101 to 100.

Thus, a population with more males than females can occur only by design. In India, consistently more females than males die in all age groups (except immediately following birth) until the late thirties because girls are not fed enough or given adequate medical care. In most Indian families, men eat first. The women eat what is left, feeding girls last. Men often leave almost nothing for the women. Some Indian construction workers I spoke to whispered that they hid a little food for themselves before they fed their husbands. They felt guilty about this, but their men never left *any* food for them. The women were spectral. Throughout this century, the proportion of women to men in India has steadily declined, from over 97 females to 100 males in 1901, to 93:100 in 1971, to 92:100 in 1991.[121] Pakistan has 94 females per 100 males—the lowest ratio of any large country except India. This disproportion is caused by attitudes toward women, not poverty. The Punjab and Haryana, two of India's richest states, have 86 women to 100 men; Kerala, which is poorer but has a matricentric tradition, has a ratio over 103:100. Indonesia and Thailand are as poor as India, and female-to-male ratios there are among the lowest in the world, yet females still substantially outnumber males.

So many females are being killed that women, until recently 51 percent of the world's population, are no longer a majority. A 1991 U.N. publication reports that the elimination of females in places like India, Pakistan, Albania, and United Arab Emirates

(*48.3* women to 100 men!) offsets the female majority in developed countries to make males the majority of the world's population.[122]

This phenomenon cannot be correlated with the wealth of a region, but may have economic roots. Sen argues that females get a larger share of a family's resources if women earn wages outside the home, if their work is recognized as productive (which usually requires cash income), or if they have economic rights or resources of their own. That is, in regions where adult women can earn wages, regardless of the region's economic state, men kill fewer baby girls. The Punjab, India's richest state, has the lowest ratio of women to men and the lowest ratio of women who work for wages in India. In economically developing regions, the life expectancy of both sexes increases, but the women's gain is less than men's because men get more and better food and medical care. Comparing the proportion of women who work for wages and female life expectancy in regions of Africa and Asia (excluding China), Sen found an almost perfect correlation. Sen lists the two scales in descending order:

PROPORTION OF WOMEN IN WORK FORCE	FEMALE LIFE EXPECTANCY
1. Sub-Saharan Africa	1. Sub-Saharan Africa
2. Southeast and Eastern Asia	2. Southeast and Eastern Asia
3. Western Asia	3. Western Asia
4. Southern Asia	4. Northern Asia
5. Northern Asia	5. Southern Asia

After the Communist revolution in China, the new leaders made an effort to improve women's lot: they forced employers to hire women for wage work, acknowledged women's contribution to society and the economy, and made health care accessible to the poor. Everyone's life expectancy grew, even during the famines of 1958–61 (after the failure of the "Great Leap Forward"). The average life span in China around 1950 was the low forties; by 1979, it was the high sixties. Chinese females could expect to live significantly longer than males—until the government introduced economic and social reforms in 1979.

China introduced reforms in 1979 to increase its rate of economic growth and end agricultural stagnation. Worried by a huge burgeoning population in a country in which only a small percentage of the land is arable, in 1980 Chinese authorities limited couples to one child. Agricultural output doubled by 1986, yet mortality rates increased—mainly because the people were killing female children. The Chinese (like most people in the world) prefer boys, and baby girls were being aborted, killed at birth, or dying from neglect. The female-to-male ratio declined drastically. By 1982, one village in Hupei province had *503 boys to 100 girls* under the age of one.[123] Wuhan, one of China's largest cities and so under more immediate government control, had 154 male to 100 female children under one that year.

But even before this decree, China had a very low ratio of women to men: the Chinese Statistical Yearbook for 1979 showed 94.32 females to 100 males. It declined to 93.42 to 100 in 1985-86. In 1989 it rose to 93.98, still below 1979 levels. Infant mortality for girls increased hugely, from an estimated 37.7 per 1000 in 1978 to 67.2 per 1000 in 1984 (Sen believes this estimate is exaggerated, but not the trend). Although China enjoyed more prosperity in this period, it cut back health services, especially in rural areas. Programs supposedly gender-neutral (affecting both sexes equally) never are in woman-hating cultures, and women suffered more than men from this cutback. The economic system introduced in 1979 reverted to the traditional division of labor: women work in the household, men outside it; fewer women were hired for wages in agriculture. Experts have also noted that since 1979, Chinese leaders no longer discuss female equality.

In trying to control population growth, both the Chinese and Indian governments concentrated mainly on women, sometimes forcibly sterilizing or aborting them. One understands the need to limit population, but the form used to do so is discriminatory. This may not be immediately apparent because we are so used to state control of female reproduction. Population control can be gender-neutral, as when China taxes or fines urban families for producing more than one child or industrial states penalize prolific couples indirectly by raising standards of care and the cost of providing it. To understand the discrimination in state policies regarding reproduction, imagine a government forcibly sterilizing men or allowing their mothers or wives or sisters to lock them up, beat them, or castrate them for sexual behavior.

Indian women are being subjected to a new atrocity. Despite laws discouraging the practice of dowry, women still need a dowry to marry. Families agree to a given sum, but after the marriage the husband's family often blackmails the bride to squeeze more out of hers—a television set, a motorcycle, a wristwatch for the groom. A woman's life is valued no more than this. A bride may commit suicide to save her family from these demands, knowing that if they are not met, her husband's family may kill her, usually by holding her over the cooking stove so her sari catches fire and she burns to death. Then they can begin the process of "buying" a new wife for their son. Indian historian Veena Oldenburg calls bride-burning a new form of capital accumulation.[124] Hundreds of thousands of young women have been murdered this way in recent years. Families whose daughters-in-law have thus perished have no trouble obtaining new ones—and new dowries—from families eager to dispose of their daughters. Nor are the police concerned with murdered women; they rarely do postmortems after suspicious deaths and almost never prosecute the murderers.

Even limiting discussion to abortion of female fetuses, murder of baby girls, or neglect unto death, Sen estimates that over 100 million females have been killed in these regions of the world. This does not include women killed in "dowry deaths," women who die of starvation because of male control of land and development policies in African countries, or women in the West killed by husbands, lovers, rapists, or fellow-workers. The total figure of women who die *unnecessarily*—felled not by disease or accident, but by men's purposeful policy—cannot be estimated. If this figure referred to a religious, ethnic, or racial group, we would be using the term "genocide." What can we call this?

Part II

INSTITUTIONAL
WARS
AGAINST
WOMEN

Women are disadvantaged in every area of life. This section surveys attitudes toward women in institutions, mainly in the United States, where discrimination remains strong despite feminist efforts to raise awareness of both overt and subtle woman-hatred. First we will examine justifications for woman-hatred offered by cultural authorities, male scientists.

SOCIOBIOLOGICAL "PROOFS" OF FEMALE INFERIORITY

During the nineteenth century, philosophers and physical scientists in many European countries devoted themselves to "proving" the inherent inferiority of women, people of color, and Jews. Using physiognomy, bumps on the skull, specious intelligence tests, and other contrived evidence, they authoritatively demonstrated that all groups other than white gentile males were subject to criminal tendencies, subnormal intellects, or other kinds of inferiority. The work of these highly respected men justified white genocidal practices in Africa and provided a scientific base for Nazism and other racist and sexist ideologies in the West. The intellectuals of today who supply the theories undergirding sexism and racism are mainly academic animal researchers and sociobiologists. The academy continues to esteem these men even though feminist scholars are quick to point out their biases.[1] Sarah Lucia Hoagland, for example, analyzes the way sexual determinists use rhetoric to reach conclusions not demonstrated by the facts.[2]

In the 1960s and 1970s, several books became highly popular for "proving" innate male aggressiveness and male dominance. While drawing their examples mainly from certain mammals, male authors did not hesitate to extend their arguments to prove "the inevitability of patriarchy" among humans.[3] A reading public that revered men touted as eminent scientists did not perceive the serious methodological flaws and factitiousness of their arguments. Authors sophisticated in using "objective" fact to mask preconceptions of male dominance, or perhaps blinded by their own overriding need, made unsubstantiated extrapolations from animal to human life. These works of pop anthropology prepared the ground for sociobiology, which arose soon after the "second wave" of the women's movement (and, Hoagland believes, in response to it). Sociobiology is evoked to challenge feminist assertions of human equality. It too tries to justify male dominance among humans by showing that male dominance, rape, and infanticide exist among animals. Again, the material is carefully selected, slanted, and often false.

Many scientists have challenged the accuracy of sociobiological data, in sophisticated technical arguments I will not summarize here.[4] This discussion is limited to sociobiologists' use of language. Sociobiological "proofs" are often only preconceptions filtered and disguised by implicit male-dominant language. The father of the discipline, E. O. Wilson, does not hesitate to make unsupported statements. In *Sociobiology* (1975), the book that provided the foundation for most later work in the field, he regularly asserts "males are dominant over females," without at any time defending the statement.[5] This is especially ironic since Wilson is an entomologist, a specialist in insects, species in which sexual domination does often occur—but is almost always *female* domination of males.

Yet Wilson treats male aggression as if it were simply normal, while dismissing female aggression as nonadaptive.[6] He also overlooks the reasons animals act aggressively—mainly when they perceive their survival or that of their young to be threatened by attack—which only occasionally motivates human aggression. Distinguishing "sexual," "territorial," and "dominance" motives for aggression, Wilson asserts that males must dominate other males to nudge them out in the contest for food, territory, or females, and claims that "the rank ordering of the males" lies "entirely *above* that of females" (my emphasis). But unless he converses with animals, it is unclear how he can know this. What he means is that male animals (of certain species—from which he extrapolates) have dominance contests with each other and females do not. For him, this makes males superior. It may give some readers the opposite impression. Such leaps from seeming fact to patriarchal interpretation are common in his work. For instance, pike blenny males are aggressive toward other males who enter their territory. Female pike blenny move through all territories, as they please. Wilson interprets this to mean males control females.

Similarly faulty logic infects his use of the word "harem." Many mammals live in all-female societies, associating with males only at mating season; other females live together with a resident male. One cannot of course be sure precisely why they do this, but it is possible that females created such arrangements to avoid, *control* male aggression. It does not do to have more than one cock in a barnyard—they fight each other. Females need males only for procreation, and for this, one will suffice. So they isolate the males or include only one in their company. Hoagland stresses the absurdity of using the term "harem" in discussing mountain sheep, who live in female-centered societies, "inherit" home ranges from other females, and "associate" with a few males during mating season. But Wilson calls such arrangements harems, as if males had *authority* over females.

But authority—the right, won and backed by power, to dictate behavior, the forms of relationships, and other activities—does not exist among animals. No animal directs the general behavior of other animals, either to constrict or empower them. Rank may lead a subordinate animal to show deference to a dominant animal, or permit a dominant animal to oust a subordinate one from a territory or away from food. But rank (which exists only in certain species) always affects *either* females or males. It never gives one sex primacy over the other. Even in insect species in which males exist mainly to service females, females do not have authority over males. Males do not prey on females in any species but the human, although in some cases, under extreme stress, males do kill infants of their own species, and females of some species may kill males after mating.

Hoagland suspects that Wilson finds sex and aggression identical. Indeed, Wilson writes that sex—which generations of poets and philosophers have seen as the force binding society, *eros*, the counterforce to aggression—is "an anti-social force in evolution. Bonds are formed between individuals in spite of sex and not because of it." Through language, Hoagland writes, "Wilson embeds the idea that by merely engaging in sex, the male dominates the female: A female who has sex with a male is, by that act, dominated by a male." To Wilson, sexual concourse is an act of war. So he describes females as taking a "receptive" or "submissive" posture (female sexual posture can be seen as meeting a male halfway or actively luring him on).[8]

Both sexes display their genitals when they want to mate, and males sometimes present a posterior position. Wilson considers males who take a posture like that of females "homosexual"! He describes them as taking a "female receptive" or "pseudofemale posture to be mounted" and approves another scientist's description of a male hamadryas baboon's display as a "homosexual appeasement ceremony" like a "military salute."[9] Hoagland concludes, "The linguistically embedded message is clear: Male penetration equals male domination." Feminist Andrea Dworkin, too, considers male-female sexual intercourse inherent subjugation. But a position that garners Wilson praise and imitation wins Dworkin male scorn and outrage. Clearly, ideas are judged not on their merits but by the sex of the person holding them.

Wilson is only one of many biologists with a patriarchal agenda. Robert R. Warner describes a fish that changes sex, the wrasse:

> A few dominant [Caribbean bluehead wrasse] males can easily *control* these sites and thus *the females* that gather at them. . . .The Pacific cleaner wrasse lives in *harems* consisting of a single male and several females. . . . In species that live and mate in larger social groups, the smaller fish produce nearly all eggs, while the largest, *dominant* individual produces mostly sperm and mates with all the *subordinates*, saving energy for *controlling his harem* rather than for making eggs."[10] [Emphasis added.]

This is odd language indeed to use about fish, especially since the male wrasse is a female who transforms herself into a sperm producer. That few males are necessary in the natural economy of wrasse life can be read as indicating the greater value of females. But Warner needs the male myth. The words "control" and "harem" confer an authority and power which the fish does not possess—all he (formerly she) does is fertilize the females' eggs. In discussing the anemonefish, whose males transform themselves into females when an older female dies, Warner omits the discomfiting fact that the male anemonefish is much smaller than the female.

The social arrangements of lions have been lovingly culled for signs of male supremacy. After all, the lion is king of the forest, king of beasts: where better to seek justifications for kingship among men? Robert Ardrey mythologizes the species:

> A lion pride is a hunting unit, and this would seem to be the sole reason for its existence. And it is the extraordinary dominance of the male lion, and little else, that welds the society together. . . . The male lion rarely makes the kill. Such entertainments he leaves to the lionesses. His normal position in a hunting pride is in the center with the lionesses spread out on either flank considerably in advance.[11]

But Evelyn Reed points out that what Ardrey calls a "lion pride" is actually a group of lionesses who *permit* a male access to their group. On his own, the male lion hunts and kills his own food, "but when he is attached to a group of females they are in charge of the hunt." Male lions neither hunt nor provide food for females; they offer only occasional use for procreation, and females for the most part keep them at a distance. Females hunt and provide food for themselves, their cubs, and any male they allow to join their group. Reed concludes, "Contrary to Ardrey's opinion, the pride of lionesses is welded together not by the extraordinary dominance of the male, but by the maternal function of the females."[12] Wilson's use of precisely the same material is almost funny: "The pride males *permit* the females to *lead* them from one place to another, and they *depend* on them to hunt and kill most of the prey. Once the animal is downed, the males move in and use their *superior* size to push the lionesses and cubs aside to eat their fill" (emphasis Hoagland's).[13]

THE WAR AGAINST WOMEN IN EDUCATION

With teachers like Wilson in our universities, it is no wonder that females are treated differently from males in education. Research at all levels shows that a paper or thesis bearing a female name gets a lower grade than precisely the same paper or thesis delivered under a male name.[14] Such tests done with official documents signed by female and male authorities showed the latter taken more seriously.[15] Other studies show that teachers of coed classes give two-thirds of their attention to boys, yet they and their students have the perception that girls and boys are being treated alike. If girls get even 40 percent of the attention, boys usually complain.[16] A male teacher who felt that girls did not ask questions as often as boys, or offer information or elaborate extensively on a topic as boys did, tried to change the situation. He found that if a girl tried to take the floor, the boys stopped her immediately, ridiculing her in an effort to silence her.

If you add to this treatment the (white) male-centered, male-exalting curriculum of our schools, you understand why a recent study showed that girls who are confident and assertive at age nine emerge from adolescence with pitiably low self-esteem and why generally, Gloria Steinem points out, the more education women have, the lower their self-esteem.[17] Interestingly, the study showed that black girls lost less self-esteem, and Hispanic girls lost it more slowly, than whites. The researchers offered no theories about Hispanic girls, but theorized that black girls draw their self-image from family and community rather than school performance, and that black families tend to provide strong female role models. But the difference could also be related to the poor education most blacks receive in the United States. (I often thank my poor early education for the fact that I retained confidence in my intellect into adulthood.)

This tendency to see women as not mattering pervades all institutions, which everywhere treat women differently from men. While some men claim to treat women differently out of protectiveness or affection, the effect of their acts is so devastating to women that they amount to a state of siege. Male campaigns against women are so concerted (government, judicial, penal, medical, and media establishments all cooperate in a way that cannot be called conspiratorial only because their aims never need to be stated) that is is sometimes hard to distinguish a single source in a particular campaign. This fact has led me to structure the following section under broad categories: war against wom-

en's personhood and war against women as mothers. Each is sub-
divided to focus on the institution primarily waging the campaign,
but you will observe the broader institutional cooperation char-
acterizing them.

WAR AGAINST WOMEN'S PERSONHOOD

The United States is unique among industrial nations in continuing to deny its people responsive social services, free advanced
education, and medical care. This omission harms the poor most,
and since four-fifths of the poorest people in the country are
women and children, they bear the greatest injury. But American
institutions do not stop at neglect; they wage out-and-out war
against women.

Judicial and Penal Systems. In 1988, Jack Hampton, a judge
in Dallas, Texas, gave a light sentence to a man convicted of
murdering two homosexual men, intimating that this was not a
serious crime. "I put prostitutes and gays at about the same level.
And I'd be hard put to give somebody life for killing a prostitute,"
he declared. Gay men protested his verdict but women did not,
yet this man was essentially defining gay men and prostitutes as
not human beings. A state commission investigated the judge for
bias and cleared him completely in a preliminary report. His lawyer explained that after all his only inappropriate act was using
the word "queer."[18] After an outcry, the commission censured
the judge, but left him on the bench.

In 1989, a jury in Grand Rapids, Michigan, convicted Clarence
Ratliff of attempted murder, which carries a possible life sentence,
for *shooting at* two officers. But he had *killed* his estranged wife,
Carol Irons, a district judge sympathetic to victims of domestic
violence. Charged with murdering Irons, Ratliff was convicted
only of manslaughter, with a maximum penalty of fifteen years
in prison. A thousand people rallied to protest. Dotti Clune, an
organizer of the protest, said, "We are outraged that the murder
of a woman is considered less serious than shooting at—and missing—two men."[19]

In 1991, an admitted rapist in Daytona Beach, Florida, accepted a plea bargain for a four-and-a-half-year sentence for rape that was accompanied by a beating. But the judge in his case, Kenneth Leffler, gave him two years' probation, justifying his leniency by accusing the *victim* of being "a victimizer of men" and "a pitiful woman." Judge Leffler has retired.

Recent studies of the legal systems of Massachusetts, New Jersey, New York, Rhode Island, Maryland, Nevada, and Connecticut show all to be pervaded by bias against women and demonstrate that male bias harms women across the board, from lawyers to litigants to court employees.[20] Refusal to see women as full human beings makes it harder for women to escape from domestic violence and makes it harder for women to practice law. Courts impose longer sentences on women, and prisons treat them more harshly than most men. Male lawyers and judges touch, yell at, harass, or speak contemptuously to women lawyers, litigants, and prisoners. They are three times more likely to address female than male lawyers by their first names or terms of endearment, and their familiarity may diminish female lawyers' effectiveness with juries. A Connecticut judge publicly complained about the "feminization of the public defenders' office," charging that since women lawyers cannot handle accused clients roughly, by "pushing them up against a wall," for instance, they mishandled criminal cases.[21]

Divorced women cannot easily find lawyers to represent them and get little help in collecting child support. Male lawyers and judges refuse to take charges of sexual assault seriously when victim and accused are acquainted. The top echelons of the judicial system are overweighted with men: women make up only 10 percent of trial judges, but 90 percent of the clerks.

The Massachusetts study showed that judges punish women unfairly, with longer sentences and probationary periods than men convicted of similar crimes. In 1984, a federal judge sentenced Susan Rosenberg to fifty-eight years in prison for illegal possession of weapons. Men who commit murder get less. Moreover, she and two other women, Silvia Baraldini and Alejandrina Torres, were kept in a specially built Women's Control Unit at the federal penitentiary in Lexington, Kentucky. The unit was underground, lit by fluorescent lamps twenty-four hours a day.

The women were under round-the-clock surveillance by eleven video cameras tended by male guards who verbally and sexually harassed them. They were given half an hour to walk to and from the shower room and take their showers. Their mail was censored, political materials removed. They were subjected to random strip searches, and humiliated by having to ask a male guard for sanitary napkins one at a time as they needed them. Their every action and every conversation was recorded in the prison logbook. They were deprived of sleep, clothes, food, medicine, exercise, fresh air, and natural light.[22]

For the government to build a special prison unit for three people was extraordinary, as was their cruel treatment. Their sin was to be *female* political prisoners, the *only* female political prisoners in federal custody. The government seemed to feel they were more dangerous than male political prisoners, who are not isolated from the general prison population. Torres, a Puerto Rican tied to a Puerto Rican revolutionary organization, is now fifty-two years old, a mother, with a heart condition that is going untreated. Baraldini, an Italian citizen, Communist Party member and political activist, was convicted of conspiracy and racketeering in connection with the Brinks armored car robbery. Rosenberg had revolutionary sympathies: she was arrested in 1979 when Joanne Chesimard escaped from prison and in 1981 in connection with the Brinks robbery. In both cases, charges were dropped because no evidence linked her to these events. She was indicted again in 1983 in the Capitol bombing. But the only crime the government could convict her of (in 1984) was for possession of weapons and explosives.

The conditions of the women's imprisonment would be labeled torture if they were inflicted on prisoners of war. These women, political revolutionaries, were involved in actions considered criminal. They did not kill anyone, yet their sentences are heavier than those of men who have. Yu Kikumura, a Japanese man who, prosecutors charge, is a member of the terrorist Japanese Red Army, admitted conveying bombs in his car on the New Jersey Turnpike in 1988. He was sentenced to thirty years in prison—twenty-eight years *less* than Rosenberg. But an appeals court ruled that the judge had overstepped the limits of federal sentencing guidelines and ordered the sentence reduced. Kikumura is now serving twenty-one years and ten months—less than half Rosenberg's sentence for an identical act.[23] A woman convicted of aiding and abetting (not committing) a bank robbery in Georgia in 1981 was sentenced to *fifty years* in prison.[24] Men's average sentence for *murder* is *six* years.

When word leaked out on the women's situation, organizations including *The Nation* initiated a campaign to remove them from the unit. In an attempt to show the three had not been singled out for this cruel treatment, prison officials hurriedly brought in two other women serving long sentences but not for "political" crimes. They promised to close the Lexington unit but as of late 1991 had not yet done so.

But the treatment of the women in Lexington is different only in degree from that of all imprisoned women. In jail, too, women are separate and unequal. In Massachusetts, men are held in county jails, women in a somewhat inaccessible central prison. Legal advisers and family have a hard time reaching the women's jail, which is squalid, "deplorable and dangerously overcrowded." A similar situation exists across the country.

The number of women in prison tripled in the 1980s. About 60 percent of women in federal prisons have been convicted of drug-related offenses like theft, prostitution, and armed robbery, writes George J. Church.[25] Many of those convicted of murder—at least 40 percent and probably more—killed men who were beating them. About 80 percent of women in state prisons have children, and 85 percent of those have custody. For them the cruelest punishment is separation from their children. Children brought for visits shriek at parting. A society really concerned with "the family" would consider children's welfare in imprisoning mothers and find some way not to separate them. But the American penal system makes no allowance for children, who are foisted on relatives (often impoverished themselves) or into state institutions, to grow up unloved, unhappy, and perhaps to become offenders themselves.

The fathers rarely take these children and do not help the women. Yet the state expects the wife of a jailed man to take responsibility for her children and charges women with neglect who do not. In this context of differential responsibility, it is par for the course that husbands, brothers, and boyfriends drop a jailed woman "like a hot potato," says Allyn Shielaff, New York City correction commissioner, although wives, mothers, and female friends throng to men's prisons on visiting days. Women inmates are visited mainly by female friends and relatives.

Society is not responsible for the fact that imprisoned women suffer more than most imprisoned men from separation from their children, but it *is* responsible for not treating them equally. Prisons train male inmates for high-paying jobs like welding and mechanics, but offer women training as homemakers, *launderers* or beauticians. The pity of it, Church reports, is that women, who are often the sole support of their families, are "more motivated career-wise than the men," according to Paul Bestolarides, director of a program at the Northern California Women's Facility that offers them training as electricians and landscapers. And health care at women's prisons is at a crisis stage. The federal system's only hospital for women, in Lexington, Kentucky, only intermittently has a full-time obstetrician/gynecologist even though one out of four women entering prison is pregnant or has recently given birth. Most pregnant inmates get little or no prenatal care—even high-risk drug users. Yet medical doctors persecute pregnant drug users under the guise of concern for the fetus. That concern for fetuses is so selective suggests that it is really controlling women that motivates men.

In 1990, men in New London, Connecticut, resuscitated an old law to prosecute their wives for adultery.[26] Simply on their husbands' statement, police arrested three women (and one alleged male lover) and charged them with adultery, punishable under the law by up to a year in prison. The police willingly went along with this. (Connecticut has since repealed the law.)

Many police departments have made efforts to be more sensitive to victims of rape and child abuse, and some are even trying to overcome prejudice against people of color. But in general, police departments show systemic prejudice against women. It is well known that police fear domestic disputes above all other calls because of the unpredictability of the men involved. Yet they have consistently shown themselves unsympathetic or incredulous toward women who kill their batterers. Of course, they themselves are often batterers. In Mexico City, they were also rapists. The Judicial Police, the equivalent of the FBI, led a gang that beat, raped, and robbed over a dozen women in 1989.[27] Some were bodyguards for the head of Mexico's anti-drug program and used government vehicles and machine guns to abduct women. Charges against many of them were dropped; others were pursued only because the victims came from prominent families.

The Medical System. The male medical profession *began* as a war on women, which continued through the late Middle Ages with campaigns against midwives. Once men dominated the healing profession (by the eighteenth century) they treated women differently from men. For example, tuberculosis in men was a lung disease; in women it was seen as caused by the uterus.[28] In this century, besides mutilating female genitals, doctors lobotomized women (two out of three lobotomies were performed on women), surgically removing part of 50,000 brains despite little evidence that it helped and considerable evidence that it harmed them.[29] Dismissing female patients' complaints as "neurotic" (men know women are unhappy), they overwhelmingly prescribed psychoactive drugs for women—67 percent of all tranquilizers and mood elevators.[30] It took a campaign initiated by a woman to restrain male physicians from removing an entire breast (mastectomy) instead of just the cancer (lumpectomy) in cases of breast cancer, and major campaigns to restrain them from performing unnecessary hysterectomies.

Medical researchers seeking preventive measures for disease focus almost entirely on men. The main killer of postmenopausal women is heart disease, but the highly touted warnings about cholesterol (for instance) are based *entirely* on studies of men. Diets promoted by the American Heart Association, among others, to reduce cholesterol may actually harm women. No one knows, because no one has tested them. Doctors tested 20,000 men and *no* women to study aspirin as a preventive of heart disease. Heart disease treatment, too, focuses on men, and significantly more women than men die after coronary bypass surgery. Pharmaceutical companies are pressuring the Food and Drug

Administration to recommend estrogen therapy for prevention of heart disease in postmenopausal women and women who have had hysterectomies, ignoring female health activists who oppose it as a preventive because so few women have been tested and it has potentially serious side effects.

Women are the fastest-growing group infected with AIDS, but no research has been done on the effects on women of AIDS therapies. Woman-specific diseases like breast and ovarian cancer have not been studied nearly as thoroughly as male-specific diseases like prostate cancer and are more likely to be fatal. Cases of breast cancer have doubled since 1960; it now kills 44,000 women each year. Yet in 1990 NIH halted a major study of the disease on economic grounds.[31] *Only 13 percent of the $7.7 million NIH budget is spent on women's health issues.* Some doctors manipulate women into having mutilating surgery for breast cancer. A 1985 report showed that doctors in Chicago charged women 37 percent more for a lumpectomy than a mastectomy, even though the former is a less serious and easier operation. In essence, the doctors bribed women to let them mutilate their bodies even when lumpectomy was a more effective treatment.

War in the Workplace. In the United States, where 55 percent of women work for wages, all face discrimination. Those in professions and managerial jobs point to a "glass ceiling" over their heads. Businesses and institutions claim they place no barrier to the promotion of women, yet few advance, and professional and managerial women earn considerably less than their male counterparts. This phenomenon has been documented in business, academia, law, and medicine.

War against women in the workplace may have a single main intention—to keep them in an inferior economic position—but it takes varied forms. For example, companies bar only women from jobs that endanger reproductive organs. In October 1990, a federal appeals court in Chicago ruled that employers may bar *all* fertile women, even those who do not want children or are through with childbearing, from jobs that pose potential risks to the reproductive organs. Companies maintained this policy for decades without even *studying* the effects of dangerous substances on men. Only recently has such research been done; predictably, it shows men to be as sensitive to toxic substances as women. Yet company policies and law have not changed to reflect these results.

A 1979 study by the National Cancer Institute found that children of fathers employed in some jobs with high exposure to lead had threee times more kidney tumors than those whose fathers lacked such exposure. Children of fathers who work with paints, solvents, automobile exhausts, and certain machines have a lower birth weight and greater rates of brain cancer and leukemia. Exposure to dibromochloropropane, a pesticide, can make a man permanently sterile. Women married to men who work in the glass, stone, textiles, and mining industries bear premature babies at twice the average rate. Those whose husbands work with vinyl chloride or waste-water treatment materials have diffculty getting and staying pregnant.[32] A 1989 British study found that children of men working at a nuclear plant in England had a higher risk of developing leukemia.[33] Companies and governments dismiss all such information; companies never bar men from jobs, nor do laws protect men from such risks. But both continue to regulate women.

We might think that such regulation is rooted in male concern for women, a wish to protect them, but male treatment of women on the job presents a different picture. Women firefighters have testified to sexual harassment so extreme that it endangered their lives. A California commission recently tried to discover why so few women worked in construction trades, despite a state policy encouraging companies to apprentice women. Female construction workers called to testify sketched a work environment of constant warfare. Men urinated beside them, and hung lewd photographs in the women's toilet. Men doused an electrician with water while she worked with live electrical wires, and grabbed and fondled her as she carried heavy loads up a ladder.[34]

One welder sued the shipyard where she worked for sexual harassment. Six women and 846 men worked as skilled craftspeople in the shipyard, which had only male supervisors, foremen, coordinators, leadermen or quartermen [sic]. The women were forced to look at pinup calendars with written comments and close-ups of female genitals; they were constantly barraged with nasty comments, teased, and pinched. Saying the shipyard maintained a "boys' club atmosphere," an unrelenting "visual assault on the sensibilities of female workers," Judge Howell Melton of Federal District Court in Jacksonville, Florida, ruled that posting pictures of nude women constituted sexual harassment.[35] His January 1991 ruling was ground-breaking, the first legal judgment labeling such actions discriminatory.

Indeed, the climate at work for women is such that the main cause of death of women workers in the United States is homicide. Catherine Bell, an epidemiologist at the National Institute for Occupational Safety and Health, asserts, "If a woman's going to die from an injury at work, she's probably going to be murdered.[36] Twice as many black women as white are killed at work (four times as many black as white women are murdered every year). But white women are more likely to be killed in the military. When white or black men and black women enter the military, their chance of being murdered drops. A 1986 study showed that male soldiers' homicide rate is one-sixth that of male civilians of comparable ages. The figures were especially striking for black men, whose civilian homicide rate was 100 out of 100,000 but military rate was 9 out of 100,000. For every 100 civilian black women murdered, 78 black women soldiers of the same age die by homicide. But for 100 white female civilians murdered, 139 are killed in the military. No explanation was offered for these findings.[37]

In 1989, male managers of the Port Authority of New York and New Jersey were charged with discriminating against women workers, and harassing them if they complained. They harassed a woman who complained of a low raise on grounds of discrimination. When a second woman complained about the men's treatment of the first, they gave her an undeserved poor performance rating and transferred her to another department.[38]

Sexual harassment exposes men's deep, unacknowledged sexual hatred of women and the censored fact that men are the agents of women's oppression. Moreover, not just supervisors but fellow workers harass women. When a supervisor harasses a woman, the act has a class dimension: the man is telling her that she holds her job at his pleasure, subduing her by both class and sex pressure. But male co-workers' derogatory comments on women's sexuality, appearance, and competence express hatred: the men tacitly threaten rape or battery and appropriate the woman's sexuality to themselves. If the supervisor tells a woman she is there at his will, fellow workers tell her she does not belong there at all.

Sexual harassment reinforces male solidarity across class lines, even if not all the men in a workplace participate or even witness in silence. By blurring class division, it splinters working-class solidarity. In the end, it reinforces class domination. This is an important factor in government fostering of sexual oppression of women. Ruling classes are always small, working classes large. To control the majority, the minority must divide it by sex, color, or class. Men who challenge women's acquiescing in male domination should ponder their long history of swallowing the line that real men disdain women, their long submission to this divisive technique, and see it for what it is: a cynical manipulation of them.

Beyond this, company policies are built on the general assumption of most societies that men support women and children, and that women do not really have to work for wages. This assumption is problematic on many grounds. In the first place, one can believe this only by blinding oneself totally to reality, *choosing* to hold on to a false idea in order to go on believing in the rightness and propriety of male dominance. Men across the world insist that women work only for "pin money," for small luxuries for themselves. In Morocco, for instance, male workers sneer that women work for "lipstick." Yet most women work to feed their children, men, and themselves; they spend almost all of their wages on necessities, while in many societies men who claim to support their families actually give them only a tiny percentage of their earnings, spending the major portion on the male equivalent of "lipstick." Even if men admit that *some* women have to work, they acknowledge only *financial* necessity as forcing women to work outside the home, as if women had no need to use talents and capacities not drawn on in the household, or to spend their days in the company of fellow workers rather than in isolation, indeed, as if only men, not women, might want, be able to earn, or deserve material comforts or status.

WAR AGAINST WOMEN AS MOTHERS

By blindly insisting that everyone lives in a family structure that *never* existed except among the well-to-do (and then only for the last two centuries), men can go on treating motherhood as a personal choice women make for their own satisfaction, and for which neither men nor society is responsible. Men act as if continuing the human race were not a basic necessity *for all human beings*, as if the re-creation and maintenance of society requires no effort, occurs "naturally." This is true in both socialist and capitalist states.

Economic War. Most American businesses neither supply nor acknowledge the need for child-care facilities. Yet women are becoming ever more important in the work force: between 1980 and 1986, employed women in the United States worked 7 percent more hours than before at their jobs, while employed men worked 7 percent fewer hours than before.[39]

In 1990, one American company fired a woman for her frequent absences to care for her child. Diane McCourtney had to tend a baby son too sick to be in day care; her husband had back problems and could not pick up the infant, so could not care for him. McCourtney understood and accepted her dismissal, but protested being denied unemployment benefits. In a case presently before the Minnesota Court of Appeals, the state of Minnesota is arguing that she is not entitled to unemployment benefits because her absenteeism was *her fault:* an attorney for the state said, "She chose her family interests over her employer's interest."[40]

By thinking and speaking about reproduction as if it were not the basis of society and the only necessary human act, men represent it as marginal. The entire system—government, legal institutions, the press, the academy—presents a false picture of family structure by using language to obscure precisely who is taking responsibility and who is not. An article reporting that after divorce children are almost twice as likely to live in poverty than before quotes a Harvard expert on child poverty: "The greatest source of insecurity in America is growing up in a single-parent home. We've done very little to see that absent parents do their share." The reporter adds, "Families that experienced a breakup had only 83 percent of the income of those that did not." Such statements obscure the fact that the responsibility for child impoverishment lies with men. While the article does report that, by four months after the breakup, only 44 percent of absent fathers were paying child support, and that women could not earn enough to make up the difference, it does not mention that men's income jumps over 40 percent after a divorce, nor assign a sex to the irresponsible "absent parent" or the impoverished "single" one.[41]

The press contributes to concealing the real power divisions in the United States. I mentioned above an article about groups less likely to be murdered in the military than in civilian life—white men, black men, and black women. White women are *more* likely to be killed in the military, yet the article was headed "Study Finds *Soldiers* Healthier Than Civilians"[42] (emphasis mine), totally ignoring white women. The headline could as easily have read "most soldiers." On the other hand, articles dealing with male irresponsibility in supporting their children all too often refer to *parents*, as if women were as likely as men to fail to support children. An article in *The New York Times* about new methods being devised to force men to pay child support was headed "Better Traps Being Built for Delinquent Parents."[43]

Men fight legal enforcement of child support; it not only costs them money, but removes a significant component of their control over women. (Some Scandinavian countries have neatly solved the problem: if a mother gets custody of the children after divorce, the state automatically deducts the father's share of their support from his paycheck.) Legislators and judges, too, resist enforcement policies, implying women can depend on men's good will. *But there is no good will.* Men are at war with women, and so, often at war with their own children.

Sexual War. All past societies constricted women's sexuality: it was a criminal act for women but not for men to have sex with someone other than a spouse, which different societies punished with varying degrees of severity, including death. Punishments from beatings to imprisonment in convents to death were inflicted on girls who lost their virginity before marriage—even if they were raped, and even if by a family member. Over the past century, many societies have revoked such laws but some have not, and custom and tradition still indoctrinate women with the belief that their bodies are men's property. Men cling to their rights over women's bodies, exerting their authority whenever they can. Nowadays, their best opportunity arises when women come under the aegis of the state in contests over child custody or applications for financial assistance. Men who cannot control the sexuality of women-in-general tighten control over the sexuality of mothers.

Because many women cannot earn enough to support their children, they fall under the power of courts or social-service agencies which assume the right to dictate their sexual lives. Welfare agencies as a matter of policy used to deny financial assistance to a mother with dependent children if a man was found in her dwelling. Now courts are intruding on the lives even of women *not* dependent on welfare, imposing a sexual morality men do not follow themselves but require of women. In 1989, Judge William Goldberg of the Rhode Island Supreme Court upheld an order prohibiting a divorced woman from having an unrelated man stay in her home when her children were present. Carha J. Parrillo, thirty-three, insisted she had the right to live her own life. The judge admitted she took good care of her three children, but forbade her from having a male guest *unless she married him*. She asked him to cite her husband for contempt for cutting back his child-support payments. The judge refused.[44] It appears that women, but not men, may if challenged lose custody of their children for having a lover. Mothers alone must be chaste.

Wars of Control: Legal System. Men are using their economic advantage over women to take their children away from them. In several countries, judicial systems and governments are colluding in an alarming new development called "fathers' rights." Presenting themselves in a new role, as caring fathers, an image built not on men's actual behavior but by media presentations of ideal fathers, men increasingly seek custody of children after divorce or children they fathered outside marriage. Fathers' rights groups are being supported by legislatures and judiciaries in the United States, the Netherlands, France, Norway, Canada, Australia, Ireland, and Great Britain. If fathers wanted closeness with their children, one would sympathize, but few men seeking custody are prepared to care for their children themselves, and legislators and judges who support male custody explicitly justify it as bolstering men's control and status vis-à-vis women.

Discussing the fathers' rights movement in Canada, Susan Crean points out that there is no evidence that men as a group are any more interested in or willing to deliver twenty-four-hour child care than they ever were, and that politicians privately acknowledge that the arguments offered by fathers' rights activists lack both logic and understanding of the law.[45] Yet they accept their representations and work for their goals. Male legislators in England see custody as an element that can raise men's legal status, writes Julia Brophy. She also shows that legal restrictions are not responsible for fathers' alienation from their children after divorce.[46]

Judges justify removing children from their mothers by citing the economic disadvantage most women suffer. They use different standards to define a "good mother" and a "good father," writes Carol Smart.[47] A "good father" need only provide economic support for his children and pay a woman or girl to care for them; quality of care is not at issue. But a "good mother" must provide economic support and care, abstain from sex, and be willing to share parental authority with her former husband. In the Netherlands, mothers' legal authority over children was not equal to fathers' until 1985. Because Catholic Ireland forbids divorce, separated people are in a legal limbo. So people live together, which almost automatically bars a woman from having custody of her children, writes Nancy D. Polikoff.[48] Indeed, the Irish Constitution defines women as maintainers of the home:

By her life in the home, woman gives to the State a support without which the common good cannot be achieved. The State shall, therefore, endeavour to ensure that mothers shall not be obliged by economic necessity to engage in labour to the neglect of their duties in the home.

Legislative or judicial movements to give fathers of "illegitimate" children authority over them exist in New Zealand, all Australian states except Victoria, Switzerland, Austria, France, the Netherlands, and Germany.[49] Scarlet Pollock and Jo Sutton discuss this trend in the United States, noting that several states have adopted the Uniform Parentage Act, to recognize men's claims on their illegitimate children. In many states, judges give unmarried biological fathers rights over children according to constitutional guarantees of "equal rights." Women could not persuade legislators to amend the American Constitution to decree women equal with men: the equality of rights judges refer to here is between single and married *men*.

In 1975, the Council of Europe drew up an agreement to abolish illegitimacy legally, not by ending the category of illegitimacy (removing the requirement that a child's father be married to its mother to legitimate its existence), but by letting biological fathers claim the children of women they had not married. The children would still be illegitimate in that their parents were not married, but a father's rights and obligations could be established "by voluntary recognition or by judicial decision." The United Kingdom signed this agreement, and in 1979 and 1982 the British Law Commission issued reports exploring legal options for securing men rights and obligations as fathers and held discussions under the rubric "changing the status of illegitimacy." But the all-male Law Commission acknowledged that its major concern was men's rights.

Legislators everywhere justify such laws by the familiar excuse—"breakdown of the family"—citing high divorce rates, increased illegitimacy, and single-parent families, most headed by women. Insisting that it wants to support "the family," the British Law Commission cites with alarm the growing number of illegitimate births in England and Wales and the fact that "a greater number of mothers than in the past now accept their illegitimate children and bring them up themselves."[50] Aware that contraception and abortion are available, the commission acknowledges that these mothers probably want their children; nevertheless, intending to end the "social problem" of women choosing to bring up children without men, they created a proposed Family Law Reform Bill that makes it almost impossible for women to raise children without men. At present in Britain, unmarried men cannot "establish paternity to a child or claim rights of guardianship, custody, or access, without the consent of the child's mother."[51] The proposed bill would allow a man to declare himself a child's father *against the mother's will.*

But women choosing to raise their children alone is not a social problem unless it is accompanied by severe poverty. It seems to be a male problem. Even the statistics used to breed such alarm are doubtful: Pollock and Sutton point out that because methods of collecting data changed between 1976 and 1982 more illegitimate births are reported, that there are a greater number of women of childbearing age, and that many women registered as having illegitimate children were separated from their legal husbands and living with their future husbands while awaiting a divorce. Most illegitimate children in the United Kingdom are born into relatively stable unions; 41 percent live with their biological parents by the age of eleven, and 65 percent live with two parents of some sort. It is also true that almost one in three marriages ends in divorce, that 90 percent of one-parent families are headed by women, and that 7 out of 10 divorces are initiated by women. But most women do not choose to raise children without a father or father figure. In 1982, only 4 percent of households in Britain consisted of single female parents with dependent children. Yet the law being considered would allow men to take children away from their mothers.

Wars of Control: Medical and Judicial Systems in League. The medical establishment is indifferent to women's health, but not if the women are mothers. Increasingly, medical practitioners, judges, and self-appointed morality police seek to take control of female reproduction. Some are trying to force them *not* to be mothers whether they want to or not, some try to force mothers to act in prescribed ways or face the consequences in court. We have discussed campaigns aimed at criminalizing abortion or coercing sterilization. Judicial decisions show a trend to force women to be the kind of mothers physicians and judges want them to be; biologists are trying to take over reproduction. Here are some examples of the first phenomenon:

- In 1988, a female Arizona judge sentenced a seventeen-year-old Catholic mother of two to use birth control *for the rest of her reproductive life.* She had left her babies alone in a hot apartment for two days and they nearly died. The mother used drugs and was herself abused as a child. But the judge had to revoke the sentence as unenforceable when the mother became pregnant again a few months later.

- As part of a plea bargain presented to her by the authorities after her four-year-old son died of an overdose of the psychiatric drug she was taking, an Indiana woman agreed to be sterilized.

- After a seventeen-year-old admitted smothering her newborn daughter in 1990, a Florida judge sentenced her to two years in prison and birth control for ten years after her release. The American Civil Liberties Union *and* the right-wing Family Research Council both protested the sentence, which was handed down despite a 1942 Supreme Court decision revoking a sentence ordering a man castrated for repeated "moral turpitude." The Supreme Court asserted that the state *may not control reproduction.*[52] But that judgment applied to a man. (To underscore the interest of the right wing in such decisions, a male anti-abortion advocate tried to kill a California Superior Court judge who had ordered a woman who abused her child to use birth control.)[53]

- In 1990, a California judge ruled that a woman convicted of child abuse must use a new contraceptive that is implanted in the body and prevents conception for five years.[54]

Judges and medical experts persecute mothers who use drugs or alcohol, even though it has never been proven that moderate use of alcohol harms a fetus, and even though no one would think of punishing male alcoholics for damaging their sperm. In the campaign to force mothers to uphold standards of behavior not demanded of men, the judicial and medical establishments have the eager cooperation of the press. *The New York Times* made much of the "fact" that a single drink during pregnancy can cause intellectual and physical defects in a fetus, although the research on which the report was based asserted fetal damage could not be shown under *three drinks a day*, and that poverty and lack of education were more serious and widespread causes of birth defects.

Jeanne Mager Stellman and Joan E. Bertin discuss an editorial in the prestigious *New England Journal of Medicine* asserting that women metabolize alcohol less efficiently than men. The editorial was based on a study of twenty men and twenty-three women alcoholics hospitalized for gastric dysfunction.[55] Medical judgments about men are never based on such skimpy evidence, nor are they used to deprive men of their children. But increasingly, judges impose "medical" regulation of women who drink or take drugs, as some recent examples show:[56]

- A Nevada woman who drank some beer the day she went into labor lost custody of her child because hospital workers smelled alcohol on her breath.

- A Wyoming woman trying to escape an abusive partner was put in jail because the police smelled liquor on her breath.

- A California woman was advised by her obstetrician to stay off her feet, eschew sex and "street drugs," and go immediately to the hospital if she started to bleed. She did not follow this advice. Her baby was born brain-damaged, and soon died. Authorities arrested her for failing to support her child under an old law intended to force men to support their children—and rarely used for that purpose.

- Prodded by "pro-life" advocates, a hospital sought the court's advice on whether to perform a caesarian section on a woman who was seriously ill with cancer, against her wishes and those of her husband, parents, and doctors. Everyone knew the operation would probably kill her and might not save the twenty-five-week-old fetus, but the judge ordered the operation, which was performed before the woman's lawyers could appeal. The woman and the baby both died. (Yet judges often refuse to order people removed from torturous life-support systems when families wish it. The existence of a fetus seems to unleash judges' appropriative emotions.)

- When this incident was dramatized on *L.A. Law*, the show's writers had a woman lawyer, Ann Kelsey, argue for the hospital and had the baby live. Television also casts women as defense attorneys for men accused of woman-hating acts like rape, battering, and murder: this no doubt is the television version of equal rights.

- The Seventh Circuit Court of Appeals upheld a decision to bar fertile women from jobs that would expose them to lead, discounting the workers' testimony (many wanted no more children or were celibate) averring that no child born to them showed ill effects traceable to lead exposure and testimony from experts averring that lead is just as dangerous to male fertility.

- Judges throughout the United States are placing women in "preventive detention," giving them jail terms for minor offenses, charging them with child abuse or neglect, and threatening them with manslaughter charges should they miscarry—all for *drinking* while pregnant, which is not a crime.

- Mothers are being arrested in their hospital beds if their babies test positive for drugs. Social workers are increasingly taking such babies away from their mothers on the assumption that a single use of drugs makes them unfit mothers—even if the mother had sought and been unable to get treatment for drug use.

- A Chicago woman who used cocaine was charged with involuntary manslaughter when her two-day-old baby daughter died. A grand jury refused to indict her, but the State Attorney's office considered charging her with possession, which carries a sentence of one to three years in prison.[57] Yet persecution by the

legal system frightens drug addicts away from treatment and prenatal care.

Poverty and lack of education are often not within individual
control; ameliorating them requires state intervention. Moderate
drinking—a relatively innocuous factor compared to mothers so
starved they give birth to two- or three-pound babies—*is* within
individual control. Like Muslim men who focus on women as the
one element they can control when they feel their societies changing under their feet, men in Western societies that are collapsing
under inequality and racism persecute women. Stellman and Bertin ask why there are no stories about the effect on childhood
development of fathers abandoning mothers or about chronic
drinking in men, which leads to the production of abnormal
sperm. The offspring of male animals that were given alcohol
show testicular atrophy or behavioral abnormalities.

In a courageous article in *The Nation*, Katha Pollitt pointed out
this persecution of women (her courage was underscored by the
vicious letters protesting it).[58] She asks if pregnant women will
now be arrested for eating junk food, smoking cigarettes, taking
aspirin, or traveling by air, and notes that judges imprison pregnant addicts but do not order drug treatment programs to accept
them. Authorities punish poor women (most of those arrested are
of color and poor) but do not try to extend Medicaid to cover crack
addiction (it pays for heroin addiction) or state funding of the
supplemental feeding program for women, infants, and children.
Judges do not stop landlords from evicting poor pregnant women
or force obstetricians to treat them, nor do physicians who warn
women against addictions offer their services. When judges jail
women, they ignore the children they have, who are cast on the
state or impoverished relatives. It is a major irony that the only
developed nation in the world without free medical care, govern-
ment-funded day care, home health visitors for mothers, or al-
lotments to subsidize childrearing is jailing *women* for improperly
caring for the babies in their wombs.

While it is surely not beneficial to a fetus for its mother to use
drugs or drink heavily, such behavior cannot be controlled by
society, and no society should try to control it. Like men, women

in despair, unhappy women, behave in self-destructive ways. A society that was really concerned about this behavior would address the causes for the hopelessness. Most of the babies harmed by self-destructive maternal actions are part of the underclass that society condemns to death every time it chooses to spend money on weapons rather than social programs. We turn our backs on these babies when we move our families to the suburbs, snatch our children out of public schools, refuse to hire people of color, or simply see them as inferior beings. We as a society do not care if these babies die—indeed, there are people who wish the poor and people of color would *not* procreate—yet we punish mothers whose actions acknowledge our indifference. Remember that in each minute that passes, the governments of the world spend $1.3 million of wealth produced by the public (between two-thirds and three-quarters of it by women) on military expenses. That government does not try to help but only to punish poor mothers, that it spends our money on weapons that kill children, not on nourishing them, is another sign of its war against women.

Wars of Control: Scientific Researchers. The campaign to control female reproduction does not stop there. To enable *them* to control reproduction, men have devised new technologies such as embryo transfer, in vitro fertilization, and artificial insemination of breeder women—"surrogate mothers." Since these techniques allow men to reproduce in the same way they get sex, by leasing women's reproductive capacities just as they lease sexual capacities in brothels, Andrea Dworkin writes they want to create a "reproductive brothel."[59] Genoveffa Corea describes methods currently used on animals that can be transferred to women and some already transferred.[60] Here are a few:

- In artificial insemination, the fresh or frozen sperm of a "superior" male animal is placed in a "gun," which is inserted in a rod, which is inserted into a female animal for insemination. Reproductive engineers artificially inseminate a "superior" cow with the sperm of a "superior" bull, remove the embryos from her body, and transfer them into "inferior" cows for gestation. There are fewer "superior" than "inferior" cows, and this transfer enables men to reproduce "superior" genes more quickly, using "inferior" gestators. Midas-like, they transform cows they consider valuable into gold, forcing them to produce embryos every two months instead of a calf a year. They can even use female bodies to hatch embryos of an alien species: in 1981, they had a Holstein dairy cow at New York's Bronx Zoo gestate a gaur, a wild endangered species.[61]

• Superovulation: Animals normally produce one egg a month. But reproductive engineers want many eggs for "efficient operation." Knowing that hormones produced by the pituitary gland affect the ovaries, they inject such hormones into a female, forcing her to ovulate from an abnormally large number of follicles (the small sacs enclosing eggs). This is superovulation. They have used hormones to force newborn animals with immature ovaries to produce eggs; they can also use them to force very old females to produce eggs.

To transfer a fertilized egg, engineers superovulate and artificially inseminate a female, but then must retrieve the fertilized egg. At first, they killed her, cutting into her oviducts, which one research team defended thus: "Slaughter of donor animals augments the consistency of [egg] recovery."[62] But killing the animal lost them an investment, so they began trying to recover eggs by surgery. Because this often left the animal sterile or a "problem breeder," they tried other methods and now use a two-way-flow catheter to flush fluids into the uterus, and collect the fluids with the eggs in a receptacle. We have no report on whether this process causes the female pain.

• Twinning: A doctor has devised a way to divide an embryo in half, producing identical twins, two animals from one fertilized egg. By twinning "you double—reliably, easily, fast, cheaply— the number of embryos a valuable donor produces."[63] Three sets of females, not necessarily of the same species, are needed: egg donors, and primary and secondary recipients in whose bodies the divided embryos are, respectively, cultured and gestated.

Applying such techniques to humans made possible what is called the "surrogate motherhood" industry. The first attempt to transfer a fertilized egg to a human incubator was made in 1977. The mothers—who are real, not surrogates—are paid a small fee; the lawyers, doctors, and middlemen who arrange the implantation receive large fees. The huge profits to be made in this industry have led lawyers, physicians, legislators, and ethicists to address ways to institutionalize "surrogate motherhood" by state regulation and certification of the *women*, not the profiteers. Attorney Russell Scott wrote a book offering ideas for making professional breeding commonplace, suggesting men offer "healthy young host mothers" money, Social Security, educational opportunities, and other signs of public approval.[64] Bio*ethicist* George F. Kieffer insists "there are certainly enough women available to form a caste of childbearers, especially if the pay was right," commending the example of an unemployed nurse who offered to bear a child for a couple so she could take herself and her young daughter off welfare.[65]

Indeed, men wax enthusiastic about the opportunities womb-leasing offers women presumed to have no other skills. Vance Packard suggests it could offer young women an undemanding career: "It would help if the hired mother was of an easygoing nature and enjoyed pregnancy and TV-watching." She could even take another job if it were not physically arduous—he suggests selling tickets at a movie theater. If the "mercenary mother" gestated an embryo conceived with another woman's egg, little would be required of her "in the way of education, family background, good looks, or even skin color. If the woman is simply to be an incubator, the price would certainly be lower than if she contributed half the baby's heredity. . . . Pleasant, conscientious Mexican-American girls" in south Texas might leap at the chance to earn $5000 merely for being pregnant for nine months; Mexican "girls" might leap at half that.[66] Corea notes that several writers have suggested the "host mother's" fee be adjusted to the economy of her country.

California Superior Court judge Richard Parslow handed down a decision declaring that a woman who bore a baby was not its "rightful" mother.[67] A woman born without a womb provided an egg, which was fertilized in vitro by her husband's sperm, and placed in another woman's womb for gestation. The second woman, having spent nine months with the fetus, nourishing it from her body, sending and receiving emotional communications, going through labor and birth, felt connected to the baby. The judge declared she was not. A similar judgment was rendered Mary Beth Whitehead, who *did* provide the egg for the baby she carried. In both cases, male judges simply declared inoperative, null and void, the *most profound* connection on earth—between a woman and the baby she gives birth to.

Men's language in these cases shows that unlike women, to whom motherhood is essentially emotional, men see procreation as primarily economic. For example, except in matrilineal societies, women never got custody of children after divorce until the industrial revolution, when children were no longer economic assets, but burdens. Contemporary men's neglect of children is partly a response to this fact. Women not only carry the physical and emotional burden of childbearing but almost always take responsibility for raising the children. A woman's view of motherhood involves labor—of all sorts—which is arduous and long-term and requires sacrifice. The only thing that can make the sacrifice worthwhile is connection, feeling, loving responsibility. Some men have a similar attitude to parenthood, but the men in the forefront of reproductive technologies see reproduction from a strictly economic perspective. Marilyn Waring cites Paul Samuelson, a Nobel Prize winner in economics, who was excited by the economic promise implicit in the use of amniocentesis to abort females.

> With knowledge may come power to control. . . . if one learns by amniocentesis that an embryo is female, and if one prefers a male, an abortion might be decided on. If such customs become common, some far-reaching sociological changes could occur. And these would have economic ramifications. . . . Scarcity tends toward value. The more women there are, all things equal, the lower might be expected to be their relative wages and lifetime earnings. Feminists might therefore look with some approval upon a future trend toward more sons rather than daughters. . . . If some people indulge a strong enough preference for sons, that will skew the adult sex ratio upwards, tending to raise female wage

rates and lower male rates. . . . One past reason for preferring sons may have been their superior earning power. Although daughters may perhaps be counted on to be more nurturing to you in your old age, sons may have the greater where-withal to support you. Or the vanity of having the family name carried on may, under our patriarchal culture, be better served by sons. But now that the contrived scarcity of fe-males raises their earnings, you have a new economic motive to indulge your preference for males less.[68]

Physicist William Shockley, another Nobel Prize winner, came up with a plan to control population. First, propaganda will con-vince people that population limitation is desirable and necessary for survival. Then, after the census bureau calculates the number of children each woman may produce (2.2, if one-third of a 1 percent increase in population is allowed each year), the public health department will sterilize every girl as she enters puberty by subcutaneous insertion of a contraceptive capsule, which pro-vides a slow seepage of contraceptive hormones until it is re-moved. (This plan, devised many years ago, may sound fantastic. But note that such a contraceptive has indeed been invented and that judges are already ordering it implanted into unwilling women who have come under their courts' jurisdiction.)

At marriage, a woman will be issued twenty-two "deci-child certificates." (Note that she is precluded from reproducing until married, that is, firmly under the control of the patriarchy.) When she hands over ten of them, a doctor removes the contraceptive capsule, replacing it after she has a baby. After two babies, the *couple* may sell their remaining two certificates on the stock exchange (!) or try to buy eight more on the open market to have a third child. Those who do not want children may sell all twenty-two certificates.[69] (Thus, only the well-to-do will have the priv-ilege of producing more than two children: this plan has every-thing!) Jalna Hanmer and Pat Allen remark that the plan puts female reproduction under the control of a state that is male-dominated—as Shockley presumably expected it to remain.

War by Blame. In a patriarchy, women must be mothers and they, not men, are held responsible for failures in parenting. But women are also blamed for *not* bearing children. The biological facts of reproduction have been known for centuries and treatment has changed in line with new medical techniques and discoveries, but both scientific and popular thinking still focuses on females as the cause for infertility: women who do not bear children are bad.[70] Over the last two centuries, scientists have persisted in asserting that women's natural maternal urges are subverted by educational, occupational, or political aspirations, equal rights, divorce, and birth control. Medical literature portrays childless women as the ultimate bad mothers, who by withholding mothering altogether are responsible for the downfall of national morality, home and family, the human race itself.

The issue of infertility was revived in the 1980s to become the subject of hosts of professional and popular books and articles and television news and dramas. A prominent specialist on infertility called it a public health problem of epidemic proportions. *Yet there is no substantive evidence that the overall incidence of infertility in the United States has grown in the past decade.* Margarete Sandelowski believes the focus on infertility is a response to women's greater autonomy and expanded freedoms; infertility looms as a price women will have to pay for reproductive freedom, that young upwardly mobile couples pay for concentrating on their careers, acquiring material goods, and pursuing sexual pleasure. It is another part of the worldwide war against women waged in the knowledge that egalitarianism—or, put another way, female autonomy—threatens "the family," i.e., male prerogatives.

Delaying childbearing can reduce fertility in some women; contraception and abortion can sometimes lead to ovulatory irregularities, pelvic infections, and pelvic adhesions impeding conception. And sexually active women are more likely to use contraception, to have had one or more abortions, and to contract sexually transmitted diseases. In addition, today's natural environment and many work environments expose people to injuries and toxic agents that affect reproductive organs, preventing conception or causing miscarriage. But many of these factors affect men too. Though doctors know about sperm deficiencies and how men cause female sterility by transmitting gonorrhea, they are reluctant to hold men responsible, "tending to exonerate the man if only one sperm cell could be shown to be viable." Contemporary literature on infertility continues to harp on female volition, writes Sandelowski, conflating two notions: that infertility is a result of a deliberate effort to thwart nature and that it expresses a woman's unconscious or disguised will.

Simply scanning the many forms of control men try to exert on female procreation produces a picture of total nonfreedom for women. No matter what they do or do not do, they can never be right by these male standards, are always open to criticism and sometimes to state or institutional intervention between them and their own bodies, them and their children. The web of regulation and interpretation men weave around women works to allow them to intervene whenever they want to, yet take no responsibility for the consequences. While men often couch their actions in the language of good intentions, their real goal is power over women: to deny women their right not to have a child, or their right to raise their children as they see fit.

Part III

THE
CULTURAL
WAR
AGAINST
WOMEN

The real attitudes of a society often lie buried from view, and can be extricated only by close analysis of behavior, language, and images. One cannot "prove" male hatred for women by citing statistics about female poverty everywhere in the world, because men can counter by impugning women's intelligence or competence, arguing that women *deserve* to be poor. That wars kill the children to whom most women devote their lives does not prove them inimical to women in particular: men may shrug and say that, sadly, the world is a harsh place for men too and women must accept it. But men who fight each other with fists often embrace afterward; enemy nations too may develop deep ties after a war. The purpose of war is to prove certain men's superiority to others, to "make a woman of" or "unman" another society (many early myths make this intention explicit) and to extirpate or transcend the "feminine" in the male. This attitude pervades the language spoken in the military and the "defense" industry.

WAR AGAINST WOMEN AS REVEALED IN MILITARY LANGUAGE

Carol Cohn spent a summer studying with male experts in nuclear strategy.[1] To understand them—and speak so they could understand her—she had to learn their language, one made up largely of invented words, acronyms impenetrable to most of us. Cohn found it a "sexy" language, offering the delight in power that comes from knowing things ordinary people don't know, that shows ones intimacy with the most secret, highest reaches of state policy. Appalled by her pleasure in this language, she acknowledges it to suggest how seductive the power of such knowledge can be. She not only found its words fun to say, but was gratified at knowing the language of priests privy to god, designed to mystify and awe. Indeed, from its inception, nuclear science has used religious imagery. The inventors of the atomic bomb called its first test "Trinity" after the Holy Trinity, the united Father, Son, and Holy Spirit, "the male forces of Creation." As it exploded in its first test, its main inventor, Robert Oppenheimer, thought of Krishna's words to Arjuna in the *Bhagavad Gita:* "I am become Death, the Shatterer of Worlds." And the men who today devise strategic doctrine call their community "the nuclear priesthood."[2]

Nuclear scientists use another set of images—images of birth, birth through the male as in male initiation rituals. Scientists at Los Alamos called the atom bomb "Oppenheimer's baby"; those at Lawrence Livermore called the hydrogen bomb "Teller's baby." Those who wanted to disparage Edward Teller argued that "he was not the bomb's father but its mother," and attributed fatherhood to Stanislaw Ulam, who "had the all-important idea and inseminated Teller with it. Teller only 'carried it' after that." A briefing officer, excitedly describing the technical capabilities of a new satellite system, added self-effacingly, "We'll do the motherhood role—telemetry, tracking, and control—the maintenance."

As in religious hierarchies, birth through the male produces only males. The perversity of patriarchal thinking is such that these men felt the bombs that wreaked such human horror on Hiroshima and Nagasaki were their babies, "Little Boy" and "Fat Man." Cohn remarks that the bombs were not only the atomic scientists' progeny, but emphatically male progeny: in early tests, before they were sure the bombs would work, the scientists expressed their anxiety by saying that "they hoped the baby was a boy, not a girl—that is, not a dud." After the success of the first test, General Leslie Groves cabled Secretary of War Henry Stimson: "Doctor has just returned most enthusiastic and confident that the little boy is as husky as his big brother. The light in his eyes discernible from here to Highhold and I could have heard his screams from here to my farm." Stimson then wrote Churchill: "Babies satisfactorily born." In 1952, after the hydrogen bomb (named "Mike") tested successfully at Eniwetok Atoll in the Marshall Islands, Teller triumphantly telegraphed Los Alamos: "It's a boy." Cohn comments: "The entire history of the bomb project . . . seems permeated with imagery that confounds man's overwhelming technological power to destroy nature with the power to create."

The view of life as a struggle for power generates a language in which life has no significance and only power matters. So nuclear scientists refer to the killing of human beings not on their own "side" as "collateral damage." Military men, who adopted this parlance, used it in their television appearances to describe Iraqis killed in the 1990–91 gulf war (whose actual number remains a state secret). Eighteenth-century physicians in Britain's Royal Society began to use euphemisms in writing up their experiments because simple language made clear the horrifying pain they were inflicting. This policy is now followed in every discipline that attacks, mutilates, and kills humans (even those supposedly intended to help them, like medicine). The term "collateral damage" also suggests that human beings were not the targets of attack, but simply in the way of the important business. So defense analysts call the incineration of cities "countervalue attacks."

Cohn's article was published in 1987, but we are all now familiar with some of the terminology she describes. We know that "surgically clean strikes" (shortened to "surgical strikes") are "counterforce" attacks (attacks by weapons on weapons or militarily useful installations) that are supposed to "take out" (accurately destroy) an opponent's weapons or command centers without causing significant damage to anything else. War is waged between weapons systems, not human beings, as if "enemies" sat at opposite sides of the globe playing video games. An MX missile carries ten warheads, each with the explosive power of 300–475 kilotons of TNT—a destructive power about 250–400 times that of the bomb that leveled Hiroshima. This is the weapon Ronald Reagan dubbed "the Peacekeeper." While the defense analysis community mockingly scorned his euphemism, they themselves call the MX a "damage limitation weapon." They also discuss "clean bombs"—nuclear devices that work largely by fusion rather than fission and therefore release *more* energy not as radiation but as blast, destructive explosive power. They are "clean" because they do not emit as much radiation, but they have a greater potential to kill and destroy.

Men have appropriated not just birth but "women's work," using nursery and domestic images to mask the horror of what they do. They approve "clean" bombs and speak longingly of "patting" bombs and missiles. They named an electronic system designed to prevent the unauthorized firing of nuclear warheads

"PAL" (permissive action links), a "carefully constructed, friendly acronym"; they called an early version of an antiballistic missile system "BAMBI," an acronym for ballistic missile boost intercept. They call the president's Annual Nuclear Weapons Stockpile Memorandum, listing short- and long-range plans to produce new nuclear weapons, "the shopping list." They choose from a "menu" of options when selecting targeting plans. Scientists call one model of nuclear attack the "cookie cutter," and the pattern MIRVed missiles' nuclear warheads make when they land a "footprint." Men do not drop nuclear bombs; they are "delivered" by a "bus." They do not use the terms "nuclear bombs" or "warheads," but call them "reentry vehicles" or "RVs"—as if they were recreational vehicles, trailers.

Cohn's summer seminar included nine other women. She expected such highly educated, knowledgeable men, faced with ten women in their midst, to feel discomfort about their more macho expressions. But, she writes, she was wrong. They seemed innocent of feminist critique of male behavior and openly said that for the American military, nuclear weapons were "irresistible, because you get more bang for the buck." They told her that scientists would never seriously contemplate disarmament because disarmament is emasculation: "to disarm is to get rid of all your stuff." One professor explained that the MX missile would not replace older, less accurate missiles, but be placed in the silos of the newest Minuteman missiles, "because they're in the nicest hole—you're not going to take the nicest missile you have and put it in a crummy hole." Scientists lectured on "vertical erector launchers, thrust-to-weight ratios, soft lay-downs, deep penetration, and the comparative advantages of protracted versus spasm attacks"—defined by one military adviser to the National Security Council as "releasing 70 to 80 percent of our megatonnage in one orgasmic whump." They expressed serious concern about "the need to harden our missiles and the need to 'face it, the Russians are a little harder than we are.' "

Cohn found *Air Force Magazine*'s advertisements for new weapons a rival to *Playboy* in cataloging men's sexual anxieties and fantasies. Ads promote weapons as "big sticks" or "penetrators," or for their "cratering" powers. When French military men do nuclear tests on the Mururoa Atoll in the South Pacific, they give every crater they gouge out of the earth a woman's name. Phallic imagery is common in descriptions of nuclear blasts. Cohn cites one by journalist William Laurence, who witnessed the bombing of Nagasaki: "Then, just when it appeared as though the thing had settled down into a state of permanence, there came shooting out of the top a giant mushroom that increased the size of the pillar to a total of 45,000 feet. The mushroom top was even more alive than the pillar, seething and boiling in a white fury of creamy foam, sizzling upward and then descending earthward, a thousand geysers rolled into one."[3]

A Pentagon target analyst explained that plans for "limited nuclear war" were doomed because "it's a pissing contest—you gotta expect them to use everything they've got." When India exploded a nuclear bomb, a professor remarked that "she" had lost her "virginity"; when New Zealand parliamentarian Marilyn Waring forced her government to bar nuclear-armed or nuclear-powered warships from its ports, a retired U.S. Air Force general, Ross Milton, wrote an angry column in *Air Force Magazine* called "Nuclear Virginity." Cohn found the world of nuclear weaponry pervaded by friendship and even romance: "enemies 'exchange' warheads; one missile 'takes out' another; weapons systems can 'marry up' "; the wires linking warning and response mechanisms allow "coupling." But this sex and romance aim at murder. If one of ones own warheads "kills" another of ones own warheads, that is "fratricide." And while these men devoted considerable discussion to "vulnerability" and "survivability," they were concerned not with the vulnerability and survival of people but of weapons systems.

Cohn quotes two descriptions of the aftermath of a nuclear attack. One, by Hisako Matsubara, who was a child in Kyoto when the atomic bomb was dropped, is based on survivors' memories:

Everything was black, had vanished into the black dust, was destroyed. Only the flames that were beginning to lick their way up had any color. From the dust that was like a fog, figures began to loom up, black, hairless, faceless. They screamed with voices that were no longer human. Their screams drowned out the groans rising everywhere from the rubble, groans that seemed to rise from the very earth itself."[4]

The second is in nukespeak, by an Army general on the National Security Council during the Carter administration:

You have to have ways to maintain communication in a nuclear environment, a situation bound to include EMP blackout, brute force damage to systems, a heavy jamming environment, and so on.[5]

The most appalling and profound truth about all this is that these men are not even concerned with their own survival. Only power matters: it is god, an exalted disembodied force more important than humankind. It is difficult to plumb such absurd and perverse thinking. Cohn stresses that men's reference point in technostrategic discourse is not themselves or even white men, is not human beings at all; it is the weapons. These men call human death "collateral damage" less to conceal human suffering than because human death *is* collateral to what matters to them— weapons themselves. But, Cohn points out, when men create a discourse that excludes human life in its calculus, it is impossible to include humans and illegitimate to expect the discourse to reflect human concerns. She realized that knowledge of this language did not enable one to introduce such concerns or influence political decisions. She even questioned whether the discourse was part of the process by which political decisions are made. Cohn believes that technostrategic discourse functions as a gloss, an "ideological curtain" disguising the real reasons for political decisions. It is however likely that those decisions are based on the same assumptions, the same values, as the discourse. Terrifyingly.

WAR AGAINST WOMEN IN ART

No comprehensive study has yet been done of the attitudes toward women underlying twentieth-century art, but John Berger's important *Ways of Seeing* links the depiction of women in Western painting and advertising with capitalism's obsession with commodities.[6] The god of capitalism (which Berger shows to be almost a religion) is money. Only money and money alone can bring a man status, love, and happiness (defined as the envy of others). Arguing that the tradition of Western painting was picked up by advertising in this century, Berger demonstrates that not just the art itself but also the subject matter of most Western art are commodities designed to appeal to a male buyer. The ultimate consumer is always presumed to be male, even in ads directed at women: they are urged to buy things that will make them more attractive commodities to male buyers. In themselves, women are only the most important goods the world has to offer to male buyers. Their sexuality, motherhood, beauty, and labor are displayed as items available to men with enough money. But Berger's brilliant, fascinating argument does not even touch men's hatred for those same commodities.

Feminists do point out the woman-hatred in the work of painters like Willem de Kooning, Picasso, or Balthus's portrayals of shockingly lascivious little girls, but a feminist analysis of art is impeded by the fact that we are pledged in our souls to freedom of expression. Artists appropriate the female body as their subject, their possession. Whether they paint women with hatred or idealize them or vapidly sentimentalize them (like Renoir, say) or appropriate them with cold superiority (like Degas, say), they are implicitly assaulting female reality and autonomy.[7] But we cannot deny artists their right to their own vision. Jerome Robbins had the right to create a ballet ("The Cage") in which insect-like females eviscerate two men, although in reality women rarely attack men. Depictions of threatening women are common in all the arts and presumably express a real male terror of women. And no wonder! Having subjugated women in every realm of life, they naturally fear retaliation.

Acclaimed modern sculptors depict women with small vacant heads and prominent or hugely enlarged sexual organs. Visiting galleries and museums (especially the Pompidou Center in Paris), I feel assaulted by twentieth-century abstract sculpture that resembles exaggerated female body parts, mainly breasts. These huge body parts seem intended to mock and dismember prehistoric sculptures of female bodies.

It is not the eroticization of the female image that disturbs, but the fact that it is eroticized *in order to be appropriated*, by one sex taking a superior position, buyer to commodity. Many women are repelled at seeing their own bodies so appropriated or transformed into commodities in commercial art and fashion. Most swallow their distress; many, having been taught to "see" this way, deform themselves to fit that mold, like Cinderella's stepsisters butchering their feet to fit a prince's glass slipper. None of us can do more than try to see clearly and say *what* we see. And what we cannot fail to see in art is men's hatred of women—and a cannibalistic male psyche. Women who analyze or depict this male psyche are usually accused of "male-bashing." A society complacent about negative female imagery in the arts grows absurdly censorious when women attack male values, behavior, and images.

The debasement of women in art and advertising is echoed in cinematic images. Women are treated so shabbily in film that *New York Times* critic Janet Maslin, not notably a feminist, was moved to protest the bimboizing of women like Madonna in *Dick Tracy*, Jennifer Jason Leigh in *Last Exit to Brooklyn* and *Miami Blues*, Victoria Abril in Pedro Almodóvar's *Tie Me Up! Tie Me Down!*, and Goldie Hawn in *Bird on a Wire*. In the last, Hawn is a lawyer, yet is not only ditsy but spends much of the film in a negligee.[8] The most popular film of 1990, *Pretty Woman*, is a Cinderella story about a prostitute. Advertisements for films often show their lead female character near naked, even if she does not appear that way in the film, or men handling women as prey, like Gérard Depardieu with a smiling Andie McDowell slung over his shoulder (*Green Card*). Rape or near-rape is becoming as obligatory in violent films in the United States as it has long been in India.[9] Add to this a tendency in film and books to portray career women as mean and selfish (Sigourney Weaver in *Working Girl*) or utterly evil (*Fatal Attraction* or *Presumed Innocent*, which as a novel topped the best-seller list for two years), and the diminishment and hatred of women in popular entertainment (consider Andrew Dice Clay, Sam Kinison, Jason and Freddy, 2 Live Crew), and you have an anatomy of men's feelings toward women in our age without even mentioning pornography.

Pornography. Actual male violence toward women will be discussed in Part IV; here we will discuss artistic representations of it. I define art as symbolic expression, without distinguishing high or low, serious or popular. I do not accept the word "pornography," but use it to be understood. I would prefer to refer to "erotic" art, art intended to arouse desire; I find erotic art in principle inoffensive. But any art that degrades women does offend me.

Years ago, few women were upset about pornography. Sadistic porn was rare. Only educated men read the Marquis de Sade or *The Story of O* (which some attribute to André Malraux), and my male friends insisted educated men were somehow immune to such work. But some women felt "popular" pornography to be dangerous. Questioning this, I read some. It was not sadistic; it centered on intercourse and was extremely, tediously repetitive, clearly designed to aid male masturbation. It seemed harmless, maybe even a boon to women if it kept men from rape—which at the time everyone thought was a crime rooted in frustrated desire. I dismissed pornography. As a writer, I opposed censorship of any sort.

Those were days of innocence. Not only did we accept snobbish class-bound distinctions as part of the natural order, but we did not yet know what twenty-odd years of feminism have revealed: the dimensions, cruelty, and pervasiveness of men's unconscionable treatment of women in actual life, concealed behind the lace curtains of the home generations of male-supremacists called sacred. Moreover, after the male "sexual revolution," pornography changed, growing far more widespread and moving from books to film to video. When it began to portray children as well as women, we discovered that men were sexually molesting children and always had (ones personal experience was not in fact merely a personal experience). In the late 1960s, pornography reached staggering depths of violence, hatred, and cruelty. Films featured lynching, mainly of Asian women; it is believed that the actresses in some "snuff" films were actually killed to make the film:

mutilation and murder tilted men into orgasm. But feminist analysis has taught us that even mild pornography degrades women and teaches men to see them through a distorted, deforming lens.

In the early 1980s, people in a poor Minneapolis neighborhood plagued by shops filled with pornography asked lawyer Catherine MacKinnon and Andrea Dworkin, well-known anti-pornography activists, to draft a bill prohibiting pornographic presentation of women or "men, children or transsexuals in the place of women." The code they drafted defined pornography as "graphic, sexually explicit subordination of women," in pictures or words, that also includes the following:

   (i)   women are presented dehumanized as sexual objects, things or commodities; or
   (ii) women are presented as sexual objects who enjoy pain or humiliation; or
   (iii) women are presented as sexual objects who experience sexual pleasure in being raped; or
   (iv) women are presented as sexual objects tied up or cut up or mutilated or bruised or physically hurt; or
   (v)   women are presented in postures of sexual submission, servility or display; or
   (vi) women's body parts—including but not limited to vaginas, breasts, and buttocks—are exhibited, such that women are reduced to those parts; or
   (vii) women are presented as whores by nature; or
   (viii) women are presented being penetrated by objects or animals; or
   (ix) women are presented in scenarios of degradation, injury, torture, shown as filthy or inferior, bleeding, bruised, or hurt in a context that makes these conditions sexual.[10]

The city of Minneapolis passed this code in 1983 and 1984; both times the mayor vetoed it.

In 1984, a member of the Indianapolis City Council introduced a different version of the code, which was signed into law by the mayor. A coalition of book, magazine, and video sellers immediately obtained an injunction against it. The Federal District Court declared it unconstitutional, and the case went to the Seventh Circuit Court of Appeals. Two judges, agreeing that "depictions of subordination tend to perpetuate subordination" of women and lead to "affront and lower pay at work, insult and injury at home, battery and rape on the streets" and that "pornography affects how people see the world, their fellows, and social relations," nevertheless concluded that these effects simply demonstrate the power of pornography as speech, which may not be leashed.[11] The Supreme Court declined to hear the case. In 1988, the code was voted in on a referendum in Bellingham, Washington, but was again ruled unconstitutional.

The campaign to pass this code was supported by the religious right in an uneasy alliance with feminists. MacKinnon distinguishes between right-wing and feminist anti-pornography positions, arguing that the right wing wants to pass obscenity laws and feminists political laws. Obscenity laws, she holds, focus on "morality," morals seen from a male point of view, the standpoint of male dominance; the feminist critique of pornography is "politics, specifically politics from women's point of view," the standpoint of women's subordination to men. Morality deals with good and evil, politics with power and powerlessness: "Obscenity is a moral idea; pornography is a political practice. Obscenity is abstract; pornography is concrete."[12]

MacKinnon sees right-wing notions of obscenity as based on a 1973 law outlawing obscenity defined as whatever an "average person applying contemporary community standards" finds "taken as a whole, appeals to the prurient interest . . . [which] depicts or describes, in a patently offensive way, sexual conduct specifically defined by the applicable state law; and [which], taken as a whole, lacks serious literary, artistic, political, or scientific value."[13] Doubting the existence of an "average person, gender neutral," MacKinnon suspects community standards more than deviations from them, and asks why "prurience counts but powerlessness doesn't," why "sensibilities are better protected from offense than women are from exploitation." She believes that sexuality, "including its violation and expropriation," is broader than state laws suggest, and asks why a body of law that cannot in practice distinguish rape from intercourse should be entrusted with distinguishing pornography from art.

Most insightful is her argument that both the legal obscenity standard and pornography derive from the male standpoint, so that obscenity laws reproduce the pornographic point of view on the level of constitutional jurisprudence. "Pornography institutionalizes the sexuality of male supremacy, which fuses the erotization of dominance and submission with the social construction of male and female." Patriarchists present men's war against women as erotic, a turn-on for both sexes, and use pornography to teach each their mutually exclusive dominant and submissive roles. MacKinnon claims defenders of pornography, whether "feminists, lawyers, or neo-Freudians," believe they are supporting "human sexual liberation" but are really defending sexual terrorism and the subordination of women.

But both positions—the patriarchal and the feminist—are political *and* moral. The difference between them lies elsewhere. Both try to use the same means but to achieve different ends. Anti-pornography feminists want to alter the American cultural climate so as to reduce violence against women and eliminate a force that undermines women's self-esteem and confidence. Anti-pornography conservatives want to alter the American cultural climate to make sexuality a taboo subject, to keep it utterly hidden. If they succeeded in censoring sadistic and degrading erotic art, they would campaign to censor all public expression of eroticism. Most feminists do not find this a desirable goal.

Anti-pornography feminists, however, believe that the safety and well-being of over half the human race is of greater value than the freedom to create degrading images of women that, at the least, legitimate and, at worst, promote sadistic violence against them. But when they protest the publication of such works, men accuse them of being puritanical censors who would have silenced Flaubert, Lawrence, Joyce, and Henry Miller, and scornfully lump them with fundamentalists who remove classics from the shelves of local libraries. Those who cite the First Amendment are treating freedom of expression as more important than eliminating a force that injures women. Yet freedom of expression *is* a vital right.

Both these positions are untenable; they are legalistic and do not reflect people's actual feelings. People of both sexes who loathe sadistic or degrading portrayals of women and sexual power relations find themselves silenced by this impasse. But all parties to this irresolvable conflict start from the assumption that expression *is* free in the United States. This assumption is false. Expression is, and always has been in this and every state since patriarchy began, subject to taboos.

Taboos are political. They exist to keep people from thinking independently, which might make them aware they are oppressed. They are aimed at precluding solidarity in groups that threaten the elite, mainly people oppressed *by* the elite. Taboos are enforced by power.[14] In the United States, *private* expression is free, although small communities censor speech by pressure, shunning or harassing those who express unpopular views. People opposed to the gulf war felt silenced in many communities. Private expression of unpopular views can possibly earn one an FBI dossier, but is unlikely to get one hauled off to a Lubyanka.

However, public expression is censored *everywhere:* either directly (by laws defining dissent as treason, or by state terrorism—persecution of dissenters) or indirectly, under the euphemism of "the market." The United States uses both methods: it has made dissent illegal and used state terrorism to silence socialists and organizers of black political movements. But the power of money usually suffices to censor public expression. Opposers of the gulf war watched television networks censor their reportage of protest marches we were part of or knew had occurred elsewhere. The more popular a medium, the more it is subject to censorship: television, film, and glossy magazines are most censored. In the United States, censorship is imposed not by a religious body or the government, but by corporations that sponsor television productions and advertise in the print media. Newspaper publishers who shape the presentation of "hard news"—supposed objective fact—often share the interests of corporations.

Filmmakers and book publishers are freest from interference, yet even before writers start to draft a work, long before it is distributed to the public, they know what they cannot say. Some people in the West scorned writers in Eastern European countries where censorship was open and heavy for colluding with the government to produce acceptable "art." Yet self-censorship is even more insidious: restraints have been internalized and writers may not be aware they are censoring themselves. Most do not even think about writing what they know will not be published. It takes an extraordinarily courageous and assured writer to dissent without legitimation by a political movement.

In the United States, since the emergence of the civil rights and feminist movements, blacks, feminists, and gay people can write or make art containing taboo material, *if* they are willing to distribute it themselves, selling Xeroxed copies from sidewalk pushcarts (which many do), live in poverty (which most writers do anyway), and give up hope for a larger reputation. No secret police will descend to imprison the authors of such *samizdat* (underground self-published books).

But even mass-market black magazines modify or launder the dissenting or revolutionary ideas of black thinkers. To spread their ideas, feminists must maintain their own journals—their work never appears *undistorted* in the major media; lesbians have opened their own publishing houses. An individual has the freedom to work in comparative obscurity and poverty in order to write freely, but with a few exceptions, her or his ideas do not penetrate the larger culture. America's ruling class has found a solution to the problem of freedom of expression: it is not necessary to maintain a KGB and gulags when you can simply keep dissenting ideas from being widely diffused.

Therefore it is easiest to discover a society's taboos by looking at the most popular media. A thorough analysis of the attitudes being promoted or censored in film or television would require a book to itself, but two recent articles on the reborn *MS.* magazine expose the effect of corporate power on women's magazines. *MS.* was never radical: it carefully avoided "male-bashing" and limited its political agenda to empowering women. It informed women as no other women's magazine did, about their own bodies, emotions, activities, and accomplishments, and never challenged capitalist notions beyond refusing to present women as commodities for male purchase. But even that was too much for the male establishment that controls all the money—and the advertising on which magazines depend for their life.

All magazines are to some degree controlled by advertisers; even supposedly independent news magazines use "soft" cover stories to sell ads; all censor articles that might disturb big advertisers or the government. Peggy Orenstein observes that many advertisers, terrified of controversy, avoid political magazines like *Mother Jones, The Nation, Harper's,* and *The Atlantic,* which need private contributions to stay afloat.[15] Women's magazines generally cannot attract such private backing because few women have money. And, Gloria Steinem writes, advertisers exert terrific pressure on women's magazines, dictating or at least guiding almost their entire content.[16]

Makers of products for women require women's magazines (called "cash cows" in the trade) to print recipes and articles on beauty and fashion to highlight their ads, and further, to promote a *certain kind* of beauty, food, and fashion—the accoutrements of woman-as-commodity. Leonard Lauder refused to place ads for Estée Lauder products in *MS.* because, he told Steinem, Estée Lauder was selling "a kept-woman mentality." Steinem protested that 60 percent of his customers work for wages and resemble *MS.* readers. He was unmoved. He knows his customers, he said, "and they would *like* to be kept women."

MS. did receive a little advertising from Clairol—until it mentioned a congressional hearing on chemicals used in hair dyes which, absorbed through the skin, may be carcinogenic. Although newspapers also reported on this hearing, Clairol removed its ads from *MS.* (It also changed its formula.) Learning that four women in the Soviet Union who produced feminist *samizdat* had been exiled (feminist ideas, considered dissent, were illegal in the Soviet Union), the *MS.* editors solicited contributions so Robin Morgan could go to Vienna to interview them. The cover story Morgan wrote, Steinem recalls, was a coup, offering "the first news of a populist peace movement in Afghanistan, a prediction of *glasnost,*" and an intimate glimpse of Soviet women's lives. It won a Front Page award. But it lost the magazine one of its few advertisers: Revlon withdrew its ads because the Soviet women pictured on the cover *were not wearing makeup.*

Many advertisers avoid women's magazines entirely, fearing that a product that becomes associated with women will be devalued for men. When Steinem visited a trade fair to drum up advertising she found VCR manufacturers demonstrating their product with pornographic videos. Some advertisers felt an irrational hatred for *MS.*: a food producer made reservations for dinner with the *MS.* editors at an expensive restaurant they could not afford, sat through their pitch, and after dinner threw the magazine on the table and said, "I wouldn't advertise in this fucking piece of shit if it were the last magazine on earth." A publisher of other women's magazines visited advertisers seeking ads and gratuitously urged them not to put ads in that "dyke" magazine.

The story has—so far—a happy ending: *MS.* is publishing again in a new format, without advertising, depending on subscriptions alone. But its editors' experience demonstrates the double standard in the magazine world: advertisers demand more control over women's magazines than over men's magazines or other publications, Steinem writes. They stipulate that ads be placed next to "compatible" material or that they not appear near controversial features. Among the issues they consider "controversial" are sickness, large body size, or *disillusionment.* Women must be happy all the time. Procter and Gamble, a giant conglomerate and major advertiser, stipulated that its products not be advertised in any issue that mentioned gun control, abortion, the occult, or cults, or that disparaged religion. Is this censorship?

To be assured of advertising revenue, women's magazines must be vapid, contentless. Steinem chose random issues from early 1990 and counted the pages of actual content—including even letters to the editor and horoscopes—versus pages of ads and "complementary copy" (articles written to advertisers' specifications). She found that the April *Glamour* had 65 pages of real copy out of 339; May *Vogue,* 38 pages of copy out of 319; April *Redbook,* 44 out of 173; March *Family Circle,* 33 out of 180; May *Elle,* 39 out of 326; and November 1989 *Lear's,* 65 out of 173.

Underlying advertisers' constraints is the fear shared by the male establishment generally, that women with a stronger self-image might no longer be willing to remain a servant class, might even unite against exploitation. To keep a group subordinate, an elite must persuade it that it deserves subordination because of *innate* inferiorities. A person of an inferior group cannot be the author of her or his own life but must center on the superior group. Thus women must be presented as mainly sexual, indeed heterosexual, beings who have no life apart from men. And it is essential that a subordinated group not perceive its dominators as oppressors. The primary taboo forbids portraying men-as-a-caste as responsible for women's problems: if one man appears as a woman's oppressor, another must appear as her savior.

When this taboo is broken, men protest. Consider, for instance, male reaction to the female-buddy film *Thelma and Louise.* Most male characters in this film are unexceptional, men most women are familiar with—a selfish, contemptuous husband, an uncommitted lover, a predatory rapist, a predatory truck driver. Two are unlikely—a sexy thief and a sympathetic police officer. Except for a Rastafarian with a sense of humor who never meets them, all the men exploit the female heroes in some way. But the film is not primarily concerned with men. It focuses on the women as oppressed human beings who liberate themselves joyously.

Thelma and Louise take violent revenge on the predatory men, but the film contains much less violence than almost any male film these days: only *one* person is murdered. But *Thelma and Louise* is radical; it breaks two major taboos: it shows men at war on women, and women retaliating against men. It is more realistic than films about violent men, who are always reabsorbed into the community if sometimes as marginal figures. But retaliating turns women into outlaws—women's real identity in a male-supremacist world, according to writers like Flora Tristan, Mary Wollstonecraft, and Virginia Woolf—and makes it impossible for them to go on living in such a world. Yet it is in the outlaw role that they discover themselves. The film addresses *human* liberation, and at the showing I attended, men as well as women were exhilarated by the heroines' discovery of freedom.

But other men were outraged by this film. Ralph Novak in *People* magazine wrote, "Any movie that went as far out of its way to trash women as this female chauvinist sow of a film does to trash men would be universally, and justifiably, condemned." He calls its male director a "gender quisling," tacitly acknowledging the existence of a sex war.[17] *Time's* Richard Schickel allows others to bear the onus of condemnation, opening his review with this sentence (emphasis mine): "It is 'the first movie I've ever seen which told the downright truth,' says Mary Lucey, *a lesbian activist* in Los Angeles." Schickel quotes John Leo of *U.S. News & World Report:* it is "a paean to transformative violence . . . an explicit fascist theme," and Richard Johnson in the New York *Daily News:* "It justifies armed robbery, manslaughter and chronic drunken driving."[18] Considering the acts male movies "justify," one can only laugh. Despite its considerable success, the movie has endured a chorus of condemnation hard for anyone to bear, and the movie's courageous writer, Callie Khouri, will need even more courage to write anything so "female" again. And other female writers know that the battle lines have been drawn.

The taboo on portraying the real sexual power relations in society affects all cultural forms to some degree. For instance, many published works contain hideous *fictional* male violence toward women, but it is hard to publish a book that discusses *actual* male violence toward women. There is little market for books on battering or rape. The cultural establishment is in the position of refusing to hinder the diffusion of works depicting male sadism toward women (on grounds a bar would be censorship) while hindering the diffusion of those depicting male oppression of women (on grounds of "the market"). This situation clearly has to do with sexual politics, not freedom of expression.

There are taboos on the cultural presentation of other groups and situations; taboos on the depiction of black men, for example, resemble those on women, for similar reasons. But some taboos work to benefit society. Anti-Semitism is not unknown in the United States, and some people consider it acceptable to hate Jews. But no film or television drama could show an approving attitude toward anti-Semitic acts. Producers self-censor such material—as they should: hatred of any group for its identity is evil. It is a moral imperative to show it as an evil. If the real dimensions of white persecution of blacks, especially in the economic realm, never appear in popular culture, neither does it focus gloatingly on the rape, mutilation, and murder of blacks. Yet popular works do dwell lovingly on the rape, mutilation, and murder of women. People disagree about morality, but certain acts are so blatantly cruel and evil that almost every human being finds them repugnant. Is not hatred and violent abuse of women such an evil? Why is it permitted to be portrayed?

The opponents of the anti-pornography feminists demand proof that pornographic works foster or inspire male violence against women. But the intersection of culture and life is not quantifiable or provable. One cannot *prove* that violence against women in pornography leads to violence against women in life any more than one can *prove* that the disparagement of blacks and Jews pervasive in nineteenth-century culture *caused* the horrors of African colonialism and the Holocaust. The mere suspicion of a connection is considered sufficient reason to refuse to legitimate hatred of groups. Only when it comes to women does our culture suspend this restraint.

Most films and television shows are produced by men for men. Their main purposes are to show white males triumphant, to teach gender roles, and to cater to men's delight in male predation and victimization of women, especially young, pretty, near-naked women with highly developed breasts and buttocks (parts that are usually the locus of attack). Like the men of the proto-Nazi German Freikorps that waged war between the wars, shooting women between the legs because they carried grenades there (!), American men's most satisfying target is women's sexuality, the area of men's greatest fear. Pornography is a systemic abuse of women because the establishment colludes in this male sadism toward women, which fits its purposes. Case in point: the Indian government, which does censor films for political content, *forbids scenes of lovemaking or kissing but allows rape;* indeed, a rape scene has been "all but requisite" in Indian films for some years, writes Anita Pratap.[19]

Since the first male leader imagined the first state, men who wanted to dominate—as priests, soldiers, or both—needed war to establish their supremacy. But war requires fighters, and people who have not been indoctrinated into a gender cult, have not been taught that aggression equals identity, do not want to fight. To get men to fight rather than flee, male leaders had to turn them against life, identified with women, sensual pleasure, children, the growing and eating of food.

Male leaders pursue the same policy today. Sexual harassment of women asserts male solidarity *across* class lines and divides working-class men from working-class women and reinforces class domination. An elite's primary need in establishing and maintaining domination is to divide men from women. Fostering male sadism promotes this division. American culture—movies, books, songs, television—teaches men to see themselves as killers, to identify the act of murder with sex, and the sex act with violent conquest. This is why so many men find it difficult to distinguish between rape and lovemaking.

A new biography of J. Edgar Hoover, the power-driven FBI director, reveals that he entertained his aides with screenings of pornographic films.[20] A news item revealed that on the nights before they bombed Iraq in the gulf war, fighter pilots on the USS *John F. Kennedy* watched pornographic movies featuring sadistic male violence toward women.[21] When an AP reporter on the ship, Neil MacFarquar, filed this story, the ship's public affairs officer censored it. Perhaps he felt it revealed a military secret.

Indeed, among the most repellent examples of woman-hatred appear in military songs and slogans. Klaus Theweleit's brilliant analysis of the sexual hatred motivating the Freikorps included a number of war songs and cartoons explicitly equating the mutilation of women with male prowess.[22] Christopher Hitchens describes a more recent work he accidentally came across—the recreational songbook of the 77th Tactical Squadron of the U.S. Air Force based outside Oxford, England. He was horrified by what he read and refused to print stanzas that he says were too tough for him.[23] Here are some examples of what he did print:

The Ballad of Lupe

Down in Cunt Valley where Red Rivers flow,
Where cocksuckers flourish and whoremongers grow,

There lives a young maiden that I do adore
She's my Hot Fuckin' Cocksuckin' Mexican Whore.

Oh Lupe, oh Lupe, dead in her tomb.
While maggots crawl out of her decomposed womb
But the smile on her face is a mute cry for more!!!
She's my Hot Fuckin' Cocksuckin' Mexican Whore.

Intercourse with dead women is a recurrent theme, Hitchens writes, quoting only one stanza of "I Fucked a Dead Whore":

I fucked a dead whore by the road side,
I knew right away she was dead.
The skin was all gone from her tummy,
The hair was all gone from her head.

Sadistic violence is not inherent in men's natures; it is indoctrinated in men by a host of institutions. Government bodies do not merely tolerate male sexual sadism against women, they foster and endorse it—in every male-dominated culture in the world.

Part IV

MEN'S
PERSONAL
WAR
AGAINST
WOMEN

From boyhood, males are bombarded with the message that "real" men dominate women, which means they control women's behavior and may abuse them verbally and physically. So powerful and pervasive is this formula for the *appearance of manhood* that a man with an equal, mutual relationship with a woman may adopt a posture of dominance toward her when other men are around. Such behavior suggests men believe "manhood" is not inherent in a man, but depends on both the opinion of other men and the existence of a subjected person or group. Male identity is therefore extremely unstable, and this instability creates anxiety, often expressed as rage.

Females have enormous power in this dynamic because the appearance of virility depends on them. Women are its center: domination of a woman is supposed to make a man feel like a man—that is, superior. Still, to justify abusive treatment of women in their own minds (after all, most men love some women), men must view them as a separate species, like pigs or dogs or cows (terms often applied to women); and dominating a lowly "dog" or "cow" can hardly be very satisfying. The formula, superstitious at its root, achieves its goal only fleetingly, unsatisfyingly. Yet instead of abandoning this unsuccessful road to self-worth, men walk it over and over again, as if enough repetition will somehow bring them to the end—blessed relief from self-doubt.

Other men, too, have power in this formula. This form of self-esteem can only be achieved by being witnessed by other men, who alone can confer manhood on a man. Moreover, men *cannot* dominate women without maintaining solidarity against them. Even a woman who accepts the status of obedient dog or brood cow has capacities for independent thought, action, speech, and creativity that militate against easy consignment of her to inferior status. To suppress these qualities, men must ally solidly against women, creating institutions that foreclose all roles to women except breeder-servanthood, thrust them into and keep them in the position of subhuman inferiors. That even a united male front has never totally succeeded in keeping women silent and subordinate does not deter men from continuing in this effort either.

Most men do not make policy in governments, churches, or

other powerful institutions. Most men serve as dogs, bulls, or robots to *their* masters. A man reading this book's indictment of global economic, political, and religious policies detrimental to women may feel his sex is being maligned, believing himself innocent of any complicity. Men continually remind women that they too are victims, are not responsible for government policy or economic disadvantage or war, that like women, they are oppressed. This is true. I question why they do not join the feminist movement or create a parallel movement. Nonetheless, the entire system of female oppression rests on ordinary men, who maintain it with a fervor and dedication to duty that any secret police force might envy. What other system can depend on almost half the population to enforce a policy daily, publicly and privately, with utter reliability?

As long as some men use physical force to subjugate females, *all* men need not. The knowledge that some men do suffices to threaten all women. Beyond that, it is not necessary to beat up a woman to beat her down. A man can simply refuse to hire women in well-paid jobs, extract as much or more work from women than men but pay them less, or treat women disrespectfully at work or at home. He can fail to support a child he has engendered, demand the woman he lives with wait on him like a servant. He can beat or kill the woman he claims to love; he can rape women, whether mate, acquaintance, or stranger; he can rape or sexually molest his daughters, nieces, stepchildren, or the children of a woman he claims to love. *The vast majority of men in the world do one or more of the above.*

Most information in this section on male violence describes the situation in the United States, because this data is most accessible to me. But a similar situation exists throughout the world, in equal or greater severity. The section is divided into two parts: daily war against women by ordinary men, economically and physically. Male violence toward women could not be as epidemic as it is without the cooperation of the entire social system—the press, police, courts, legislatures, academia, welfare agencies, the professions, and other institutions. Personal violence against women is a tissue of individual acts given firm backing by entrenched institutions. Just as women's problems are circular, so is male oppression: systemic war against women could not succeed without the cooperation of individual men, and individual men's wars on women require the cooperation of the system.

INDIVIDUAL MEN'S ECONOMIC WAR AGAINST WOMEN

The majority of men who leave their families do not support their children adequately or at all; few support the wives they insisted become dependent upon them. These facts have become well known in the past decade as the huge number of destitute women and children became a national problem—but a problem blamed on *women*. People blame welfare mothers, not irresponsible men or the arms budget, for the inflated national budget. Yet only a tiny percentage of the national budget is devoted to welfare aid. As a result of perverse national priorities, children comprise the single largest segment of the population living in poverty.

The statistics are staggering: judges do not order men to support their children in over 40 percent of cases when mothers get custody; when they do, they award them roughly $10 to $40 a week— a laughable amount considering what it costs to house, feed, clothe, provide medical care, and educate a child.[1] Even if judges do order men to support their children, the overwhelming majority of men fail to do so. In 1985, only 25 percent of the 8.8 million men required to pay child support paid it; another 25 percent sent lesser amounts; *half* paid nothing at all.[2] They simply abandon the fruit of their bodies. Women have little recourse: at most, they can file charges against the men and have them imprisoned. Not only does this defeat their purpose—a man in jail loses his wages—but most women cannot find lawyers who will help them in suing for nonsupport. The innumerable single mothers unable to obtain child support have no recourse at all.

Men are better off financially after divorce. Men have always been paid more than women, an inequity justified by their support of families. Yet on average in the first year after divorce, men have 42 percent more to spend on themselves, while their families live on 73 percent less. Children of divorced parents are almost twice as likely to live in poverty than before. Mothers who give up their children often do so because they cannot support them.

One man went so far as to declare bankruptcy to avoid paying his ex-wife anything. When Jeanne Farrey and Gerald Sanderfoot divorced in 1986, a Wisconsin court ordered Sanderfoot to pay Farrey alimony and child support and divided the marital property, giving him the house but ordering him to pay the debts and give Farrey $29,000. To enforce his compliance, the court gave Farrey a lien on the property for that amount. Eight months later, Sanderfoot declared bankruptcy. Farrey recalled his warning that if she divorced him, he would "see to it that I got nothing, that he was going to file for bankruptcy." In 1988, a female judge accused Sanderfoot of manipulating bankruptcy law and ordered him to pay his debt to Farrey, but her judgment was overturned by an appeals court which held that Sanderfoot had acted within the law. The case is being taken to the Supreme Court. (*The New York Times* reported this case under the headline "Can Bankruptcy Reduce the Price of a Divorce?" The headline brings the perspective of a male addressing men to a piece largely sympathetic to Farrey.)[3]

Middle-class whites often shrug off the statistics on female poverty, assuming such things only happen to the poor and non-white—who indeed make up a disproportionate percentage of unsupported mothers. But the majority of the destitute in the United States are white women and their children, many formerly middle-class. About 22 million women today remain dependent on their husband's income. Never having worked or not in decades, they are "just a man away from poverty," as the Displaced Homemakers Network in Washington, D.C., puts it.[4] More and more, judges award no-fault and equitable distribution divorces with little or no alimony, thrusting middle-class women into destitution. Many are still responsible for children, but 58 percent of displaced homemakers are over sixty-five, with no way to support themselves.[5]

Not that having a man in the house ensures women a more equitable deal. More than half the married women with children who work outside the home do all or most of the household maintenance—although surely all able-bodied persons in a household should take care of themselves and their own living space. A 1985 study showed that American men still refuse to take responsibility for themselves and their surroundings.[6] The only household tasks more men than women take responsibility for are yard work and home repairs. The stereotype has men handling money, but only 32 percent of men paid the bills until 1985, when 52 percent did so.

This study, conducted over decades, reveals that in 1965 American men worked in the household 4.6 hours a week, while women put in 27 hours; in 1975, men contributed 7 hours a week, women 21.7; and in 1985, men averaged 8.8 hours a week, women 19.5. If we continue at this rate, we may expect men to share maintenance tasks by 2025. In Eastern European countries, where marketing involves queuing for almost everything, household appliances are primitive (and not everyone has them), and take-out fast food is nonexistent, women spend endless hours on maintenance work after their work days—and most work outside the home. In Hungary, for instance, 80 percent of women work for wages. Men in most Eastern European countries, in India, and in most of Africa do no household work and take little responsibility for raising their children.

These statistics suggest why polls invariably show men happier than women after marriage: in 1965, women did housework 15.5 hours a week before marriage, but 31.6 after it; men put 4.7 hours into household tasks before marriage, but 4.5 after it. This situation too has improved: in 1985, single women worked in the household 14.9 hours and married women averaged 22.4 hours; single men put in 7.9 hours, married 11.1. Women with children under five have the greatest burden, averaging 22.5 hours a week of housework; those with children over five average 19.9.[7]

Marilyn Waring discusses a survey of recreation conducted in New Zealand that defined recreation as things people enjoy doing and become deeply involved in—hobbies, sports, social or cultural activities. Women overwhelmingly—nine out of ten, as opposed to five out of ten men—re-created themselves at home. Far more women were involved in cultural activities, men in sporting activities. But the most interesting finding was that children limited women's recreational participation to an extreme degree, but men spent *more* time at sporting events *after* the birth of their children.

Housework is not entirely unpleasant. Many people, women and men, enjoy cooking an occasional meal, putting wash in the machine, or straightening a closet. Some even claim to enjoy housecleaning. But it is arduous when money and space are tight, when one has young children, when one alone has to do it after putting in eight or more hours at another job. Women protest their exclusive responsibility for housework because they are overworked but also because the division of labor sets up an uneven power arrangement: the person responsible for maintenance automatically becomes a servant to the others. And since housework is unpaid, the woman serves without reward or respect.

Men's expectation that women will take responsibility for maintaining them is a carryover from infancy. Women perpetuate the system out of habit and inculcate their daughters with guilt. Men enforce the system by laws or customs that force women into economic dependence on men and by the ever-present threat: she who does not care for her man, does not mother him like a baby, will lose him and his economic support. Women are subjected by fear; men foster their own infantilization, believing it demonstrates their superiority. Yet even women's caretaking and service are not enough to keep men from being violent toward them. And beneath women's fear of losing economic support is their fear of men's physical violence.

INDIVIDUAL MEN'S PHYSICAL WAR AGAINST WOMEN

The extent of male violence against women is even more staggering than men's irresponsibility toward their children. No statistics compile all forms of male violence against women; when records are kept, they separate incidents by type—such as rape, beatings, or incest—reported to the police. Most such incidents are not reported, and harassment almost never. Women travelers in Italy have traditionally been harassed and even raped or injured. No one helped the victims—Italian men prided themselves on this behavior. Men harass, molest, rape, and beat women travelers

in South Asia, especially India. No one offers to help the victims—
Asian women are only beginning to fight back themselves. A
young European woman in India, attacked by a mob of men, threw
herself into the sea; only other tourists saved her from drowning.[8]

Because male attacks on women are not categorized as a class,
we cannot estimate the number of women physically injured by
men in any given year. The statistics we have are frequently
flawed, and women often do not report skirmishes in men's war
against them. But in an article entitled "The Global War Against
Women," Lori Heise reports that half the married men in Bangkok, Thailand, regularly beat their wives; in Quito, Ecuador, 80
percent of all women report having been physically beaten; in
Nicaragua, 44 percent of men admit they beat their wives and
girlfriends.[9] In Papua, New Guinea, wife-beating "is an accepted
custom" not worth discussing, a government minister argued during parliamentary debate over making it illegal. One parliamentarian stormed, "I paid for my wife, so she should not overrule
my decisions, because I am the head of the familiy." In Brazil
over the last twenty years, men's severe beating or murder of
wives and female lovers was so common that "defense of honor"
became a legitimate and widespread legal defense.[10]

Barbara Roberts' article "No Safe Place: The War Against
Women" cites social scientists' estimate that over 1.8 million
husbands in the United States badly batter their wives; she also
cites a survey in which 28 percent of couples admitted physical
violence had occurred in their relationship.[11] Researchers believe
that the true rate of men *ever* beating a wife or female lover in
the life of a relationship is closer to 50 percent for all couples.[12]
Roberts concludes that in the privacy of the "sacred" home, a war
is being waged against women, and adds that "so long as men are
at war against women, peace for all of humankind cannot exist,
and there is no safe place on earth for any of us."

In the United States, a man beats a woman every twelve sec-
onds, and every day four of these beatings reach their final con-
summation, the death of the woman.[13] About 20 percent of
women who report beatings by their husbands, former husbands,
or male lovers have been beaten so often in the three months
preceding that they cannot recall each incident distinctly. Men

often threaten to kill the women they beat (although they might later claim they were speaking in "the heat of the moment" or "under the influence"), yet until a few years ago women could not plead self-defense if they killed their abusers even if they killed them *while* the beating was going on—another example of the legal system being used to injure women. The entire social system, including the police and courts, closes ranks to protect *the violent man.*

Policemen fear calls on domestic violence above all (and *they* have guns), and do no more than end the beating momentarily. Many policemen are themselves wife-beaters. In 1989, a former New York City police officer suspected of murdering his first wife was arraigned on charges of sexually abusing his twelve- and thirteen-year-old stepdaughters and raping one of them.[14] Madelyn Diaz, accused of murdering a husband who had regularly beaten, threatened, and tortured her, was asked why she did not go to the police. "He *was* the police," she replied.[15]

Battered women have almost no recourse. Many men (and women) blame the *women* whose husbands beat them, asking why they did not leave their abuser. But even if a woman has enough money to leave and someplace to go, there is no escape from a man obsessed. You can move, you can hide, you can change your name, but they follow. They are obsessed: they have turned a woman into the cause of all their problems or an answer to them. Almost every day, a man kills a woman who has left him for beating her, who has struggled *within the system*, getting a court order enjoining him from approaching her. He also often kills her children, and anyone else who happens to be near her at the time—a mother, sister, friend—and sometimes himself. Indeed, Department of Justice statistics show that 75 percent of reported assaults against wives or lovers are committed *after* separation.

We believe we live in an enlightened time, but the situation for battered women reminds me of women's situation in Japan after about the twelfth century. A Japanese wife could escape an intolerable marriage only by fleeing to a temple that gave women sanctuary. There were few, and it might be hard for a woman to reach one—and she would have to abandon her children. Escape had to be well planned, for if a husband's servants caught her before she reached sanctuary, she was dragged back. Common law came to hold that if a woman managed to throw her shoe through the gate, she would not be forcibly returned home. Battered women today have women's shelters for sanctuary, but they are few and endangered. If conservatives had their way, even their small state subsidies would be stopped.

So powerful and pervasive is the taboo against blaming men-as-a-class in our society that even social scientists who deplore male violence against women perpetuate a sense of male blamelessness for these acts. Male language generally—the language used by those who work in military, engineering, computer, and or other "masculine" enterprises—is characterized by a lack of agency. Like the nuclear strategy analysts discussed earlier, social scientists who write about male violence toward women and whose work may be aimed at ameliorating the situation use locutions suggesting either that no one is responsible for what is happening, that "things" happen as it were by themselves, or that both parties are equally responsible.

Sharon Lamb, who analyzes the language used in academic descriptions of male violence, writes that all social scientists use "the ubiquitous passive voice . . . which presents acts without agents, harm without guilt." When men smash women with their fists, hammers, or other heavy objects, twist their arms back, break their bones, smash their skulls, kick them, slash them with knives, shoot them, and harm them in other inventive ways, social scientists refer innocuously to "domestic" or "spousal" violence.[16] Spousal? Lamb finds family systems theorists particularly given to conceptualizing the problem as if a man and woman shared responsibility for it, not as men preying on women. She cites a passage from a book in which the authors describe a brutal scene of a husband beating his wife over the head with a cane and whipping her arms and legs with a hose, then ask, "How could a couple inflict such a situation upon one another?"[17]

Like men who rape women, men who beat women claim the women provoked them and bear all or most of the responsibility for the aggression. Male social scientists are complicit in this attribution. Lamb found that men writing alone or with women were over half again as likely to write without assigning agents to actions as women who wrote alone or with other women. Indeed, assigning men responsibility for aggressive acts may keep a paper from being published in social science journals—or in newspapers or magazines, for that matter. Articles naming men as agents of violent acts were so rare, Lamb did not tally them. Here are some of Lamb's examples:

- Acts without agents (passive voice): "Black women are abused at a disproportionately higher rate than white women."

- Acts without agents: "the violent behavior," "the battery," "the abuse" with no reference to *whose*.

- Victims without agents: "battered" or "abused" women; abused/battered "wives."

- Gender obfuscation: "She may be beaten when the assailant comes calling"; "Why do battered women remain in relationships with abusive mates?"

Susan Schechter, who wrote a historical account of the movement to aid women whose men beat them, explained that in seeking funding from organizations willing to help the "needy," activists found it politic to emphasize women's victimization and consequent psychosocial problems.[18] By doing so, they unintentionally conferred on "battered women" the permanent label of helpless victim and helped generate a mental health profession claiming expertise in "family violence." Schechter believes these professionals watered down their language and shifted their focus away from "battered women" and "battering men" to "domestic violence" from fear of alienating the men involved in funding programs.

While women are less likely to be victims of violent crime than men, they are *six times* more likely to be harmed by an intimate. In 1991, Department of Justice statistics showed that violent crime against men had dropped about 20 percent between 1973 and 1987, but that violence against women remained constant; the FBI, however, found a rising incidence of rape.[19] About two and a half million women are assaulted, raped, or robbed every year and a quarter of these crimes are committed by their relatives or friends. Only 4 percent of violent crimes against men are committed by female relatives or women they have dated.

The United States has one of the highest, if not the highest, rate of rape in the world, counting only those that are reported. The National Crime Survey, conducted annually by the Census Bureau, found twice as many actual rapes as were reported to the police. Women are reluctant to report rape committed by intimates—husbands (marital rape), boyfriends (date rape), and relatives (incest).[20] It is especially difficult to counter men's sense that rape is legitimate, that it is their right. Both sexes are raised in a culture that, until recently, implicitly reinforced this idea. Rape within marriage or on a date was considered impossible; rape by a stranger was the victim's fault: she was out alone [Heb: whore—she who goes out of the house], she was wearing the wrong clothes or shoes, she had a drink.

Indeed, two recent studies of men who had committed rape demonstrate that men who rape, even those convicted of rape (a tiny minority), overwhelmingly excuse or justify the act. Diana Scully interviewed in depth convicted rapists in prison.[21] She found they fell into two categories which she labeled *admitters* and *deniers*. Neither took responsibility for their act but admitters acknowledged that rape was wrong. They excused their own performance of it on grounds that they were not fully responsible—they were drinking or taking drugs, the woman had led them on. Their versions of the rape either downplayed or omitted the degree of force they had exerted. Deniers denied either that rape was wrong or that their particular performance of it was inappropriate; they acknowledged their acts but justified them by claiming the woman lured them on, the woman wanted it, she didn't resist "enough," she enjoyed it, she was loose, a prostitute, or high. Deniers minimized their responsibility and revised the story from one of rape to one of seduction. Men of both types, if they were high on alcohol or drugs when they raped a woman, used this fact to excuse their violence. But if the woman was high on alcohol or drugs, they used this fact to justify their violence, claiming she was "out of control." Seventy percent of admitters but only

40 percent of the deniers said substance abuse had affected their behavior; 56 percent of the deniers but only 15 percent of the admitters said the victim's behavior was affected by drugs or alcohol.

Most important to our argument here, neither category felt guilt or empathy for their victims during or after the rape. Both types considered rape a "low-risk, high-reward" act: they assumed they would not be arrested, or if so, not punished. Rape was a reward— a kind of revenge, a bonus during the commission of another crime, a form of recreation or adventure. Most infuriating, given women's heartrending guilt after a rape—their constant questioning of what they did or wore or where they went or how they acted that could have precipitated this action—is that *all* the men in this survey, asked why they had chosen a particular woman, replied, "It could have been any woman," or "It didn't have to be her, she was just there at the wrong time."

Peggy Reeves Sanday questioned three thousand college women about rape.[22] Twenty-five percent said they had had unwelcome sex under men's bullying, their pressure or arguments; 15 percent had come close to succumbing to threats of force; and 9 percent had been threatened or forced into having sex. The main focus of Sanday's investigation, however, was gang rape: between 1982 and 1988, there were seventy-five documented cases of gang rape on college campuses. But members of a fraternity in which a girl was gang-raped said such incidents occurred once or twice a month on their campus. Sanday suggests rape is part of male socialization. Many American men are initiated into "manhood" by fraternity initiations during which they are brutalized and degraded, "treated as polluted and despised women and as 'pansies.'" Brutalization teaches them the nature of the social order and their possible places in it: they can be men or they can be women. They in turn visit their learned "misogynist subjectivity" on the next generation of fraternity pledges and on "party women," Sanday writes. These men do not consider sexual coercion *rape*; they call it "working a yes out"—talking a girl into sex or getting her high. Afterward they say she "was asking for it."

Pauline Bart reports that before the jury withdrew to deliberate in rape trials, judges commonly recited Hale's dictum: "Rape is an accusation easily to be made and hard to be proved and harder to be defended by the party accused, tho' never so innocent."[23] Sir Matthew Hale (1609–1676), a famous British jurist, is quoted by every legal writer on rape. Only as a result of feminist efforts did judges in California stop routinely reading his instruction to juries before they deliberate.

Marital rape is still legal in many states, and at least one in seven husbands rapes his wife. Most marital rape goes unreported, like 90 percent of date rapes, but feminists have pressed thirty states to abolish or modify legal language exempting men from prosecution for raping their wives. Some have modified the phrase "against her will" to "without her consent"; in Illinois the phrase has been eliminated, which means the prosecution no longer has to prove a woman did *not* consent, the defense has to prove that she agreed "by word or deed." Men are currently challenging the constitutionality of marital rape laws on grounds that the terms "force" and "bodily harm" are vague and *too broad*. We have noted several cases in which police or judges were unwilling to take action against rapists. The United States Navy, too, is reluctant. The Navy received twenty-four reports of rape or sexual assault of students at the Orlando Naval Training Center between January 1989 and June 1990: it failed to prosecute five of these cases, and only one case resulted in a court-martial.[24]

Feminist experts on rape like Pauline Bart and Susan Brownmiller agree that rape is "a conscious process of intimidation by which all men keep all women in a state of fear."[25] Bart points out that since male sexual aggression is endemic, if any sex act against a person's will were considered rape, the majority of men would be rapists, adding, "No man ever died of an erection— though many women have." Scully concludes: "No fundamental change will occur until men are forced to admit that sexual violence is *their* problem." Yet while everyone knows that it is men who rape, few see it as men's problem. All too many women, and men who do not rape, blame women for rape, claiming that they deserve it for putting themselves at risk. We will put aside the many cases that make a mockery of such statements (like ninety-year-old women raped and killed in their own houses) to examine such a position. What are these people saying? They are assuming that men are women's natural enemies (much as one animal is another's), that all men are potential predators upon women, and that women know this and must protect themselves. If they do not, they are asking for what they get. Men's behavior is taken for granted, not judged. Only women are judged. And what is taken for granted is that men are engaged in perpetual war against women.

So automatic is society's acceptance of male rapists as a fact of life that journalists often conceal this form of male predation. Peace activist Betty Reardon points out that male-dominated media often censor the fact that murdered women were also raped. For example, the men who murdered the four American religieuses in El Salvador in 1980 raped them first—but most media did not mention this fact. One person who *did*, Reardon writes, was Mary Bader Papa in the *National Catholic Report*, who wrote: "A special message was sent us by the rapists and murderers of the four American women. They wanted to make it clear that women who step out of their place will find no special protection behind the labels of 'nun or churchworker.' Or even 'American.' "[26] Furthermore, male peace activists ignore rape and other forms of male violence toward women in discussing violence in society, according to social scientist/peace activist Birgit Brock-Utne. Citing a study that includes in a list of "peaceful" societies those in which violence against women is routine, she asks how a movement can call itself a peace movement and ignore male violence toward women.[27]

The dimensions of incest are not yet known, but what is becoming clear is that it is far more widespread than anyone had guessed. Incest is not class-linked: men of every class and educational level rape little boys and girls. Girls, however, are the primary targets. Author Betsy Peterson's father, a highly respected, much-loved physician, a surgeon, in private revealed his contempt for his female patients. (He also treated his wife contemptuously.) He began to molest his daughter, massaging her clitoris to bring her to orgasm (or whatever a baby experiences), when she was only three, lying in a crib. When her older half-sister came to live with the family, he molested her too, raping her when she reached fourteen in Peterson's sight, saying he was "making a woman of her."[28]

Such men are not out of the ordinary. Psychologists have tested men imprisoned for rape and incest and find them "normal." Bart, who finds rape a paradigm for male control in partriarchal societies, points out that there is little reason to believe that men who commit incest are mentally ill. She cites a study that concludes that incestuous fathers are neither psychotic nor intellectually defective, but are "especially hostile toward women" and "see the sex act as an act of aggression."[29] In patriarchal societies, one "makes a woman of" a girl and "makes a man of" a boy by the same method: humiliation and brutalization. But boys are humiliated by being treated as subordinates (females); girls are humiliated by being taught that their own sexuality is not in their control. My own informal survey of adult women suggests that very few reach the age of twenty-one without suffering some form of male predation—incest, molestation, rape or attempted rape, beatings, and sometimes torture or imprisonment.

Other forms of violence become sex-linked because only women are their victims. For instance, in 1990 a man stalked the streets of Manhattan shooting darts into women's buttocks.[30] Most serial killers focus on females, especially prostitutes. Police tend not to pursue prostitutes' murderers energetically. Perhaps, like the Texas judge who does not deem the murder of homosexuals or prostitutes a serious crime, they do not consider them human beings. In any case, the police themselves are part of an exclusive male club that routinely uses violence to maintain control. When women are not available, men turn other males into "women." So male prisoners regularly rape other male prisoners, and many ministers and priests betray the trust of little boys or male teenagers by molesting them.

The list could go on and on: I call these revelations the slime under the rug of patriarchy. We are hearing about it only now, but it has been there forever. In a collection of Spanish women's verse, some of the earliest poems, dating from the fifteenth and sixteenth centuries, are laments over incestuous fathers or brutal husbands. The most important accomplishment of the feminist movement may be the exposure of this secret, the hauling it out of the private darkness where it has flourished and hanging it out in the air for all to see. All patriarchists exalt the home and family as sacred, demanding it remain inviolate from prying eyes. Men want privacy for their violations of women. Women, forced to be dependent upon men, educated to believe that men care for them and will take care of them, find that the very men they were taught to trust implicitly betray, brutalize, and violate them. All women learn in childhood that women as a sex are men's prey; many also learn that the men who supposedly cherish them are the worst offenders. They learn that "love" is about power and they are the powerless.

The overwhelming majority of serial murderers are men (female serial murderers often appear in films but there are almost none in actuality). Most mass murders are committed by men as well, and many focus on women. Marc Lépine shot fourteen female engineering students to death at the University of Montreal in December 1989. He then committed suicide, leaving a note: "Even if the Mad Killer epithet will be attributed to me by media, I consider myself a rational, erudite man." Recently, on the same campus, another man bludgeoned a female engineering student on the head with a rock. She lived; he fled. *MS.*, which reported the event, found a silver lining: the tragedy had made people aware that women are engineers, raising enrollment at the school.[31] But we must take Lépine seriously. He considered himself sane, *erudite*. He felt *he had the right* to kill women because they had taken "his" place in the school. Indeed, he ranted about "feminists" before his suicide.

Like the pious Jews at the Wailing Wall who threw heavy metal chairs at women's heads (and could easily have killed one), like the pious Muslims who knifed women marching to protest the Ayatollah's decree on purdah, like the pious Protestants who bomb abortion clinics, like thousands of husbands, "dates," fraternity boys, and strangers who beat or rape or kill women because they have decided women are the cause of their troubles, like the rap musicians and comedians who spew hate at women, Marc Lépine felt he had the right to do what he chose to women.

In personal and public life, in kitchen, bedroom and halls of parliament, men wage unremitting war against women. We have examined discrimination against women in public spheres—in the workplace, the courts, and government agencies. We know that the effect of discrimination in the public sphere often leads to female (and child) impoverishment, starvation, and death. We know that, everywhere, women have lower status than men, less power, and more responsibility.

Men start repressing females at birth: only the means vary by society. They direct female babies to be selectively aborted, little girls to be neglected, underfed, genitally mutilated, raped, or molested; they sell adolescent girls to men in marriage or slavery. Around all females swirls a culture pervaded by images of female sexual organs, of female bodies being assaulted by men.

The climate of violence against women harms all women. To be female is to walk the world in fear: on tests of fearfulness, the least fearful women, the young, score the same level of fear as the most fearful men, the elderly. Women tend to lead stifling lives; they avoid going out alone after dark, avoid even necessary tasks like errands or marketing in areas or at times when they feel at risk. But women are attacked at home too, old women who draw the shades and lock their doors, young professionals, women of all ages and classes. The fact that most consistently correlates with fear of crime is femaleness.[32] Women are afraid in a world in which almost half the population bears the guise of the predator, in which no factor—age, dress, or color—distinguishes a man who will harm a woman from one who will not. Wherever they are, women are always afraid of being, as rapists say, "any woman" in the wrong place at the wrong time.

And women's fear of bodily harm carries us full circle back to the abstract public sphere of politics, where it functions to motivate women to support the very political structures that oppress them. In *The Iron Ladies: Why Do Women Vote Tory?*, Beatrix Campbell discusses the reasons so many British women support the Conservative Party. Tory women have been the backbone of the Conservative Party organization: their votes carry it to victory. Campbell points out that if the Tories had been forced to rely on the vote Labour extracts from women, "it would not have survived electorally, nor would it be able to represent itself . . . as the 'national party.' "[33] Labour presents itself as an egalitarian party, the Tories as anti-egalitarian. But the Labour Party was designed to represent *organized* labor, not working people generally, and by the twentieth century organized labor had eliminated women, defeated their demands for equal access to work and wages. The self-declared egalitarian political party was firmly tied to a masculinized political tradition (a choice that is now destroying it), while the wily party of privilege gave women a special place, "created a culture that embraced women, that celebrated their subordination."

When the Conservative Party modernized after World War II, it was faced with far more working-class than "leisure"-class voters and rapidly regrouped—around women. Labour kept its loyal female following but failed to expand it—mainly because it dismissed working-class women's demands for economic equality even though women were making a huge contribution to an economy in crisis because of the war. The Conservatives did not support economic equality either, but promised to "liberate" the housewife. Resuscitating the ideology of separate sexual spheres, they assigned women responsibility for the "domestic" organization of the party. Women, given a place of their own (which Labour did not offer), thronged to the party, gaining enough leverage by the late 1950s to challenge the party leadership with their own agenda. What Campbell calls the party's "women's agenda" associated women with an emerging "new right, an antimodernist axis which became Thatcherism," and was expressed almost entirely in the language of moral authoritarianism and "law and order."

"*Women's fear*," writes Campbell, "provided the emotional ignition for the law and order debates." While male party leaders watched in "bewildered silence," women terrified by a new level of violence that became endemic in the U.K. after the war, pressured the party to legislate their safety. If safety required separate spheres (like separate subway cars), so be it. It was largely the willingness of the Tories to include "law and order" in their agenda that accounts for the fact that historically more men than women supported the Labour Party and more women than men supported the Conservative Party. Yet Conservative women are no fools: pessimistic about the likelihood that politics will improve women's lot, strong yet subordinate, they remain idealistic only about the power of women in their own sphere. Campbell finds a "contradiction at the centre of British Conservatism": the party "provides a space inhabited by a strong feminine presence" and yet "is one of the institutions which structures women's subordination as a sex and supports the class and gender power of men." Even women's ostensible friends are their enemies at heart.

While men strut and fret their hour upon the stage, shout in bars and sports arenas, thump their chests or show their profiles in the legislatures, and explode incredible weapons in an endless contest for status, an obsessive quest for symbolic "proof" of their superiority, women quietly keep the world going. Women know that men will not do this, that either they do the job or it will not be done. They grow or buy, they carry and prepare food for the essential, inevitable, necessarily female-prepared dinner; they give birth to the children and feed them and bathe them and hold them and teach them and hope they will survive. They encourage their men, nurture them, soothe them, nag them, hoping they too will survive and help the children to survive. They do not—as a caste—want the same things men want, and so different are the motivations driving the two sexes that men shake their heads wondering "what do women want?" Women know what men want—but they too shake their heads.

Women are not selfless saints. They kill; they have been known to torture and torment; they abuse others and themselves, fight, injure, are cruel. Women have egos, selves, desires for themselves. No human emotion is alien to women and there is no human behavior they are not capable of except thrusting a penis that is naturally attached to their bodies into an opening. In this sense, they are less limited than men, who cannot menstruate, get pregnant, give birth, feed a baby from their bodies, or accept a penile object in a vagina. Women may not be identified as mothers, for not all women are or want to be mothers. But women-as-a-caste behave as they do because most are mothers.

And because women are mothers and men are not, men feel lacking, without a center. It seems not to occur to most men that they can, like women, find their center in children, in future generations, focus on maintaining the human race. Men seem unable to feel equal to women: they must be superior or they are inferior. They seek a center in other men, in male solidarity through male cults (in simple societies), priesthoods, military or paramilitary groups, academies, professions, teams, religious brotherhoods, or the new male cults. *All of these* exalt not men-as-a-caste but group members, posited as superior to most other men and all women. *All* such priesthoods teach xenophobia—hatred of strangers—and bigotry; all exalt some form of self-denial—austerity in living, denial of feelings or need—and all worship aggression and violence because all worship domination. Only the ability to dominate others makes them superior to women. And superiority to women is the very foundation of this kind of male identity.

Violence is an easy response to fear. It is also simpleminded. For the men who rule society to inculcate and foster violence in dominant males is to educate them to be truly inferior human beings. Some women today believe that men are well on their way to exterminating women from the world through violent behavior and oppressive policies. Medieval clerics used to question why their god had invented women at all, concluding sadly that women were necessary for procreation. Now new reproductive technologies can make women obsolete, and the laboratory will become a new locus of violence against women.

But so extreme is this worldwide multileveled assault on women that people are uniting against it. Men are joining together to discuss their own sense of identity. These groups are still small and scattered, but more men are beginning to realize that male supremacy may work to their practical advantage but stunts them emotionally, and that this emotional damage affects everything—thought processes, life span, health, relationships, the entire quality of a life. Some groups, like Robert Bly's male gatherings, seem to exalt the very qualities that are the problem, but others seek a new definition of manhood.[34]

Women's fight against male oppression is global and richly varied. Women everywhere are joining together in grass-roots economic projects or building clinics or schools; such projects benefit entire communities. Women everywhere are agitating against male violence toward women and founding formal groups to fight for fair laws, political representation, education, and economic justice for women. Feminists are producing an original, impressive body of scholarly work that provides a foundation for future society and alternatives to patriarchal structures. *Our Bodies, Ourselves,* produced by the Boston Women's Health Collective and widely translated, revolutionized women's way of caring for themselves. Women in Kenya adopted a holistic approach to health, self-esteem, and race/sex oppression developed by the Black Women's Health Network in Atlanta. For over a decade, the Women's Health Clinic in Geneva (Dispensaire des Femmes) has offered nonmedical feminist health care using Western and herbal treatments, and trained women who have established similar clinics in Costa Rica, Brazil, Nicaragua, and India.[35]

Feminist groups like GABRIELA in the Philippines and the Women's Information Centre in Thailand help victims of forced prostitution in their countries, and educate young women about the dangers of believing deceitful ads offering jobs abroad. They also denounce their governments for complicity in sex-tourism, which brings in foreign capital and is sometimes officially included in the budget for national development plans. A global business, it requires global action, and feminists from Japan, Thailand, Korea, and the Philippines worked the crowd at the International Tourism conference in Manila in 1982, holding demonstrations there and at national airports, embarrassing everyone involved.

Women in Wai'anae, Hawaii, which has one of the highest unemployment rates in the state, organized to deal with male domestic violence. Realizing the heightened level of violence was connected to the political situation, they decided to work for political change in their community. Among their programs was one called Peace Education, which is now offered in most Wai'anae public schools. The two-week curriculum teaches students to examine their anger and violent behavior and ways to create harmony in the family. The group holds health seminars for women and girls and drew up a grant proposal for a Women's Handi-Craft Cooperative to enable them to earn money in cottage industries. the Wai'anae women also work for nuclear disarmament, and made a film to promote it.[36]

Indian women formed Vimochana to help battered women get police or legal help.[37] But as the organization grew, it expanded to offer consciousness-raising groups to help women deal with male violence, and practical help with harassment over dowries or bigamous husbands who abandon families without support. It organizes women in slums, industries, and working women's hostels around issues of oppression and discrimination. Vimochana women also join peasant and workers' associations, which they sometimes lead in actions, and work in the peace movement.

Feminists founded Development Alternatives with Women for a New Era (DAWN), an international organization based in India that connects Third World women activists, researchers, and policymakers to develop a global perspective on women's economic and political situation.[38] DAWN's workshops and panels at U.S. Women's Conferences have influenced Third World women delegates to defy their governments and openly criticize oppressive social and political practices, including clitoridectomy. In 1984, women from twenty-four African countries held a conference in the Sudan, "African Women Speak on Female Circumcision," and issued a report advocating the total eradication of genital mutilation of women.

Women in Brazilian shantytowns told DAWN workers their main problem was reproduction. The Brazilian left, campaigning against population control, had printed a flyer showing a man on television offering women birth control pills and the women responding by demanding resources, not pills. The women of São Paulo said this falsely represented them: they wanted *both*. DAWN formed Proyecto Esse Sexo que e Nosso (Project for This Sex That Is Ours), which produced a series of simple illustrated booklets describing basic aspects of women's health, reproduction, and sexual pleasure. The most effective educational materials for poor women available in Brazil, they are now distributed by the government.[39]

Noting that 44 percent of Nicaraguan men regularly beat their wives or lovers, the Nicaraguan Women's Association launched a campaign to condemn male violence. Since Brazilian women hesitate to report abuse to policemen, who tend to treat them as criminals, the São Paulo State Council for Women's Rights introduced all-female-staffed police stations in 1984. The initiative was so successful that seventy similar stations were opened across Brazil to deal with complaints of rape and domestic violence.[40] For over a decade, Brazilian feminists campaigned to end legally sanctioned wife murder. Men could murder wives, even those who had left them, and claim a "legitimate defense of honor" on grounds the women had been unfaithful. In 1980–81 alone, 722 men in São Paulo state used this defense to win acquittal for wife murder. A campaign leader explained, "In the interior of the country, it is easier and cheaper for a man to hire a gunslinger to kill his wife than to get a divorce and to separate the property." Feminist pressure and dissemination of information on such crimes won a victory for women in March 1991, when the Brazilian Supreme Court disallowed this defense.[41]

Women attorneys started the Uganda Association of Women Lawyers and a Women's Legal Aid Clinic to help uneducated poor women.[42] Eighty percent of the Ugandan population is illiterate; many people are unaware of Ugandan laws, and women especially are caught in the intersection of tradition and modern laws. Women married in traditional fashion do not know that they are not legally married and have no protection if their husbands die. Men's families often take all their possessions, leaving their widows (men often marry more than one wife) and children destitute. Clinic lawyers go out into the countryside and sit on the grass talking to women. They teach rural women that wife-beating is illegal, help widows claim part of their husband's estate, and help women left by their husbands, who are then denied jobs on the ground that those who cannot manage their own homes cannot manage anything else.

When the Manuela Ramos Movement Women's Center in the slums of Lima, Peru, began offering courses, women asked to learn about sexuality, health, and birth control. The center held workshops to discuss women's lives on personal, informational, and organizational levels. In the first, women learn about their bodies, their sexuality, and their roles as human beings, mothers, and citizens. The informational workshops respond to women's questions about health, primary education, and neighborhood organization. For organizational sessions, the center sketches projects the women could initiate, like running child care centers, eating places, or training programs. A Lima slum woman left her house to community women when she died, for their use as a shelter from battering. Women in Peruvian shantytowns have taken to carrying whistles, which they blow if they are beaten or attacked; a whistle blown immediately draws a crowd of women ready to defend the victim.

Southeast Asian women organize projects to help victims of battery and rape and to change rape laws and community attitudes. Indian women bang pots and pans outside the houses of men most abusive to their wives. Feminist groups like Saheli agitate against widespread "dowry deaths," and have forced passage of a law requiring any "accidental death" or "suicide" of a woman in the first seven years of her marriage to be investigated for possible foul play.

In Nigeria, girls are married between eleven and thirteen (and may be genitally mutilated) and often have agonized childbirths. Obstructed birth can tear a hole between the birth canal and the bladder that without corrective surgery renders a girl incontinent for life. Twenty thousand women, mainly Muslims, in northern Nigeria suffer from this damage, VVF (vesicovaginal fistula). Their husbands divorce them and families shun them. Publicity galvanized Nigerian feminists to mount a campaign against early marriage.[43]

African-American Mildred Tudy and Mexican-American Maria Fava worked separately to improve living conditions and reduce racial enmity in the Williamsburg–Greenpoint neighborhood of Brooklyn. They forced the city to take some necessary steps, in the process introducing low-income women to feminism and enriching their own lives.[44] White women join black women to fight against the Ku Klux Klan in many localities.[45] Women lead citizens' groups to oppose nuclear power, and are the most committed and energetic agitators and the majority of leaders of community efforts to deal with toxic waste in Chicago and other cities.

In industrial societies, women are slotted into office work that often pays less than factory work. Women who may be as well educated as their male bosses are confined to a "female occupation" that allows the men to treat them like servants. Women in banking and insurance companies in Cleveland, Boston, and Washington, D.C., organized to deal with sex discrimination and poor treatment in offices. At first, organizers formed groups piecemeal to negotiate solutions. When this proved unsatisfactory, they affiliated with the Service Employees International Union as Nine to Five, the National Association of Working Women. The film *Nine to Five* inspired women across the country to form similar independent groups, like Women Employed and Working Women.[46]

Chilean women endured pressure hoses spewing garbage and risked imprisonment, as did Argentinian women, to demand return of their *desaparecidos* ("disappeared ones"), and helped bring down authoritarian military governments in both countries. Chilean women made and smuggled *arpilleras* out of the country: these embroidered or appliquéd tapestries used pictures to inform the world about torture, murder, and starvation in Chile. Soviet women dared to defy a dictatorial government by demanding information on murdered soldier sons. Korean women regularly mount protests in the name of children murdered by the tyrannical South Korean regime.

Women anxious about the arms race between the United States and the Soviet Union mounted "Women Strike for Peace" (WSP) in 1961, a grass-roots effort organized by informal networking.[47] The House Committee on Un-American Activities (HUAC), designed to suppress dissent, saw peace movements as dissent (as government still does) and summoned some WSP women for interrogation. The women's nonhierarchical organizing methods generated a huge successful action and also protected them from political persecution—because there were no designated leaders and they kept *no written lists* of members. Determined not to hold internal purges or cower before the committee, WSP members volunteered to talk, instead of refusing to testify, like 1950s radicals and civil libertarians. About a hundred women telegraphed the HUAC chairman, offering to come to Washington to talk about the movement.

The offers were refused. This original WSP tactic revealed the committee's real intent—to expose and smear those it investigated, not to get information. A typical newspaper account read:

The dreaded House Un-American Activities Committee met its Waterloo this week. It tangled with 500 irate women. They laughed at it. Klieg lights glared, television cameras whirred, and 50 reporters scribbled notes while babies cried and cooed during the fantastic inquisition.

When the first woman headed to the witness table, the crowd rose silently to its feet. The irritated Chairman Clyde Doyle of California outlawed standing. They applauded the next witness and Doyle outlawed clapping. Then they took to running out to kiss the witness. . . . Finally, each woman as she was called was met and handed a huge bouquet. By then Doyle was a beaten man. By the third day the crowd was giving standing ovations to the heroines with impunity.[48]

The WSP women ended HUAC's effectiveness and helped influence President Kennedy to sign the limited Test Ban Treaty of 1963.[49]

In 1980, the first Women's Pentagon Action, two thousand women circled the Pentagon, declaring to the world that militarism was sexism. Their powerful expression of feminist antimilitarism inspired women elsewhere, such as at Greenham Common.[50] In 1979, in a broad intensification of the nuclear arms race, NATO announced plans to place hundreds of American nuclear missiles in Western Europe. First to be installed (in 1983) were ninety-six ground-launched cruise missiles at the U.S. air base at Greenham Common, near Newbury, about sixty miles west of London. In September 1981, forty British women walked 120 miles from Wales to Greenham Common to protest and publicize this use of British soil.[51] The media ignored them, so the women decided to remain until the public grew aware of American strategy to use Europe as a shield against the Eastern bloc to keep war from American soil.

The Greenham Common women's peace camp developed from this vigil outside the gates of the base. The women, many with children, put up tents and settled in; the small stubborn group grew, and on December 11, 1982, 20,000 women formed a nine-mile human chain around the base.[52] They "redecorated" the site, adorning the barbed-wire fence with thousands of bits of fabric, poems, children's pictures, toys, and other personal treasures. The protesters' original aim was to open public debate on the new nuclear weapons, but as more and more women joined the effort and the protest started receiving international attention, they shifted their goal to blocking the deployment of missiles at Greenham.

Both governments ignored them, and missiles arrived at the base in November 1983. But the women remained, keeping a permanent vigil to protest the missiles and all nuclear weapons. The number of women actually camping out at Greenham has varied over time, but they have continued, day and night, in all seasons, in sun or rain (mostly rain in that part of England).[53] *They are still there,* if not in the same numbers. Actions involving up to 50,000 women at a time have been held at the base every year since the camp began.

The protest propelled huge numbers of women across Britain into peace activism and inspired women to build peace encampments at over a hundred sites: Molesworth, England; Comiso, Italy; Hunsrück, Germany; Nanoose, Canada; Seneca and Puget Sound in the United States; Soesterburg, Holland; Pine Gap, Australia. Shibokusa women have protested American troops occupying Japan since the 1950s. Feminists have mounted anti-militarist actions in the United States, Britain, Germany, the South Pacific, New Zealand, and Eastern Europe, actions that are not isolated protests but tied to a global network: Greenham Common women affirm solidarity with women at American peace camps; women in the American peace movement held a dialogue in San Francisco with women from Japan, the Marshall Islands, and Latin America in 1983. In 1984, thousands of New Zealand women marched in support of the Greenham Common women. Among them were women from the movement for Maori self-determination, marching against militarism and for Maori land rights.[54] Women infused the peace movement with new vitality.

After millennia of male war against them, women are fighting back on every front.

NOTES

INTRODUCTION

1. The statements made in this opening section are based on material documented in my *Beyond Power* (New York: Summit Books, 1985) and *From Eve to Dawn: A Women's History of the World*, forthcoming.

2. Many nationalist revolutions in Africa were inspired by European socialism; it is less known that Gandhi modeled his *satyagraha*, passive resistance campaign, on the British suffragist campaign. James Hunt wrote that Gandhi "was citing the women's movement more than a year before he discovered Thoreau's 'Civil Disobedience' " (James D. Hunt, *Gandhi in London* [New Delhi: Promilla, 1978]). Gandhi followed the news from England closely and was aware of the first arrests of English suffragists in Manchester, and those in London in 1905 and 1906, when he was formulating South African Indians' demands for legal, political, and human rights. In 1906, he went to England to plead his cause and was immediately caught up in the suffrage protests; three days after he arrived, eleven women were arrested for demonstrating at the House of Commons. A few days later, he published an article praising the suffragists' courage and perseverance, taking his title from their slogan, "Deeds Better Than Words." Gandhi wrote admiringly of the suffragists for choosing prison over fines, and in 1909, again in London, he attended a mass meeting celebrating the release from prison of the first group of suffrage hunger strikers. He held them up as an example to Indians: "When we consider the suffering and courage of these women, how can the Indian *satyagrahi* stand comparison with them?" (Hunt, pp. 137–138.)

3. Sylvia Ann Hewlett, "Running Hard Just to Keep Up," *Time*, Special Issue (Fall 1990).

4. For instance, Women Strike for Peace. See Amy Swerdlow, "Ladies' Day at the Capitol: Women Strike for Peace Versus HUAC," *Feminist Studies* 8, 3 (Fall 1982): 493–520.

5. Personal communication, 1986.

6. *The Trapped Woman: Catch 22 in Deviance and Control*, ed. Josefina

Figueira-McDonough and Rosemary Sarri (Newbury Park, Calif.: Sage, 1987).

7. Ibid. See especially the articles by Greer Litton Fox and Jan Allen, and Nancy R. Hooyman and Rosemary Ryan.

8. A recent editorial spoke of *women* choosing to have fewer children as if men were not part of this decision. See "The Baby Boom Boom," editorial, *New York Times*, April 24, 1991.

PART I

1. The estimate of 75 percent comes from Karin Soder, former foreign minister of Sweden, at the Center Party's convention in 1976. Cited by Berit Ås, "The Feminist University," in *Radical Voices: A Decade of Feminist Resistance*, Women's Studies International Forum, ed. Renate D. Klein and Deborah Lynn Steinberg (Elmsford, N.Y.: Pergamon Press, 1989).

2. U.S. Department of Commerce, Bureau of the Census: *Household Wealth and Asset Management: 1988.*

3. Marilyn Waring, *If Women Counted* (San Francisco: Harper & Row, 1988).

4. Statistics and quotations from Jennifer Seymour Whitaker, *How Can Africa Survive?* (New York: Harper & Row, 1988), p. 152.

5. Irene Tinker, "New Technologies for Food-Related Activities: An Equity Strategy," in *Women and Technological Change in Developing Countries*, ed. Roslyn Dauber and Melinda L. Cain (Boulder, Colo.: Westview, 1981).

6. Maria Mies, *Patriarchy and Accumulation on a World Scale: Women in the International Division of Labour* (London: Zed Books, 1986).

7. Hewlett, op. cit.

8. Kenneth B. Noble, "Low-Paying Jobs Foreseen for Most Working Women," *New York Times*, December 12, 1985.

9. Janice Castro, "Get Set: Here They Come!"; Barbara Ehrenreich, "Sorry, Sisters, This Is Not the Revolution," both in *Time*, Special Issue (Fall 1990).

10. The figures in these two paragraphs come from Elaine Sciolino, "UN Finds Widespread Inequality for Women," *New York Times*, June 23, 1985.

11. "Working Women Gained on Men," *New York Times*, February 2, 1988.

12. Tamar Lewin, "Older Women Face Bias in Workplace," *New York Times*, May 11, 1991.

13. Marilyn Power, "Falling Through the 'Safety Net': Women, Economic Crisis, and Reaganomics," *Feminist Studies* 10, 1 (Spring 1984): 31–58.

14. Ibid.

15. Ibid.

16. Cited in *MS.*, January/February 1991.

17. Amartya Sen, "More Than 100 Million Women Are Missing," *New York Review of Books*, December 20, 1990.

18. "Fewer Women in Parliaments," *New York Times*, August 25, 1989.

19. William E. Schmidt, "Who's in Charge Here? Chances Are It's a Woman," *New York Times*, May 21, 1991.

20. Nadine Brozen, "Despite Women's Gains in States, Studies Find Few in the Top Posts," *New York Times*, October 24, 1986.

21. *MS.*, January/February 1991. This vote was later annulled.

22. Bill Keller, "Raisa Gorbachev Hits Back: The Women Are All for Me," *New York Times*, May 27, 1989.

23. All information on Anna Walentynowicz is drawn from Jane Atkinson, "The Woman Behind Solidarity," *MS.*, February 1984.

24. "Solidarity's Spark Runs Strike," *New York Times*, March 29, 1991.

25. George M. Marsden ("Defining American Fundamentalism," in *The Fundamentalist Phenomenon*, ed. Norman J. Cohen [Grand Rapids, Mich.: W. B. Eerdmans, 1990] writes that the term "fundamentalist" properly describes an evangelical Protestant militantly opposed to modern liberal theologies and to some aspects of secularism in modern culture. "Fundamentalist" should denote adhering to the founding ideas of a religion. This is why the term does not apply to Islamic or Jewish movements: Muslims referred to as fundamentalist do not adhere more closely to Muhammad's teachings than other Muslims; indeed, Riffat Hassan ("The Burgeoning of Islamic Fundamentalism: Toward an Understanding of the Phenomenon," in *The Fundamentalist Phenomenon*) writes that much of what is called fundamentalist Islam is antitraditional, opposed to both spirit and letter of Islamic tradition as understood and practiced since the Qur'anic revelation. Judaism has no absolute dogma; the body of texts that forms its core is subjected to constant discussion and revision. Leon Wielseltier ("The Jewish Face of Fundamentalism," in *The Fundamentalist Phenomenon*) suggests that fundamentalism is the antithesis of normative Judaism because it proposes to abolish centuries of Jewish thought and that "restorationists" is a more accurate term for those who agitate for a return to a text or to a time.

26. John R. Rice, *I Am a Fundamentalist* (Murfreesboro, Tenn.: Sword of the Lord Publishers, 1975).

27. Richard Hofstadter, *Anti-intellectualism in American Life* (New York: Random House–Vintage, 1962).

28. Mortimer Ostow, "The Fundamentalist Phenomenon: A Psychological Perspective," in *The Fundamentalist Phenomenon*, op cit.

29. Betty A. DeBerg, *Ungodly Women: Gender and the First Wave of American Fundamentalism* (Minneapolis: Fortress Press, 1990).

30. Linda Gordon, "Voluntary Motherhood: The Beginnings of Feminist

Birth Control Ideas in the United States," in *Cleo's Consciousness Raised*, ed. Mary S. Hartmann and Lois Banner (New York: Harper & Row, 1974).

31. Daniel Scott Smith, "Family Limitation, Sexual Control, and Domestic Feminism in Victorian America," in *A Heritage of Her Own: Toward a New Social History of American Women*, ed. Nancy F. Cott and Elizabeth H. Pleck (New York: Simon and Schuster, 1979).

32. Carl N. Degler, "The Changing Place of Women in America," in *The Woman Question in American History*, ed. Barbara Welter (Hinsdale, Ill.: Dryden Press, 1973), cited by DeBerg.

33. *King's Business* 12, 1 (February 1921): 107–108, cited by DeBerg.

34. "Woman Suffrage and the Bible," *King's Business* 10, 8 (August 1919): 701, cited by DeBerg.

35. "The Mother's Reward," *Watchman* 86 (August 11, 1904); Stanley White, address to women at Moody's Northfield Young Women's Conference in 1906, cited by DeBerg.

36. DeBerg, op cit.

37. *Western Recorder* 69, 39 (August 8, 1895); Davis, "A Woman's Appeal to Women," *Western Recorder* 10 (1917), cited by DeBerg.

38. Leonard I. Sweet, *The Minister's Wife: Her Role in Nineteenth-Century American Evangelicism* (Philadelphia: Temple University Press, 1983), cited by DeBerg.

39. Douglas W. Frank, *Less Than Conquerors: How Evangelicals Entered the Twentieth Century* (Grand Rapids, Mich.: W. B. Eerdmans, 1986), cited by DeBerg.

40. "A Woman's Career," *Western Recorder* 85, 14 (February 10, 1910): 10, cited by DeBerg.

41. A. R. Funderburk, "The Word of God on Women's Dress," *Moody Bible Institute Monthly* 22 (January 1922):759, cited by DeBerg.

42. Many biblical scholars now hold this position. See in particular Julian Morgenstern, "*Beena* Marriage (Matriarchat) in Ancient Israel and Its Historical Implications," *Zeitschrift für die Altestamentische Wissenschaft* 47 (1929), and David Bakan, *And They Took Themselves Wives* (San Francisco: Harper & Row, 1979).

43. "Divorce," *Western Recorder* 86, 52 (November 2, 1911), cited by DeBerg.

44. "The Family," *Western Recorder* 86, 15 (February 16, 1911), cited by DeBerg.

45. J. F. Norris, "Address on Evolution Before Texas Legislature," *Searchlight* 6, 15 (February 23, 1923): 3, cited by DeBerg.

46. J. F. Norris, "Another Example," *Searchlight* 6, 22 (April 13, 1923): 6, cited by DeBerg.

47. J. F. Norris, "The First and Second Creations," *Searchlight* 5, 48 (October 13, 1922): 2, cited by DeBerg.

48. Nancy Ammerman, *Bible Believers: Fundamentalists in the Modern World* (New Brunswick, N.J.: Rutgers University Press, 1987), cited by DeBerg.

49. Jerry Falwell, *Eternity* 31 (July–August 1980), cited in *The Fundamentalist Phenomenon*, ed. Jerry Falwell with Ed Dobson and Ed Hinson (Garden City, N.Y.: Doubleday, 1981).

50. Sheila Ruth, "A Feminist Analysis of the New Right," in *Radical Voices: A Decade of Feminist Resistance*, Women's Studies International Forum, ed. Renate D. Klein and Deborah Lynn Steinberg (Elmsford, N.Y.: Pergamon Press, 1989).

51. All quoted in "Are We All God's People?" pamphlet of People for the American Way, project of Citizens for Constitutional Concerns, based in Washington, D.C.

52. Peter Steinfels, "6,000 Form Rival Baptist Organization," *New York Times*, May 12, 1991.

53. Fred Clarkson writing in *Mother Jones*, November/December 1990.

54. Adolph Reed Jr., "False Prophet," *The Nation*, January 28, 1991. Information for this section was also drawn from the first half of this article, published in *The Nation*, January 21, 1991.

55. Mahnaz Afkhami, "Iran: A Future in the Past—the 'Prerevolutionary' Women's Movement," in *Sisterhood Is Global*, ed. Robin Morgan (Garden City, N.Y.: Doubleday, 1984).

56. For an eyewitness description, see Kate Millett, *Going to Iran* (New York: Coward, McCann and Geoghegan, 1982).

57. Peter R. Knauss, *The Persistence of Patriarchy* (New York: Praeger, 1984).

58. Lisa Beyer, "Life Behind the Veil," *Time*, Special Issue (Fall 1990).

59. Youssef M. Ibrahim, "Algerians Choose the Protest Vote," *International Herald Tribune*, June 27, 1990.

60. The political leader is Mona Makram-Ebeid; the secretary-general, Dr. Hoda Badran. Both are quoted by Alan Cowell, the former in "Safe Haven for Women: Train Car Without Men," *New York Times*, January 15, 1990, the latter in "Egypt's Pain: Wives Killing Husbands," *New York Times*, September 23, 1989.

61. Beyer, op. cit.

62. Cowell, "Egypt's Pain."

63. John F. Burns, "Moscow Gone, Najibullah Boasts and Kabul Stands," *New York Times*, March 12, 1989.

64. Henry Kamm, "Afghan Peace Could Herald War of Sexes," *New York Times*, December 12, 1988.

65. Kathy Evans, "Afghan Edict Tells Women How to Dress," *The Guardian*, June 23, 1990.

66. John F. Burns, "Afghan-Relief Agencies Report Intimidation," *New York Times*, May 24, 1990.

67. Evans, op. cit.

68. Burns, op cit.

69. Evans, op cit.

70. Beyer, op. cit.

71. Stephen Hubbell, "Jordan Votes the Islamic Ticket," *The Nation*, December 25, 1989.

72. Leon Wieseltier, "The Jewish Face of Fundamentalism," in Cohen, op cit., argues the term is erroneously applied to Judaism, but Ian Lustick described Gush ideology as fundamentalism in *For the Land and the Lord: Jewish Fundamentalism in Israel* (New York: Council on Foreign Relations, 1988).

73. Wieseltier, "Jewish Face," p. 196 in Cohen, op cit.

74. Marcia Freedman, *Exile in the Promised Land* (New York: Firebrand Books, 1990).

75. Ibid.

76. Ibid.

77. The Israel Women's Network, a feminist organization founded by Alice Shalvi, produces a newsletter, *Networking for Women*. This information comes from the Summer 1989 issue.

78. "Officers Break Up a March in Israel," *New York Times*, December 30, 1989.

79. "Hasidim Attack Women at Prayers," *New York Times*, March 21, 1989.

80. Alice Shalvi, "The War of All Mothers," *Networking for Women*, Spring 1991.

81. Prehistoric structures often imitate the female body. See William I. Thompson, *The Time Falling Bodies Take to Light* (New York: St. Martins, 1981).

82. Jane O'Reilly, "Naming the Sacred," *MS.*, January/February 1991.

83. The history of the church's position on abortion comes from Jane Hurst, *The History of Abortion in the Catholic Church: The Untold Story* (Washington, D.C.: Catholics for a Free Choice, 1989).

84. "Actions Speak Louder," a bulletin issued by Catholics for a Free Choice, 1991.

85. Discussed in my *From Eve to Dawn*, to be published.

86. Gloria Steinem, *Outrageous Acts and Everyday Rebellions* (New York: Signet Books, 1986).

87. Robin Morgan, Introduction, *Sisterhood Is Global* (Garden City, N.Y.: Doubleday, 1984).

88. Le Anne Schrieber, "Where Are the Doctors Who Will Do Abortions?" *Glamour*, September 1991.

89. John F. Burns, "After a 20-Year Truce, Abortion Debate Is Revived in Canada as Court Strikes Down Restrictive Law," *New York Times*, February 20, 1988.

90. Michele Landsberg also provided most of the foregoing information on the abortion struggle in Canada.

91. See Katrina Vanden Heuvel, "Glasnost for Women?" *The Nation*, June 4, 1990.

92. Malgorzata Fuszara, "Abortion and the Shaping of a New Political Scene in Poland," and "Will the Abortion Issue Give Birth to Feminism in Poland?" (1991); these articles have not been published in English, but Fuszara provided most of the information for this section.

93. "Poland Ends Subsidies for Birth Control Pills," *New York Times*, May 9, 1991.

94. Stephen Engelberg, "Abortion Ban, Sought by Church, Is Rejected by Polish Parliament," *New York Times*, May 18, 1991.

95. Howard S. Levy, *Chinese Footbinding: The History of a Curious Erotic Custom* (New York: Walton Rawls, 1966).

96. "Airline Removes Agent for Not Using Makeup," *New York Times*, May 12, 1991. After an outcry, the airline offered to rehire the woman, Teresa Fischette.

97. Azar Tabari, "The Women's Movement in Iran: A Hopeful Prognosis," *Feminist Studies* 12, 2 (Summer 1986): 343–360.

98. Celestine Bohlen, "East Europe's Women Struggle with New Rules, and Old Ones," *New York Times*, November 25, 1990.

99. All statistics in this paragraph come from B. Meredith Burke, "Ceauşescu's Main Victims: Women and Children," *New York Times*, January 10, 1989.

100. Chuck Sudetic, "Romania Seeks to Reduce Abortions," *New York Times*, January 17, 1991.

101. Steven R. Weisman, "In Crowded Japan, a Bonus for Babies Angers Women," *New York Times*, February 17, 1991.

102. Angela Y. Davis, *Women, Race, and Class* (New York: Random House, 1981).

103. Adrienne Rich, "Compulsory Heterosexuality and Lesbian Existence," *Signs* 5, 4 (Summer 1980): 631–660.

104. Hanny Lightfoot-Klein, *Prisoners of Ritual: An Odyssey into Female Genital Circumcision in Africa* (New York: Harrington Park Press, 1989).

105. For an extensive discussion, see Fran Hosken, *The Hosken Report: Genital and Sexual Mutilation of Females* (Lexington, Mass.: Women's International Network News, 1979), and Lightfoot-Klein, op. cit.

106. Lilian Passmore Sanderson, *Against the Mutilation of Women* (London: Ithaca Press, 1981), p. 27.

107. E. Wallerstein, "Circumcision: Ritual Surgery or Surgical Ritual?" *Medicine and Law* 2 (1983), cited by Lightfoot-Klein.

108. E. Wallerstein, "Circumcision: The Uniquely American Medical Enigma," *Symposium on Advances in Pediatric Urology* (1985), cited by Lightfoot-Klein.

109. Sanderson, op. cit., p. 28.

110. John Money, *The Destroying Angel* (Buffalo, N.Y.: Prometheus Books, 1985).

111. R. Spitz, "Authority and Masturbation," *Psychoanalytic Quarterly* 21, 4 (1952), cited by Lightfoot-Klein.

112. V. Bullough and B. Bullough, *Sin, Sickness, and Sanity* (New York: American Library, 1977), cited by Lightfoot-Klein.

113. Sanderson, op. cit.

114. Hosken, op. cit.

115. Olayinka Koso-Thomas, *Circumcision of Women: A Strategy for Eradication* (Atlantic Highlands, N.J.: Zed Books, 1987).

116. Dr. Abu el Futuh Shandall studied female mutilation in the Sudan. See Sanderson, op. cit.

117. Lightfoot-Klein, op. cit.

118. M. B. Assad, "Female Circumcision in Egypt: Current Research and Social Implications," *WHO/EMRO Technical Publications: Seminar on Traditional Practices Affecting the Health of Women and Children in Africa* (Alexandria, Egypt, 1980), cited by Lightfoot-Klein.

119. Shandall, cited above.

120. Sen, op. cit.

121. The first two statistics come from ibid., the last from Barbara Crosette, "India's Population Put at 844 Million," *New York Times*, March 26, 1991.

122. *The World's Women: 1970–1990: Trends and Statistics* (United Nations, 1991). The report lists nations with fewer than 95 women to 100 men:

United Arab Emirates	48.3*
Qatar	59.8*
Bahrain	68.8*
Kuwait	75.2*
Saudi Arabia	84.0*
Oman	90.8*
Libyan Arab Jamahinya	90.8
Vanuatu	91.7
Pakistan	92.1
Papua New Guinea	92.8
Bhutan	93.3
India	93.5
Brunei Darussalam	93.8
Hong Kong	93.9
Bangladesh	94.1
Albania	94.3
China	94.3
Afghanistan	94.5

Jordan	94.8
Nepal	94.8
Turkey	94.8

*Oil-producing countries with large numbers of male immigrants.

123. Vern L. Bullough and Fang-Fu Ruan, "China's Children," *The Nation*, June 18, 1988.
124. Personal communication, 1986.

PART II

1. These include male feminists. See for instance Steven Rose, *Against Biological Determinism* (New York: Schocken Books, 1982) and *Towards a Liberatory Biology* (New York: Schocken Books, 1982); and R. C. Lewontin, Steven Rose, and Leon Kamin, *Not in Our Genes* (New York: Pantheon, 1984).
2. Sarah Lucia Hoagland, "Androcentric Rhetoric in Sociobiology," in *Radical Voices*, op. cit.
3. For example, Robert Ardrey, *African Genesis* (New York: Dell, 1963); Konrad Lorenz, *On Aggression* (New York: Harcourt Brace, 1966); Lionel Tiger, *Men in Groups* (London, 1969); Stephen Goldberg, *The Inevitability of Patriarchy* (New York, 1974); and Lionel Tiger and Robin Fox, *The Imperial Animal* (London, 1977).
4. See the works by Rose and Lewontin, et al., cited above.
5. E. O. Wilson, *Sociobiology: The New Synthesis* (Cambridge, Mass.: Harvard University Press, 1975). Hoagland refers especially to pp. 291, 552, 568, and 531.
6. The material in this and the next two paragraphs comes from Hoagland, op. cit.
7. Wilson, op. cit., p. 314.
8. Ibid., pp. 282, 153.
9. Ibid., pp. 281, 181.
10. Robert R. Warner, "Boys Will Be Boys—or Girls," is a separate inset in a larger article by Sarah Blaffer Hrdy, "Daughters or Sons," on the ways certain creatures are able to control their production of female and male offspring, and the reasons they do so. The entire report, edited by Rebecca B. Finnell, appears in *Natural History* 97, 4 (April 1988): 63–82. No other section of the report uses male-myth language.
11. Robert Ardrey, *African Genesis* (New York: Dell, 1963), p. 101.
12. Evelyn Reed, *Women's Evolution: From Matriarchal Clan to Patriarchal Family* (New York: Pathfinder Press, 1975), p. 55.

13. Wilson, op. cit., p. 504.

14. Berit Ås, "The Feminist University," in *Radical Voices*, op. cit. She cites a study done by Phillip Goldberg, "Are Women Prejudiced Against Women?" in *And Jill Came Tumbling After: Sexism in American Education*, ed. Judith Stacey et al. (New York: Dell, 1974), Dale Spender, *Man Made Language* (London: Routledge & Kegan Paul, 1980), and Birgit Brock-Utne and Runa Kaukaa, *Kunuskap uten maks* ("Knowledge Without Power") (Olso: University Press, 1980).

15. Ås cites a Swedish study by Einarsson, *Språk och kön i skolan* (1981).

16. Dale Spender, *Invisible Woman: The Schooling Scandal* (London: Writers & Readers, 1982).

17. The study, commissioned by the American Association of University Women and conducted by Greenberg-Lake Analysis Group Inc., surveyed 2400 girls and 600 boys at thirty-six public schools in twelve communities throughout the country in 1990. It was reported in *New York Times*, January 9, 1991.

18. Lisa Belkin, "Report Clears Judge of Bias in Remarks About Homosexuals," *New York Times*, November 2, 1989.

19. Associated Press report, November 28, 1989.

20. Allan R. Gold, "Sex Bias Is Found Pervading Courts," *New York Times*, July 2, 1989, and "Study Finds Sex Bias in Connecticut Legal System," *New York Times*, September 8, 1991.

21. "Study Finds Sex Bias in Connecticut Legal System," *New York Times*, September 8, 1991.

22. Much of this material comes from Robert T. Garrett, *Louisville Courier-Journal*, March 23, 1988.

23. "Sentence Cut for Man Caught with Bombs," *New York Times*, March 3, 1991.

24. The woman was Samantha Dorinda Lopez; her sentence was mentioned in passing in "Fugitive Lovers Are Back in Jail," *New York Times*, November 17, 1986.

25. George J. Church, "The View from Behind Bars," *Time*, Special Issue (Fall 1990).

26. "Adultery Arrests Rise to Four in Connecticut," *New York Times*, August 30, 1990.

27. Larry Rohter, "Rape Case in Mexico Fuels Outrage at Police," *New York Times*, January 31, 1990.

28. For further discussion of this subject, see Barbara Ehrenreich and Deirdre English, *For Her Own Good* (Garden City, N.Y.: Doubleday, 1983); Carroll Smith-Rosenberg, "Puberty to Menopause," and Regina Morantz, "The Lady and Her Physician," both in *Clio's Consciousness Raised*, ed. Mary S. Hartman and Lois Banner (New York: Harper & Row, 1974).

29. Stephan Chorover, *From Genesis to Genocide* (Cambridge, Mass.: MIT Press, 1979).

30. See Ehrenreich and English, op. cit.

31. Andrew Purvis, "A Perilous Gap," *Time*, Special Issue (Fall 1990).

32. Devra Lee Davis, "Fathers and Fetuses," *New York Times*, March 1, 1991.

33. William E. Schmidt, "Risk to Fetus Ruled as Barring Women from Jobs," *New York Times*, October 3, 1989; "British Study Finds Leukemia Risk in Children of A-Plant Workers," *New York Times*, February 18, 1990.

34. Katherine Bishop, "Scant Success for California Efforts to Put Women in Construction Jobs," *New York Times*, February 15, 1991.

35. Tamar Lewin, "Nude Pictures Are Ruled Sexual Harassment," *New York Times*, January 23, 1991.

36. "Homicide Is Top Cause of Death from On-Job Injury for Women," *New York Times*, August 16, 1990.

37. "Study Finds Soldiers Healthier Than Civilians," *New York Times*, November 7, 1990.

38. "Port Authority Charged in Sex Discrimination," *New York Times*, May 25, 1989.

39. Louis A. LoMothe writing in the *Stanford Lawyer* (Spring/Summer 1990).

40. The attorney was Steven B. Liss, the company was Seagate Technology in Minnetonka, Minnesota. Cited by Tamar Lewin, "Child Care in Conflict with a Job," *New York Times*, March 2, 1991.

41. Jason DeParle, "Child Poverty Twice as Likely After Family Split, Study Says," *New York Times*, March 1, 1991.

42. *New York Times*, November 7, 1990.

43. Michael deCourcy Hinds, "Better Traps Being Built for Delinquent Parents," *New York Times*, December 9, 1989.

44. "Court Limits Woman's Right to Male Guests in Her Home," *New York Times*, March 12, 1989.

45. Susan Crean, *The the Name of the Fathers: The Story Behind Male Custody* (Vancouver, B.C.: Amanita Publications, 1988).

46. Julia Brophy, "Custody Law, Childcare, and Inequality in Britain," in *Child Custody and the Politics of Gender*, ed. Carol Smart and Selma Sevenhuijzen (New York: Routledge, 1989), pp. 217–242.

47. Carol Smart, "Power and Politics of Child Custody," in ibid., pp. 1–26.

48. Nancy D. Polikoff, "Fathers' Rights, Mothers' Wrongs," *Women's Review of Books* (June 1990).

49. Scarlet Pollock and Jo Sutton, "Father's Rights, Women's Losses," in *Radical Voices*, op. cit.

50. Ibid.

51. British Law Commission Report (1982), para. 2.2.

52. All the preceding cases are discussed by Felicity Barringer, "Sentence for Killing Newborn: Jail Term, Then Birth Control," *New York Times*, November 18, 1990.

53. "Man Is Charged in Shooting After a Birth Control Ruling," *New York Times*, March 7, 1991.

54. Tamar Lewin, "Implanted Birth Control Device Renews Debate Over Forced Contraception," *New York Times*, January 10, 1991.

55. Jeanne Mager Stellman and Joan E. Bertin, "Science's Anti-Female Bias," *New York Times*, June 4, 1990.

56. These examples come from Katha Pollitt, "A New Assault on Feminism," *The Nation*, March 26, 1990, and Stellman and Bertin, op. cit.

57. Isabel Wilkerson, "Jury in Illinois Refuses to Charge Mother in Drug Death of Newborn," *New York Times*, May 27, 1989.

58. Pollitt, "A New Assault on Feminism."

59. Andrea Dworkin, *Right-Wing Women* (New York: Pedigree Books, 1983).

60. Genoveffa Corea, "The Reproductive Brothel," in *Radical Voices*, op. cit.

61. Harris Brotman, "Engineering the Birth of Cattle," *New York Times Magazine*, May 15, 1983.

62. T. L Avery and E. F. Graham, "Investigations Associated with the Transplanting of Bovine Ova," *Journal of Reproductive Fertility* (1962): 212–217.

63. S. M. Willasden, H. Lenhn-Jensen, C. B. Fehilly, and R. Newcomb, "The Production of Monozygotic Twins of Preselected Parentage by Micromanipulation of Non-surgically Collected Cow Embryos," *Theriogenology* 15, 1 (1981): 23–27.

64. Russell Scott, *The Body as Property* (New York: Viking Press, 1981).

65. George H. Kieffer, *Bioethics: A Textbook of Issues* (Reading, Mass.: Addison-Wesley, 1979).

66. Vance Packard, *The People Shapers* (New York: Bantam, 1979).

67. Katha Pollitt, "When Is a Mother Not a Mother?" *The Nation*, December 31, 1990.

68. Paul Samuelson, "Frontiers in Demographic Economics," *American Economic Review* 75 (May 1985), cited by Waring, op. cit.

69. Waring, op. cit., citing Jalna Hanmer and Pat Allen, *Feminist Issues* (Spring 1982): 57.

70. Margarete J. Sandelowski, "Failures of Volition: Female Agency and Infertility in Historical Perspective," *Signs* 15, 3 (Spring 1990).

Part III

1. Carol Cohn, "In the Rational World of Defense Intellectuals," *Signs* 12, 4 (Summer 1987).

2. All quotations from ibid.

3. William L. Laurence, *Dawn Over Zero: The Study of the Atomic Bomb* (London: Museum Press, 1974), pp. 198–199, cited by Cohn.

4. Hisako Matsubara, *Cranes at Dusk* (Garden City, N.Y.: Dial Press, 1985), cited by Cohn.

5. General Robert Rosenberg, "The Influence of Policymaking on C3I," Incidental Paper, Seminar on C3I (Cambridge, Mass.: Harvard University, Center for Information Policy Research, Spring 1980, cited by Cohn.

6. John Berger, *Ways of Seeing* (London: Penguin Books, 1972).

7. For this sense of Degas, see Arthur Danto, "Degas," *The Nation*, December 12, 1988.

8. Janet Maslin, "Bimbos Embody Retro Rage," *New York Times*, June 17, 1990.

9. Anita Pratap, "Romance and a Little Rape," *Time*, August 13, 1990.

10. Catherine A. MacKinnon, "Pornography: Not a Moral Issue," in *Radical Voices*, op. cit.

11. *American Booksellers Association, Inc., et al., v. William H. Hudnut III, Mayor, City of Indianapolis, et al.* (1985).

12. MacKinnon, op. cit.

13. *Miller v. California* (1973).

14. In some societies, it is taboo for a man to utter the name of his mother-in-law, or for people to utter the real names of certain kin; in some, it is taboo for a woman to look on the face of her sons-in-law; in some, for a woman to show her face to men who are not kin. I suspect all taboos are basically political, that is, they mystify the power relations in a society.

15. Peggy Orenstein, "*MS.* Fights for Its Life," *Mother Jones*, November/December 1990.

16. Gloria Steinem, "Sex, Lies, & Advertising," *MS.*, July/August 1990.

17. *People*, June 10, 1991.

18. All cited in *Time*, June 24, 1991.

19. Pratap, op. cit.

20. David Johnston, "Hoover: Still a Shadow Not to Be Stepped On," *New York Times*, September 9, 1991, with information derived from Curt Gentry, *J. Edgar Hoover: The Man and the Secrets* (N.Y.: W. W. Norton & Co., 1991).

21. Howard Kurtz, "Correspondents Chafe Over Curbs on News," *Washington Post*, January 16, 1991.

22. Klaus Theweleit, *Male Fantasies*, Vol. 1: *Women, Floods, Bodies, History* (Minneapolis: University of Minnesota Press, 1987).

23. Christopher Hitchens, *The Nation*, February 13, 1989.

PART IV

1. Hinds, op. cit.

2. Ibid.

3. David Margolick, "Can Bankruptcy Reduce the Price of a Divorce?" *New York Times*, March 2, 1991.

4. Janice Castro, "Caution: Hazardous Work," *Time*, Special Issue (Fall 1990).

5. Ibid.

6. "Study Says Women Still Do Most Housework," *New York Times*, December 8, 1988.

7. The figures in the *New York Times* report of the study, by John F. Robinson of the University of Maryland, imply that all married women work almost as many hours in the household (22.4) as women with small children.

8. Barbara Crossette, "Women Face Harassment at Resorts in Asia," *New York Times*, January 28, 1990.

9. Lori Heise, "The Global War Against Women," *World Watch*, reprinted in *Washington Post*, April 9, 1989.

10. *Time*, Special Issue (Fall 1990).

11. Barbara Roberts, "No Safe Place: The War Against Women," *Our Generation* 15, 4 (1983): 7–26.

12. Birgit Brock-Utne, *Feminist Perspectives on Peace and Peace Education* (New York: Pergamon Press, 1989). She cites A. Strauss, *Negotiations: Varieties, Contexts, Processes and Social Order* (San Francisco: Jossey-Bass, 1978).

13. Heise, op. cit.

14. Don Terry, "Ex-Officer Held in Girls' Sex Assault," *New York Times*, June 14, 1989.

15. *I Shot My Husband . . . and No One Asked Me Why*, a Scarlet Productions documentary with Beatrix Campbell (London, 1988). A jury acquitted Diaz on grounds of self-defense.

16. Sharon Lamb, "Acts Without Agents: An Analysis of Linguistic Avoidance in Journal Articles on Men who Batter Women," *American Journal of Orthopsychiatry* 61, 2 (April 1991).

17. M. Straus, R. Gelles, and S. Steinmetz, *Behind Closed Doors* (New York: Doubleday, 1980), cited by Lamb.

18. Susan Schechter, *Women and Male Violence: The Visions and Struggles of the Battered Women's Movement* (Boston: South End Press, 1982).

19. Tamar Lewin, "Women Found to Be Frequent Victims of Assaults by Intimates," *New York Times*, January 17, 1991.

20. Robin Willis Knowlton, "Rape in the United States Continues at One of the Highest Rates in the World," *In These Times*, September 23, 1987, p. 15.

21. Diana Scully, *Understanding Sexual Violence: A Study of Convicted Rapists* (Boston: Unwin Hayman, 1990).

22. Peggy Reeves Sanday, *Fraternity Gang Rape: Sex, Brotherhood, and Privilege on Campus* (New York: New York University Press, 1990).

23. Pauline B. Bart, "Rape as a Paradigm of Sexism in Society—Victimization and Its Discontents," in *Radical Voices*, op. cit.

24. *MS.*, January/February 1991.

25. Susan Brownmiller, *Against Our Will: Men, Women, and Rape* (New York: Simon and Schuster, 1975), p. 114.

26. Cited by Betty Reardon, "Sex and the War System," paper for the Institute for World Order (1982), the basis for *Sexism and the War System* (New York: Teachers College Press, 1985).

27. Brock-Utne, *Feminist Perspectives*, op. cit. The study she cites is David Fabbro, "Peaceful Societies: An Introduction," *Journal of Peace Research* 15, 1 (1978).

28. Betsy Peterson, *Dancing with Daddy* (New York: Bantam, 1991).

29. J. Herman and L. Hirschman, "Father-Daughter Incest," *Signs* 2, 4 (1977): 735–757.

30. Over fifty-five women were attacked by the dart-shooter in 1990; the attacks started up again in February 1991, but the police do not think they are the work of the same man.

31. *MS.*, January/February 1991.

32. Knowlton, op. cit.

33. Beatrix Campbell, *The Iron Ladies: Why Do Women Vote Tory?* (London: Virago, 1987).

34. Fred Pelka, "Robert Bly and Iron John," *On the Issues*, Summer 1991, writes that Bly "lays the blame for men's 'grief' on women." This fits into the twentieth-century tradition of blaming men's psychological problems on their mothers and wives, as Philip Wylie did in *Generation of Vipers* (1955).

35. Most of these examples and many that follow come from Charlotte Bunch, *Bringing the Global Home: Feminism in the '80s* (Denver, Colo.: Antelope Publications, 1985), and personal communications.

36. Alice Yun Chai and Ho'oipo De Cambra, "Evolution of Global Feminism Through Hawaiian Feminist Politics," in *Women's Studies International Forum*, ed. Berenice A. Carroll and Jane E. Mohraz (New York: Pergamon Press, 1989).

37. Madhu Bhushan, "Vimochana: Women's Struggles, Nonviolent Militancy and Direct Action in the Indian Context," in *Women's Studies International Forum*, op. cit.

38. Amrita Basu, "Reflections on Forum '85 in Nairobi, Kenya: Voices from the International Women's Studies Community," *Signs*, 11, 3 (Spring 1986): 584–608.

39. These examples were provided by Bunch, op. cit.

40. Ibid.

41. James Brooke, " 'Honor' Killing of Wives Is Outlawed in Brazil," *New York Times*, March 29, 1991.

42. Jane Perlez, "When the Trouble Is Men, Women Help Women," *New York Times*, June 5, 1989.

43. James Brooke, "A Nigerian Shame: The Agony of the Child Bride," *New York Times*, July 17, 1987.

44. Anne Witte Garland, *Women Activists: Challenging the Abuse of Power* (New York: Feminist Press, 1988).

45. Patricia A. Gozemba and Marilyn L. Humphries, "Women in the Anti–Ku Klux Klan Movement, 1865–1984," in *Women's Studies International Forum*, op. cit.

46. Michele Hoyman, "Working Women: The Potential of Unionization and Collective Action in the United States," in *Women's Studies International Forum*, op. cit.

47. Amy Swerdlow, "Ladies' Day at the Capitol: Women Strike for Peace Versus HUAC," *Feminist Studies* 8, 3 (Fall 1982): 493–520.

48. Bill Galt, *Vancouver* (B.C.) *Sun*, December 14.

49. "Wiesner [Jerome Wiesner, President Kennedy's science adviser] gave the major credit for moving President Kennedy toward the limited Test Ban Treaty of 1963, not to arms controllers inside the government but to the Women Strike for Peace and to SANE and Linus Pauling." *Science* (1970).

50. Laurie Cashdan, "Anti-war Feminism: New Directions, New Dualities: A Marxist-Humanist Perspective," in *Women's Studies International Forum*, op. cit.

51. Garland, op. cit.

52. Amanda Sebestyen, "Britain: The Politics of Survival," in *Sisterhood Is Global*, op. cit.

53. Garland, op. cit.

54. Cashdan, op. cit.

About the Author

MARILYN FRENCH is one of the country's leading feminist philosophers and theorists. Her best-selling novel, *The Women's Room*, is generally considered a watershed work in contemporary women's fiction. She has written two other novels, *The Bleeding Heart* and *Her Mother's Daughter*, and several works of nonfiction, including *Shakespeare's Division of Experience* and *Beyond Power: Women, Men, and Morals*. She received her Ph.D. from Harvard.